the

ART

of

PROBLEM

SOLVING

Volume 2:
and BEYOND
Solutions

Richard Rusczyk
Sandor Lehoczky

Cover: "Niagara Falls" by Vanessa Rusczyk.

Sixth Edition; printed September, 2004.

Published by AoPS Incorporated, P.O. Box 2185, Alpine, CA 91903-2185.

ISBN: 1-885875-02-9

This book was produced as camera ready copy using the TeX and LaTeX typesetting systems.

Chapter 1

Logarithms

Solutions to Exercises

1-1 Let $\log_a b = x$, $\log_a c = y$, and $\log_c b = z$. For Property 3, we must prove $x - y = \log_a b/c$. Writing our first two equations in exponential notation, we have $b/c = a^{x-y}$, so that $\log_a b/c = x - y$ as required. For Property 5, we wish to show that $x/y = z$. Once again writing the three equations in exponential notation, we have $a^x = b$, $a^y = c$ and $c^z = b$. Raising the second equation to the z power, we have $a^{yz} = c^z = b = a^x$. Hence, $yz = x$, or $x/y = z$ as desired. Finally, for the final property, let $\log_{a^n} b^n = w$, so $a^{nw} = b^n$. Raising this to the $1/n$ power, we have $a^w = b$, so that $w = x$ (since $a^x = b$ also) and Property 6 is proven.

1-2 Let $a = d$ in Property 4; then we have

$$(\log_a b)(\log_c a) = (\log_a a)(\log_c b) = \log_c b,$$

proving the chain rule for logarithms.

1-3 First, we write all expressions in the simplest base possible. Since $\log_3 4 = \log_3 2^2 = 2\log_3 2$, we can write $\log_3 2 = x/2$. For the first problem, we note that $10 = 5 \cdot 2$, and we can write

$$\log_3 10 = \log_3 2 + \log_3 5 = \frac{x}{2} + \frac{1}{\log_5 3} = \frac{x}{2} + \frac{1}{y}.$$

For the second problem, note that $6/5 = 1.2$ and $3(2) = 6$, so

$$\log_3 1.2 = \log_3(6/5) = \log_3 3 + \log_3 2 - \log_3 5 = 1 + \frac{x}{2} - \frac{1}{y}.$$

1-4 Writing Property 5 backwards, we have $\log_2 3 = (\log_{10} 3)/(\log_{10} 2)$. My calculator can do everything on the right side of this, so my calculator can figure out $\log_2 3$.

1-5 Let $\log_x y = z$, so $x^z = y$. Hence,

$$x^{\log_x y} = x^z = y.$$

Solutions to Problems

1. Applying the chain rule repeatedly, we have $(\log_2 3)(\log_3 4) = \log_2 4$, $(\log_2 4)(\log_4 5) = \log_2 5$, and so on, until finally we are just left with $\log_2 8 = \mathbf{3}$.

2. Writing the given information in the simplest base possible, we find $\log 6 = a/2$ and $\log 5 = b/3$ (since $\log 36 = \log 6^2 = 2\log 6 = a$, for example). Thus,

$$\log(1/12) = \log(1/6) + \log(1/2) = -\log 6 - \log 2 = -\frac{a}{2} - (\log 10 - \log 5) = -\frac{a}{2} + \frac{b}{3} - \mathbf{1}.$$

Make sure you see why $\log 1/2 = -\log 2$.

3. If the graphs intersect, then $2\log x = \log 2x$, or $\log x^2 = \log 2x$, from which we find $x^2 = 2x$ and $x = 2$ or $x = 0$. The expressions in the given equation are clearly not defined for $x = 0$, so we discard that solution and we are left with only **1** point at which the graphs intersect.

4. We've got messy expressions in our exponents. One sure way to get them out of the exponents is to take logarithms. Taking the logarithm base 10, we find

$$\log x^{\log x} = \log \frac{x^3}{100}$$
$$(\log x)(\log x) = \log x^3 - \log 100$$
$$(\log x)^2 = 3\log x - 2.$$

If we let $y = \log x$, we have a quadratic in y, for which the solutions are $y = 2$ and $y = 1$. Solving for x ($x = 10^y$), we find the solutions $x = \mathbf{100}$ and $x = \mathbf{10}$.

5. From Property 5, $p = \log_a(\log_b a)$. Hence, $a^p = \log_b a$.

6. From the given information, we note that $2^{10} > 10^3$, so that $\log 2^{10} > \log 10^3$, or $10\log 2 > 3$. We also find that $10^4 > 2^{13}$, and taking the logarithm of this base 10, we find $4 > 13\log 2$. Hence, the best we can do is $\mathbf{3/10} < \log 2 < \mathbf{4/13}$.

7. Since $1/\log_a b = \log_b a$, the sum is $\log_x 3 + \log_x 4 + \log_x 5 = \log_x 60$.

8. Taking the logarithm base 10 of a number will tell us how many digits the number has. For example, a number y with 25 digits, when written in scientific notation, is of the form

$x \cdot 10^{24}$, where x is some number from 1 to 10. The logarithm of this number is $24 + \log x$. Since x is between 1 and 10, $0 < \log x < 1$, so that $\lfloor \log y \rfloor = 24$. Similarly, the integer part of the logarithm of any positive integer is 1 less than the number of digits it has (remember, y above has 25 digits). (Can you make this proof rigorous? Try using n instead of 25.) Thus, we take the logarithm of 5^{44} in base 10, yielding

$$\log 5^{44} = 44 \log 5 = 44(\log 10 - \log 2) = 44(1 - 0.3010) = 30.756,$$

so 5^{44} has $30 + 1 = \mathbf{31}$ digits.

9. First, we use the simplest bases possible. Since $8^P = 3$, we have $2^{3P} = 3$ and $\log_2 3 = 3P$. Since there are no factors of 3 in our desired expression, but 3's occur in both our known expressions, we want to introduce 3's into $\log_{10} 5$ somehow. Looking over our properties, we see that division is a good way to do this. Let's try it:

$$\log_{10} 5 = \frac{\log_3 5}{\log_3 10} = \frac{Q}{\log_3 5 + \log_3 2} = \frac{Q}{Q + 1/(3P)}.$$

Simplifying this, we find $\log_{10} 5 = \mathbf{(3PQ)/(1 + 3PQ)}$.

10. Set all the given logarithms equal to t. Writing these as exponential equations, we have $9^t = p$, $12^t = q$, and $16^t = p + q$. Taking the quotient of the first two, we have $12^t/9^t = (4/3)^t = q/p$. Now we note that $16^t/9^t = [(4/3)^t]^2 = (q/p)^2 = q^2/p^2$. Going back to the original equations, we find $16^t = p + q = 12^t + 9^t$. Dividing this by 9^t, we have $16^t/9^t = 12^t/9^t + 1$, or

$$\left[\left(\frac{4}{3} \right)^t \right]^2 = \left(\frac{4}{3} \right)^t + 1$$

since $16/9 = (4/3)^2$. Letting $q/p = x$, this equation becomes $x^2 = x + 1$. Solving for x (and recalling that we want the positive value since p and q are both positive), we find $x = \mathbf{(1 + \sqrt{5})/2}$.

11. Letting the two logarithmic expressions equal x and writing them in exponential notation, we have $(4n)^x = 40\sqrt{3}$ and $(3n)^x = 45$. Dividing these gives $(4/3)^x = 8\sqrt{3}/9$, from which we find $x = 3/2$. Thus, $(3n)^{3/2} = 45$, $(3n)^3 = 45^2$, and $n^3 = 45^2/27 = \mathbf{75}$.

12. Attack this just like the previous similar problem. Writing the given logarithms, all set equal to x, in exponential form, we have $9^x = a$, $15^x = b$, and $25^x = a + 2b$. As before, $b/a = (15/9)^x = (5/3)^x$ and $b^2/a^2 = [(5/3)^2]^x = 25^x/9^x$. Combining the exponential equations, we find $25^x = a + 2b = 9^x + 2(15^x)$. Dividing by 9^x and letting $y = (5/3)^x = b/a$, we have $y^2 = 1 + 2y$, which has solutions $y = 1 \pm \sqrt{2}$. Finally, we find $b/a = 1 + \sqrt{2}$ since a and b are both positive.

13. From the given information, we have $a = \log_{60} 3$ and $b = \log_{60} 5$. Using these and many of our logarithmic properties, we have

$$12^{[(1-a-b)/2(1-b)]} = 12^{[(1-(\log_{60} 3 + \log_{60} 5))/2(1 - \log_{60} 5)]}$$

$$= \quad 12^{(\log_{60} 60 - \log_{60} 15)/(2\log_{60} 60 - 2\log_{60} 5)}$$

$$= \quad 12^{(\log_{60} 4)/(\log_{60} 60^2/5^2)}$$

$$= \quad 12^{(\log_{60} 4)/(\log_{60} 144)}$$

$$= \quad 12^{(\log_{144} 4)} = 12^{(\log_{12} 2)} = \mathbf{2}.$$

Make sure you see how we have applied our properties at each step.

Chapter 2

Not Just For Right Triangles

Solutions to Exercises

2-1 $30°$ is in quadrant **I**. Since $700° = 700° - 360° = 340°$, it is in quadrant **IV**. $5\pi/3$ is in quadrant **IV** as well. Finally, $-3\pi/5 = -3\pi/5 + 2\pi = 7\pi/5$, which is between π and $3\pi/2$. Hence, $-3\pi/5$ is in quadrant **III**.

2-2   If $(1, \theta)$ is on the x axis then it is either $(1, 0)$ or $(-1, 0)$. In either case, $\sin \theta = 0$. In the former case, $\cos \theta = 1$ and in the latter $\cos \theta = -1$. Similarly, if $(1, \theta)$ is on the y axis, $x = 0$ and therefore $\cos \theta = 0$, and $\sin \theta$ is either 1 or -1. If the point is on the x axis, θ is an integral multiple of π. If it is on the y axis, it is $\pi/2$ more than a multiple of π, or $2n\pi + \pi/2$.

2-3   Evaluate each of these as described in the text. Pay close attention to your signs! You should find that

$$
\begin{aligned}
\sin 300° &= -\sqrt{3}/2 \\
\cos 215° &= -\sqrt{2}/2 \\
\csc 150° &= 1/\sin 150° = 1/(1/2) = 2 \\
\cot 5\pi/3 &= (\cos 5\pi/3)/(\sin 5\pi/3) = (1/2)/(-\sqrt{3}/2) = -\sqrt{3}/3 \\
\tan \pi &= (\sin \pi)/(\cos \pi) = 0/(-1) = 0 \\
\sec 5\pi/6 &= 1/(\cos 5\pi/6) = 1/(-\sqrt{3}/2) = -2\sqrt{3}/3.
\end{aligned}
$$

2-4   Have fun!

2-5   Any angle in the first or fourth quadrant has a positive cosine (since x is positive there) and any angle in the second or third has a negative cosine. For similar reasons, sine is positive in the first and second quadrants (corresponding to positive y) and negative in the other two.

2-6   Let $\theta = \angle AOC$. Since B is on the negative x axis, $\cos\theta = -OB = -\cos\angle AOB = -\cos(\pi - \theta)$.

2-7   Are you convinced? If not, keep working on it. Plug in some points.

2-8   The parent function is $g(x) = \sin ax$, so $f(x) = g(x + b/a)$, and the phase shift is $-b/a$.

2-9   The answer is not π because the period of $\tan x$ is not 2π! Look at the graph of $\tan x$. It repeats every π, so its period is π. Hence, the period of $\tan 2x$ is $\boldsymbol{\pi/2}$. (Graph it and see!)

2-10   While $\sin^{-1} 1 = \pi/2$, $\sin^{-1} 1$ is not single valued! For example, we can write $\sin^{-1} 1 - \sin^{-1} 1 = 5\pi/2 - \pi/2 = 2\pi$, so the given statement is not always true.

2-11   Since $\csc x = 1/\sin x = -1$ when $x = 3\pi/2 + 2n\pi$,

$$\operatorname{arccsc} -1 = \boldsymbol{3\pi/2 + 2n\pi}.$$

Since $\cos \pi/4 = \sqrt{2}/2$, $\cos^{-1}\sqrt{2}/2 = \boldsymbol{\pi/4}$. The last is a bit trickier. We seek an x such that $(\sin x)/(\cos x) = -\sqrt{3}/3$, or $\sin x = (-\sqrt{3}\cos x)/3$. Substituting this into $\sin^2 x + \cos^2 x = 1$, we find that $(4\cos^2 x)/3 = 1$, so $\cos x = \pm\sqrt{3}/2$. Since $\arctan x$ is between $-\pi/2$ and $\pi/2$, $\cos x = \sqrt{3}/2$ and $\sin x = -1/2$ so $x = \boldsymbol{-\pi/6}$.

2-12   Any function for which $f(x) = f(-x)$ is even and those for which $f(x) = -f(x)$ are odd. Thus, $\sin x$, $\tan x$, $\cot x$, and $\csc x$ are all odd. We can see this just by noting that $\sin x$ and $\tan x$ are odd. The other two are just reciprocals of these. Finally, $\cos x$ and $\sec x$ are even. Query: How could we deduce that $\tan x$ is odd just by knowing that $\sin x$ is odd and $\cos x$ is even?

2-13   Since $\sec(270° + x) = 1/\cos(270° + x)$, we examine cosine. Shifting $\cos x$ (solid line) to the left by $270°$ gives $\cos(270° + x)$ (dashed line), which we see is the same as $\sin x$. Thus, $\sec(270° + x) = 1/(\sin x) = \csc x$.

Shifting $\cos x$ to the left by π results in $\cos(x + \pi)$, which we see is the reflection of $\cos x$ in the x axis, so $\cos(x + \pi) = -\cos x$.

Shifting $\tan x$ (dashed line) to the left by $450°$ (resulting in the dotted line), we see that the resulting graph is the graph of $\cot x$ (bold line) reflected in the x axis, so $\tan(450° + x) = -\cot x$.

Finally, for $\sin(3\pi - x)$, we shift $\sin(-x)$ to the right by 3π, and the resulting graph is the

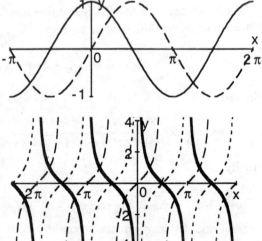

same as $\sin x$. Thus, $\sin(3\pi - x) = \sin x$.

2-14 Let $\angle BAD = \alpha$, $AD = 1$, and $\angle CAD = \beta$. Thus, $AB = 1/(\cos\alpha)$ and $AC = 1/\cos\beta$, $BD = \tan\alpha$, $DC = \tan\beta$, and

$$
\begin{aligned}
[ABC] &= [ABD] - [ACD] \\
(1/2)(AB)(AC)\sin\angle BAC &= (1/2)(AD)(BD) - (1/2)(AD)(DC) \\
\left(\frac{1}{\cos\alpha}\right)\left(\frac{1}{\cos\beta}\right)\sin(\alpha - \beta) &= \frac{\sin\alpha}{\cos\alpha} - \frac{\sin\beta}{\cos\beta}
\end{aligned}
$$

Multiplying both sides by $\cos\alpha\cos\beta$ yields

$$\sin(\alpha - \beta) = \sin\alpha\cos\beta - \sin\beta\cos\alpha.$$

2-15 Use the addition formula on α and $-\beta$:

$$\sin[\alpha + (-\beta)] = \sin\alpha\cos(-\beta) + \sin(-\beta)\cos(\alpha) = \sin\alpha\cos\beta - \sin\beta\cos\alpha,$$

where we have used $\sin(-x) = -\sin x$ and $\cos(-x) = \cos x$.

2-16 We use the same approach as above:

$$\cos[\alpha + (-\beta)] = \cos\alpha\cos(-\beta) - \sin\alpha\sin(-\beta) = \cos\alpha\cos\beta + \sin\alpha\sin\beta.$$

2-17 Let's try this in terms of sines and cosines:

$$\cot(\alpha - \beta) = \frac{\cos(\alpha - \beta)}{\sin(\alpha - \beta)} = \frac{\cos\alpha\cos\beta + \sin\alpha\sin\beta}{\sin\alpha\cos\beta - \sin\beta\cos\alpha} = \frac{\cot\alpha\cot\beta + 1}{\cot\beta - \cot\alpha},$$

where we have divided top and bottom of the fraction by $\sin\alpha\sin\beta$.

2-18 We try to write these as differences or sums of angles with which we are familiar. Since $\sin 15° = \sin(45° - 30°)$, we have

$$\sin 15° = \sin 45°\cos 30° - \cos 45°\sin 30° = \frac{\sqrt{6} - \sqrt{2}}{4}.$$

Similarly,

$$\sec(5\pi/12) = \frac{1}{\cos(\pi/6 + \pi/4)} = \frac{1}{\cos\pi/6\cos\pi/4 - \sin\pi/4\sin\pi/6} = \sqrt{6} + \sqrt{2}.$$

Finally,

$$\cos(-345°) = \cos 15° = \cos(45° - 30°) = \cos 45°\cos 30° + \sin 45°\sin 30° = \frac{\sqrt{6} + \sqrt{2}}{4}.$$

2-19 Using the half angle formula,

$$\sin 15° = \sin(30°/2) = \sqrt{\frac{1 - \frac{\sqrt{3}}{2}}{2}} = \sqrt{\frac{1 - \cos 30°}{2}} = \frac{\sqrt{2 - \sqrt{3}}}{2}.$$

2-20 Since $(\sqrt{6} + \sqrt{2})^2 = 4(2 + \sqrt{3})$, we have $\sqrt{2 + \sqrt{3}} = (\sqrt{6} + \sqrt{2})/2$. Putting this in one expression for $\sin 15°$ yields the other, so the two expressions are equivalent.

2-21 We write $\tan x/2$ in terms of sine and cosine:

$$\tan \frac{x}{2} = \frac{\sin(x/2)}{\cos(x/2)} = \frac{\sqrt{1 - \cos x}}{\sqrt{1 + \cos x}}.$$

We can get rid of the square roots by multiplying top and bottom by either $\sqrt{1 - \cos x}$ or $\sqrt{1 + \cos x}$. The former yields

$$\tan \frac{x}{2} = \frac{1 - \cos x}{\sqrt{1 - \cos^2 x}} = \frac{1 - \cos x}{\sin x},$$

and the latter gives

$$\tan \frac{x}{2} = \frac{\sin x}{1 + \cos x}.$$

2-22 Yes, this is true in general. Go through the derivation in the example with a in place of 3 and b in place of 1 to see so.

2-23 Since $\sin(ax/b)$ repeats every $2b\pi/a$ and $\cos(cx/d)$ repeats every $2d\pi/c$, both functions complete and integral number of periods from $x = 0$ to $x = z$ if $z/(2b\pi/a)$ and $z/(2d\pi/c)$ are integers. Since $az/2b\pi$ and $cz/2d\pi$ are both integers, the numerator of z must be divisible by 2, π, b and d. Thus the numerator of z is at least π times the least common multiple of 2, b, and d. Since az and cz must both be integers, the denominator of z can be no greater the greatest common factor of a and c. Putting this together, we find the minimum z when the numerator is minimized and the denominator is maximized, or

$$z = \frac{\pi \cdot [2, b, d]}{(a, c)}.$$

2-24 We use our double angle formulas and other identities:

$$\sqrt{\frac{2 \sin x - 2 \cos^2 x \sin x}{(2 \sin x \cos x)/\cos x}} = \sqrt{\frac{2 \sin x (1 - \cos^2 x)}{2 \sin x}} = \sqrt{1 - \cos^2 x} = \sin x.$$

Solutions to Problems

14. Using $\sin x = \cos(90° - x)$ on the first four terms, our sum is

$$\cos^2(80°) + \cdots + \cos^2(50°) + \sin^2(50°) + \cdots + \sin^2(80°) + \sin^2(90°) = \mathbf{5},$$

where we have used $\sin^2 x + \cos^2 x = 1$ four times.

15. $\csc\left(\text{Arcsin}\,\frac{1}{2} - \text{Arccos}\,\frac{1}{2}\right) = \csc(30° - 60°) = \csc(-30°) = 1/\sin(-30°) = \mathbf{-2}$.

16. Taking sines of the given equation, we have $\sin y = x$. To find $\tan y$ we need to find $\cos y$. From $\sin^2 y + \cos^2 y = 1$, we find $\cos y = \sqrt{1 - x^2}$. Thus, $\tan y = \boldsymbol{x/\sqrt{1-x^2}}$.

17. For each period of sine, the value c is attained twice. (look at a graph of $\sin x$ to convince yourself of this. Since the period of $\sin nq$ is $2\pi/n$, there are n periods of the graph between 0 and 2π. Thus, the value c is attained $\mathbf{2n}$ times.

18. The sides are sides of a right triangle since they satisfy the Pythagorean Theorem. Thus, $\sin A = a/c = 3/5$, $\sin 2B = 2\sin B \cos B = 2(4/5)(3/5) = 24/25$, and $\sin 3C = \sin 3\pi/2 = -1$. Our desired sum is then $\mathbf{14/25}$.

19. Take tangents of both sides, yielding

$$1 = \tan\frac{\pi}{4} = \tan(\text{Arctan}\,\frac{x}{2} + \text{Arctan}\,\frac{2x}{3}) = \frac{x/2 + 2x/3}{1 - (x/2)(2x/3)} = \frac{7x/6}{1 - x^2/3} = \frac{7x}{6 - 2x^2}.$$

Solving this quadratic, we find the roots $x = (-7 \pm \sqrt{97})/4$. The two principal inverse tangents in the sum will have the same sign as x. Since their sum is positive, x must be positive, so $x = \mathbf{(-7 + \sqrt{97})/4}$.

20. The period of the first term in the sum is $1/2$ and that of the second is $2/5$. Let z be the period of the given sum. Thus, z is the smallest positive real number such that $z/(2/5) = 5z/2$ and $z/(1/2) = 2z$ are both integers. Clearly the smallest such z is $z = \mathbf{2}$. Notice that the phase shifts and amplitudes of the terms in the sum are irrelevant.

21. This is good practice in the use of the identites $\sin^2 x + \cos^2 x = 1$ and $\cos 2x = 2\cos^2 x - 1$:

$$
\begin{aligned}
\sin^4 x &= (1 - \cos^2 x)^2 = \left(\frac{1 - \cos 2x}{2}\right)^2 \\
&= \frac{1 - 2\cos 2x + \cos^2 2x}{4} = \frac{1 - 2\cos 2x}{4} + \frac{1 + \cos 4x}{8} \\
&= (3 - 4\cos 2x + \cos 4x)/8.
\end{aligned}
$$

Note that we have used the cosine double angle formula 'backwards,' as $\cos^2 x = (\cos 2x + 1)/2$ and $\cos^2 2x = (\cos 4x + 1)/2$.

22. Express the sum in terms of sines and cosines and find a common denominator:

$$\cot 10 + \tan 5 = \frac{\cos 10}{\sin 10} + \frac{\sin 5}{\cos 5} = \frac{\cos 10 \cos 5 + \sin 10 \sin 5}{\sin 10 \cos 5}.$$

The numerator is the expansion of $\cos(10 - 5)$! Thus our sum is

$$\frac{\cos 5}{\sin 10 \cos 5} = \csc 10.$$

23. Writing the equation in terms of $\sin x$ we have $\sin x = 1 - 2\sin^2 x$. Solving this as a quadratic in $\sin x$, we find $\sin x = 1/2$ or $\sin x = -1$. Given that $0 \le x \le \pi/2$, $x = \pi/6$.

24. Seeing that the angles often have ratios of 2 or 1/2, we use the sine double angle formula, forwards and backwards, and $\sin x = \cos(90° - x)$. For the first, $\sin 100° = \sin(180° - 100°) = \sin 80° = \cos 10°$, so

$$\begin{aligned}
\sin 10° \sin 10° \sin 100° &= \sin 10° \sin 10° \cos 10° = (\sin 10°)(\sin 20°)(1/2) \\
&= \sin 10° \sin 20° \sin 30°.
\end{aligned}$$

For the second,

$$\sin 10° \sin 20° \sin 80° = \sin 10° \sin 20° \cos 10° = (\sin 20° \sin 20°)(1/2) = \sin 20° \sin 20° \sin 30°.$$

For the third,

$$\begin{aligned}
\sin 10° \sin 40° \sin 50° &= \sin 10° \sin 40° \cos 40° = (\sin 10°)(\sin 80°)(1/2) \\
&= (\sin 10°)(\cos 10°)(1/2) = (\sin 20°)(1/2)(1/2) = \sin 20° \sin^2 30°.
\end{aligned}$$

25. We repeatedly factor the equation and apply double angle formulas:

$$\begin{aligned}
8 \sin x \cos^5 x - 8 \sin^5 x \cos x &= 8 \sin x \cos x \, (\cos^4 x - \sin^4 x) \\
&= 4 \sin 2x \, (\cos^2 x - \sin^2 x)(\cos^2 x + \sin^2 x) \\
&= 4 \sin 2x \, (\cos 2x) = 2 \sin 4x.
\end{aligned}$$

Thus, $2 \sin 4x = 1$ and $\sin 4x = 1/2$. Since we want the smallest solution, we solve $4x = 30°$, so $x = 7.5°$.

26. Square the given equation to find $\sin^2 x + 2 \sin x \cos x + \cos^2 x = 1/25$, so $1 + \sin 2x = 1/25$ and $\sin 2x = -24/25$. Using $\sin^2 2x + \cos^2 2x = 1$ and noting that $2x$ is in the fourth quadrant, we solve for $\cos 2x$ and $\cos 2x = 7/25$.

27. As before, squaring the given equation gives $1 + \sin 2x = 1/4$, so $\sin 2x = -3/4$. Thus, x is in quadrant II. (If it were in quadrant I, $\sin 2x$ would be positive.) Note that $(\cos x - \sin x)^2 = \cos^2 x - 2 \sin x \cos x + \sin^2 x = 1 - \sin 2x = 7/4$. Since x is in quadrant II,

$\cos x - \sin x = -\sqrt{7}/2$. (Why can't it be positive?) Adding this to the given equation gives us $\cos x = 1/4 - \sqrt{7}/4$, so $\sin x = 1/4 + \sqrt{7}/4$. Thus, $\tan x = (1 + \sqrt{7})/(1 - \sqrt{7}) = -(4 + \sqrt{7})/3$, and $(p, q) = (\mathbf{4, 7})$.

28. Since $AB = BC$, $\widehat{AB} = \widehat{BC}$, so $\angle BDA = \angle BDC$. Thus, BD is the angle bisector of $\angle CDA$. Let $\angle BDA = x$, so $\angle CDA = 2x$. From right triangle DBA (since $\angle DBA$ is inscribed in a semicircle), $\sin x = AB/AD = 1/4$. Thus, $\cos \angle CDA = \cos 2x = 1 - 2\sin^2 x = 7/8$. From right triangle CAD, $CD/AD = \cos \angle CDA = \cos 2x$, so $CD = \mathbf{7/2}$.

29. The key here is to recognize that $1 - \sin 2x = (\sin x - \cos x)^2$. (Why?) Thus we have

$$\frac{\sin^2 x}{3} + \frac{\cos^2 x}{7} = \frac{(\sin x - \cos x)^2}{10}.$$

Since we seek $\tan x$, we divide both sides by $\cos^2 x$, yielding

$$\frac{\tan^2 x}{3} + \frac{1}{7} = \frac{(\tan x - 1)^2}{10}.$$

Rearranging this and factoring the resulting quadratic in $\tan x$, we have $49 \tan^2 x + 42 \tan x + 9 = (7 \tan x + 3)^2 = 0$, so $\tan x = \mathbf{-3/7}$.

30. Since

$$1 = \tan(20° + 25°) = \frac{\tan 20° + \tan 25°}{1 - \tan 20° \tan 25°},$$

we have $1 - \tan 20° \tan 25° = \tan 20° + \tan 25°$. Thus, $\tan 20° + \tan 25° + \tan 20° \tan 25° = 1$. Expanding the given product, we have

$$(1 + \tan A)(1 + \tan B) = 1 + \tan A + \tan B + \tan A \tan B = 1 + 1 = \mathbf{2}.$$

31. Since $\sin \theta/2 = \sqrt{(1 - \cos \theta)/2}$, we find $\cos \theta$ as

$$\cos \theta = 1 - 2\sin^2(\theta/2) = 1 - \frac{x - 1}{x} = \frac{1}{x}.$$

Since $\tan^2 \theta + 1 = \sec^2 \theta$, we find $\tan \theta = \sqrt{\sec^2 \theta - 1} = \sqrt{x^2 - 1}$, where we take the positive square root since θ is acute.

32. Draw altitude DE to AB. Thus,

$$\tan x = \tan(\angle EDB + \angle EDA) = \frac{\tan \angle EDB + \tan \angle EDA}{1 - \tan \angle EDB \tan \angle EDA}.$$

$EBCD$ is a rectangle, so $EB = 6$ and $ED = 4$. Hence, we find $\tan \angle EDB = 3/2$ and $\tan \angle ADE = (y - 6)/4$. Substituting this in the above yields

$$\tan x = \frac{y/4}{1 - 3(y - 6)/8}.$$

Solving this equation for y gives us our answer,

$$y = \frac{26 \sin x}{2 \cos x + 3 \sin x}.$$

The moral of this problem is that making rectangles is often very useful.

33. Using the cosine double angle formula backwards we can write

$$\cos 72° = 2 \cos^2 36° - 1 \quad \text{and} \quad \cos 36° = 1 - 2 \sin^2 18°.$$

Since $\sin 18° = \cos 72°$, we can write the latter equation as $\cos 36° = 1 - 2 \cos^2 72°$. Adding this to the first equation above yields

$$\cos 36° + \cos 72° = 2(\cos^2 36° - \cos^2 72°) = 2(\cos 36° - \cos 72°)(\cos 36° + \cos 72°).$$

Dividing both sides by $2(\cos 36° + \cos 72°)$ gives us $\cos 36° - \cos 72° = \mathbf{1/2}$. This may seem a bit contrived, but there is a method involved. We try to express each term in the initial expression in terms of the other.

34. We find the area of $ABCDE$, where $AB = 1$, in two different ways. In the first diagram, $\angle ABC = 3\pi/5$ and $\angle ACB = \pi/5$ (since $\triangle ABC$ is isosceles). Thus, $\angle ACF = 3\pi/5 - \pi/5 = 2\pi/5$, $AF = CF \tan \angle ACF = (1/2) \tan(2\pi/5)$, and

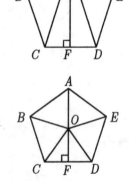

$$
\begin{aligned}
[ABCDE] &= 2[ABC] + [ACD] \\
&= 2(1/2)(1)(1) \sin 3\pi/5 + (CD)(AF)/2 \\
&= \sin 3\pi/5 + (1)(\tan 2\pi/5)/4 \\
&= \sin 3\pi/5 + (\tan 2\pi/5)/4.
\end{aligned}
$$

Since $\sin 3\pi/5 = \sin 2\pi/5$, we have $4[ABCDE] = 4 \sin 2\pi/5 + \tan 2\pi/5$. In the second diagran, $\angle COF = 2\pi/10 = \pi/5$, so $OF = CF \cot(\pi/5) = (\cot \pi/5)/2$, and

$$
\begin{aligned}
[ABCDE] &= 10[OCF] = 10(OF)(FC)/2 \\
&= 5(1/2)(1/2)(\cot \frac{\pi}{5}) = \frac{5}{4} \cot \frac{\pi}{5}.
\end{aligned}
$$

Combining this with the first expression for $[ABCDE]$, we have our desired expression.

35. Shown is triangle ABC with $\angle ABC = \angle ACB = 2\angle BAC = 72°$. We draw angle bisectors CF, BE, and AD. Since $\angle ABI = \angle CBI = \angle BCI = \angle ACI = 36°$, we have

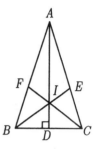

$$\triangle AEB \sim \triangle AFC \sim \triangle BIC$$

and $\triangle ABC \sim \triangle CFB \sim \triangle BEC \sim \triangle BFI \sim \triangle CIE$. If we let $AB = y$ and $CB = x$, we have $FB/FC = BC/AB$, so $FB = x^2/y$ (since $FC = BC = x$). From $FI/FB = BC/AB$, we find (since $IC = IB = FB$ and $FI = FC - IC$)

$$\frac{x - x^2/y}{x^2/y} = \frac{x}{y}.$$

Thus, $yx - x^2 = x^3/y$, or $y^2 - yx - x^2 = 0$. Applying the quadratic formula, we find $y = (x \pm \sqrt{5x^2})/2 = x(1 + \sqrt{5})/2$, where we take the positive square root since y and x are both positive. From right triangle ABD, we have

$$\sin \angle DAB = \sin 18° = BD/AB = x/2y = (\sqrt{5} - 1)/4.$$

Similarly, $\cos \angle ICD = \cos 36° = CD/IC = (x/2)/(x^2/y) = y/2x = (1 + \sqrt{5})/4$.

Chapter 3

More Triangles!

Solutions to Exercises

3-1 First, when B is on the circle centered at A with radius AC, we have $b = a$ and $\cos C = CB/DC = a/2b$

$$a^2 + b^2 - 2ab\cos C = a^2 + b^2 - 2ab\left(\frac{a}{2b}\right) = b^2 = c^2$$

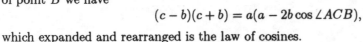

For B outside the circle, we will address the case where BC extended intersects the circle on the opposite side of AC with respect to B as shown. Since $\angle ECD$ and $\angle ACB$ are supplementary, $\cos\angle ECD = -\cos\angle ACB$ and $EC = 2b\cos\angle ECD = -2b\cos\angle ACB$. Since $BF = c - b$ ($AF = AC = b$), from the power of point B we have

$$(c - b)(c + b) = a(a - 2b\cos\angle ACB),$$

which expanded and rearranged is the law of cosines.

3-2 Since $2R = AC/\sin B = 12$, $R = 12/2 = \mathbf{6}$.

3-3 When angle A is right, BC is the diameter of the circumcircle. Since $\sin 90° = 1$, $BC/\sin A = 2R$ is true. For the case of obtuse $\angle A$, consider the diagram where CD is the diameter of the circumcircle of $\triangle ABC$. Since $\sin D = BC/CD = a/2R$ and $\angle D = \overset{\frown}{BC}/2 = 180° - \overset{\frown}{BDC}/2 = 180° - \angle A$,

$$\frac{a}{2R} = \sin D = \sin(180° - A) = \sin A,$$

which completes our proof.

3-4 If one of the angles is obtuse, the proof is clear from the shown diagram, where $AB < DB < BC$. The first inequality can be seen from the Pythagorean Theorem. If both angles are acute, we have $BC/AC = \sin A/\sin B$ from the law of sines. If $\angle A > \angle B$, then $BC/AC = \sin A/\sin B > 1$, so $BC > AC$. Similarly, if $BC > AC$, we can deduce $\sin A > \sin B$, from which $\angle A > \angle B$ follows.

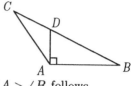

3-5 Let $AB = x$ and $AC = y$. Since $\angle ADB = 180° - \angle ADC$, $\cos \angle ADB = -\cos \angle ADC$, and

$$\frac{x^2 - 52}{-48} = -\frac{y^2 - 45}{-36}.$$

Rearranging this we find $3x^2 + 4y^2 = 336$. From the Angle Bisector Theorem we have $x/y = 4/3$, and our equation becomes $21x^2/4 = 336$, so $x = \mathbf{8}$.

3-6 Continuing from the previous example, we write $a = 2R\sin A$, from which the desired result follows.

3-7 From Heron's formula, we have $[ABC] = \sqrt{21(8)(7)(6)} = 84$. The shortest altitude is the one drawn to the longest side, so $\frac{1}{2}(15)(x) = 84$, and our shortest altitude has length **56/5**.

3-8 Since $\angle ABC$ and $\angle BCD$ are supplementary, $\cos \angle ABC = -\cos \angle BCD$, and

$$\frac{AC^2 - AB^2 - BC^2}{-2(AB)(BC)} = -\frac{BD^2 - BC^2 - CD^2}{-2(BC)(CD)}.$$

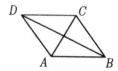

Since $CD = AB$, we can rearrange this as the desired $AC^2 + BD^2 = AB^2 + BC^2 + CD^2 + DA^2$.

3-9 Solving $4AD^2 + BC^2 = 2(AB^2 + AC^2)$ for AD, we find

$$AD = \frac{1}{2}\sqrt{2(AB^2 + AC^2) - BC^2}.$$

3-10 Solving for d in Stewart's Theorem, we find

$$d^2 = \frac{bmb + cnc - man}{a} = b^2\left(\frac{m}{a}\right) + c^2\left(\frac{n}{a}\right) - mn.$$

writing a as $m + n$ and noting that $m/(m+n) = 1/(1 + n/m) = 1/(1 + b/c) = c/(b + c)$ (remember, $n/m = b/c$ from the Angle Bisector Theorem), we have

$$\begin{aligned} d^2 &= b^2\left(\frac{c}{b+c}\right) + c^2\left(\frac{b}{b+c}\right) - mn \\ &= \frac{bc(b+c)}{b+c} - \left(\frac{m}{m+n}\right)\left(\frac{n}{m+n}\right)a^2. \end{aligned}$$

Using our aforementioned expressions for $m/(m+n)$ and $n/(m+n)$, we have

$$d = \sqrt{bc - \left(\frac{c}{b+c}\right)\left(\frac{b}{b+c}\right)a^2} = \sqrt{bc\left(1 - \frac{a^2}{(b+c)^2}\right)}.$$

3-11   Since AD is a median, $m = n = a/2$ and Stewart's Theorem provides

$$\frac{a^3}{4} + ad^2 = \frac{ab^2}{2} + \frac{ac^2}{2}.$$

Solving for d, we find

$$d = \sqrt{\frac{b^2 + c^2}{2} - \frac{a^2}{4}}.$$

Solutions to Problems

36. Since $6^2 + 8^2 > 9^2$, the triangle is **acute**.

37. From Heron's formula, the area of the triangle is $\sqrt{21(8)(7)(6)} = 84$. Alternately, we can express the area as $(14)(h)/2$. Setting these equal, we find $h = \mathbf{12}$.

38. From the Angle Bisector Theorem, $CB/AB = CD/AD = 4/3$, so $BC = 4$ and $AC = 7$. Thus,

$$BD = \sqrt{(8)(6)\left(1 - \frac{49}{196}\right)} = \mathbf{6}.$$

39. Let the sides be $4x$, $6x$, and $8x$. Since the smallest angle is opposite the smallest side, we apply the law of cosines to find

$$16x^2 = 36x^2 + 64x^2 - 2(6x)(8x)\cos\theta.$$

Solving for $\cos\theta$, we find $\cos\theta = \mathbf{7/8}$.

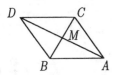

40. Extend median AM past M to D as shown so that $ABDC$ is a parallelogram. Since $AB = CD$, $AC = BD$, and $AD = 2AM$, we have

$$\begin{aligned} AD^2 + BC^2 &= AC^2 + CD^2 + DB^2 + AB^2, \text{ so} \\ 36 + BC^2 &= 2(64 + 16). \end{aligned}$$

Finally, $BC = \mathbf{2\sqrt{31}}$.

41. Shown is $\triangle ABC$ with angle bisector AD. Applying the law of sines to $\triangle ADC$ and $\triangle ADB$ and noting that $\sin \angle ADC = \sin \angle ADB$ and $\sin \angle CAD = \sin \angle DAB$, we have

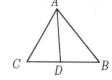

$$\frac{AC}{CD} = \frac{\sin \angle ADC}{\sin \angle CAD}$$
$$= \frac{\sin \angle ADB}{\sin \angle BAD}$$
$$= \frac{AB}{BD}.$$

42. Multiplying both sides by $a + b + c$, we find $a^3 + b^3 = c^2(a + b)$. Factoring the left side, we find $(a + b)(a^2 + b^2 - ab) = c^2(a + b)$, so dividing by $a + b$ gives $c^2 = a^2 + b^2 - ab$. Since from the law of cosines we have $c^2 = a^2 + b^2 - 2ab \cos C$, we know $\cos C = 1/2$ by comparison to the above equation. Thus $\sin C = \sqrt{3}/2$ (why?) and $\tan C = \sqrt{3}$.

43. Drawing the altitude from A to BC, we can use the Pythagorean Theorem to determine the altitdue has length $\sqrt{49 - 1} = 4\sqrt{3}$. Thus, the triangle has area $(2)(4\sqrt{3})/2 = 4\sqrt{3}$. Since $abc = 4KR$, we find $R = AO = 49\sqrt{3}/24$.

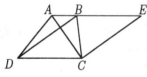

44. Extend AB to E so that $BECD$ is a parallelogram. Thus, $AE = AB + BE = AB + CD$ and applying the law of cosines to $\triangle ACE$ gives

$$AE^2 = (AB + CD)^2 = AC^2 + EC^2 - 2(AC)(CE) \cos \angle ACE.$$

Since $EC = BD$ and $(AB + CD)^2 - (AC^2 + BD^2) = 0$, we have $\cos \angle ACE = 0$. Thus, $\angle ACE = 90°$. Since $BD \parallel EC$, $BD \perp AC$ and $ABCD$ is orthodiagonal.

45. Seeing sines, we consider the law of sines. Writing $\sin A = a/2R$ and likewise for the other two angles, our fraction becomes

$$7 = \frac{a^3 + b^3 + c^3}{\sin^3 A + \sin^3 B + \sin^3 C} = 8R^3.$$

Thus, $R = \sqrt[3]{7}/2$. Since the triangle is inscribed in a circle with diameter $\sqrt[3]{7}$, the maximum length a side can have is $\sqrt[3]{7}$.

46. Writing $\sin(A/2) = \sqrt{(1 - \cos A)/2}$ and applying the law of cosines yields

$$\sin\left(\frac{A}{2}\right) = \sqrt{\frac{1 + \frac{a^2 - b^2 - c^2}{2bc}}{2}} = \sqrt{\frac{a^2 - (b - c)^2}{4bc}}$$
$$= \sqrt{\frac{(a - b + c)(a + b - c)}{4bc}} = \sqrt{\frac{(s - b)(s - c)}{bc}}.$$

47. Rather than using the half angle formula for cosine and the law of cosines, we note that

$$2\sin\frac{A}{2}\cos\frac{A}{2} = \sin A = \frac{2[ABC]}{bc} = \frac{2\sqrt{s(s-a)(s-b)(s-c)}}{bc}.$$

Using our expression for $\sin(A/2)$ from the previous problem, we find

$$\cos\frac{A}{2} = \sqrt{\frac{s(s-a)}{bc}}.$$

48. Since $\cot(A/2) = \cos(A/2)/\sin(A/2)$, we have from the previous two problems

$$r^2\cot\frac{A}{2}\cot\frac{B}{2}\cot\frac{C}{2} = r^2\sqrt{\frac{s^3}{(s-a)(s-b)(s-c)}} = r^2 s\sqrt{\frac{s}{(s-a)(s-b)(s-c)}}.$$

Noting that $r = \sqrt{(s-a)(s-b)(s-c)/s}$, we recognize the right side of the above as $r^2 s(1/r) = rs = [ABC]$, as desired.

49. By connecting both B and C to the center, O, of the circle we can use SSS congruency to show $\triangle OXB \cong \triangle OXC$, so $\angle BXD = \angle DXC$. Using SAS we can then show $\triangle BXA \cong \triangle CXA$ ($\angle BXA = \angle CXA$, $BX = CX$, and $AX = AX$) so that $\angle BAX = \angle CAX = 6°$ (since $\angle BAC = 12°$). From right triangle ABD, $AB = AD\cos\angle BAD = \cos 6°$. Since $\angle BXD = 18°$, $\angle BXA = 162°$ and $\angle ABX = 12°$. Finally, we apply the law of sines to $\triangle ABX$ to find

$$\frac{AX}{\sin 12°} = \frac{AB}{\sin 162°}.$$

Since $\sin 162° = \sin 18°$ and $AB = \cos 6°$, $AX = \cos 6° \sin 12°/\sin 18°$.

50. Like many times before, we extend AD past D to M so that $ABMC$ is a parallelogram. From the law of cosines applied to $\triangle ACM$, we have

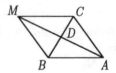

$$AM^2 = AC^2 + CM^2 - 2(AC)(CM)\cos\angle ACM.$$

Since $CM = AB$, $AM = 2AD$, and $\cos\angle ACM = \cos\angle(180° - \angle CAB) = -\cos\angle CAB$, this equation becomes

$$4AD^2 = AC^2 + AB^2 + 2(AC)(AB)\cos\angle BAC.$$

51. For this problem, we apply the fact that if in $\triangle DEF$ we have $\angle D > \angle E$, then $EF > DF$. We use this on $\triangle AXC$, then $\triangle BYC$, then $\triangle CZB$. We can then relate the cevians of $\triangle ABC$ to the sides. Since $c \le b \le a$, we have $\angle C \le \angle B \le \angle A$. Since $\angle AXC > \angle B \ge \angle C$, $AC > AX$. Similarly, since $\angle BYC > \angle A \ge \angle C$, $BC > BY$, and since $\angle CZB > \angle CAB \ge \angle B$, $BC > CZ$. Hence, $AX + BY + CZ < AC + BC + BC = 2a + b$.

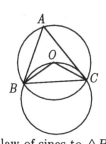

52. First we apply the law of sines to $\triangle ABC$ to determine BC, the common side of $\triangle ABC$ and $\triangle OBC$. We find

$$\frac{BC}{\sin A} = 2OB.$$

Since $OB = 1$ and $\sin A = \sin 60° = \sqrt{3}/2$, we have $BC = \sqrt{3}$. Since $\angle A = 60°$, $\overparen{BC} = 120°$. Thus, $\angle BOC = 120°$. We can now apply the law of sines to $\triangle BOC$, finding $R_{\triangle BOC} = BC/2\sin \angle BOC = 1$.

53. Let the desired length be x. We attack this problem by finding the area as $[ABC] = (ab/2)\sin C$ and $[ABC] = [ACD] + [BCD] = (ax/2)\sin(C/2) + (bx/2)\sin(C/2)$. Since $\sin C = 2\sin(C/2)\cos(C/2)$, we have

$$(ab/2)(2\sin(C/2)\cos(C/2)) = (ax/2)\sin(C/2) + (bx/2)\sin(C/2).$$

Solving this for x, we find

$$x = \frac{2ab\cos\frac{C}{2}}{a+b}.$$

54. Let $\angle ACD = \angle DCB = \theta$ and $CD = x$. We solve this problem by finding $[ABC]$ in two ways:

$$[ABC] = [ACD] + [BCD]$$
$$(ab/2)\sin \angle ACB = (ax/2)\sin \theta + (bx/2)\sin \theta.$$

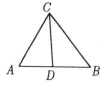

Since $\sin \angle ACB = \sin 2\theta = 2\sin\theta\cos\theta$, the above becomes

$$ab\sin\theta\cos\theta = (ax/2)\sin\theta + (bx/2)\sin\theta.$$

Dividing by $\sin \theta$ and by ab (so we can get $1/a$ and $1/b$ terms as in the desired expression), we find

$$\frac{2}{x}\cos\theta = \frac{1}{a} + \frac{1}{b}.$$

We are given $x = 6$ and $\cos\theta = 1/3$, so we find $1/a + 1/b = \mathbf{1/9}$.

55. Let $x = AD$ and $y = AE$. From the Angle Bisector Theorem applied to triangles ABE and ADC, we find $AB = 2y/3$ and $AC = 2x$. Since we have angle bisectors of triangles ABE and ADC, we apply the angle bisector formula $d^2 + mn = bc$ proved in the text to them to get equations in x and y:

$$x^2 + 6 = 2y^2/3 \quad \text{and} \quad y^2 + 18 = 2x^2.$$

Solving these, we find $(x, y) = (3\sqrt{6}, 3\sqrt{10})$. Hence the sides of the triangle are $AB = 2y/3 = 2\sqrt{10}$, $AC = 2x = 6\sqrt{6}$, and $BC = 11$. The shortest of these is $\mathbf{2\sqrt{10}}$.

56. First, $\triangle AMD \cong \triangle AME$ by ASA ($\angle EAM = \angle DAM$, $AM = AM$, and $\angle AMD = \angle AME$). Similarly, $\triangle C'DM \cong \triangle CEM$. Hence, $AD = AE = 6$, $DC' = EC = 12$, and $C'M = CM = BM = DM + 10$. Since $[ABM] = [ACM]$ and $[ADM] = [AEM]$, we have $[ABM] - [ADM] = [ACM] - [AEM]$, or $[ABD] = [CEM] = [C'DM]$. Hence,

$$[ABD] = \frac{(10)(6)}{2} \sin \angle BDA = \frac{(12)(DM)}{2} \sin \angle C'DM = [C'DM],$$

so $DM = 5$ since $\angle BDA = \angle C'DM$. Applying the law of cosines to $\triangle ABD$ and noting $\angle ADB = \angle C'DM$, we have

$$
\begin{aligned}
AB^2 &= 100 + 36 - 2(10)(6) \cos \angle ADM \\
&= 136 - 120 \cos \angle C'DM \\
&= 136 - 120 \left(-\frac{225 - 144 - 25}{2(12)(5)} \right) = 192.
\end{aligned}
$$

Thus, $AB = 8\sqrt{3}$, and $k = \mathbf{8}$.

57. Seeing three angles which add to π, we let these be the angles of triangle ABC, where $\angle A = \alpha$, $\angle B = \beta$, and $\angle C = \gamma$. Drawing the circumcircle of $\triangle ABC$ centered at O, we have $\angle BOC = 2\alpha$, $\angle AOB = 2\gamma$, and $\angle AOC = 2\beta$. Letting $AO = OB = OC = 1$, we have

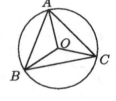

$$[ABC] = \frac{1}{2} \sin 2\alpha + \frac{1}{2} \sin 2\beta + \frac{1}{2} \sin 2\gamma.$$

Expressing the area as $(ab/2) \sin C$ and using the law of sines we have

$$[ABC] = \frac{ab}{2} \sin C = \frac{(2R \sin A)(2R \sin B)}{2} \sin C = 2 \sin \alpha \sin \beta \sin \gamma.$$

Setting these two expressions for $[ABC]$ equal we have the desired expression.

Chapter 4

Cyclic Quadrilaterals

Solutions to Exercises

4-1 Since their sides satisfy the Pythagorean Theorem, both $\triangle ABC$ and $\triangle ACD$ are right triangles. Hence, $\angle ABC + \angle ADC = 180°$, and $ABCD$ is a cyclic quadrilateral. Since

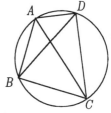

$$\tan(\alpha + \beta) = \frac{\tan \alpha + \tan \beta}{1 - \tan \alpha \tan \beta},$$

we need only find $\tan \alpha$ and $\tan \beta$. The first is simply AB/BC since $\angle ACB$ is in a right triangle. For the second, note $\angle ABD = \angle ACD$, so $\tan \beta = \tan \angle ACD = AD/CD = 24/7$. Using these values in the above expression yields $\tan(\alpha + \beta) = -4/3$.

4-2 Rearranging the given equation as $AO/DO = BO/CO$ and noting that $\angle AOB = \angle COD$, we have $\triangle AOB \sim \triangle DOC$ by SAS similarity. Hence, $\angle CAB = \angle BDC$ and $ABCD$ is cyclic.

Solutions to Problems

58. In an isosceles trapezoid the opposite interior angles are supplementary; thus, an isosceles trapezoid is cyclic. This proves the 'if' part. To show the 'only if' part, we note that any inscribed trapezoid has supplementary opposite interior angles and is thus isosceles.

59. Since $\angle BAC = \angle BDC$ and $\angle AEB = \angle CED$, we have $\triangle ABE \sim \triangle DCE$. Hence, $AB/BE = CD/CE$ and $CE = 42/5$.

60. Let $\angle ABM = \angle ACB = x$ and $\angle ADM = \angle ACD = y$. Hence, $\angle BAD = 180° - x - y$ from $\triangle ABD$ and $\angle BCD = x + y$. Since $\angle BAD + \angle BCD = 180°$, $ABCD$ is a cyclic quadrilateral; thus, $\angle ABM = \angle ACD = \angle ADM$. From this, $\triangle ABD$ is isosceles and $AB = AD$.

61. The diameter of the circle has length 17. Since $\triangle ABC$ is right, its sides must satisfy the Pythagorean Theorem so we deduce that AB and BC are 8 and 15. Since $CD = 12$, $AD = \sqrt{145}$. Applying Ptolemy's Theorem, we find $BD = (96 + 15\sqrt{145})/17$.

62. In general, we apply the law of cosines to find the diagonals as shown in an example in the text. If we try this here, we find that the cosine of the angle between the sides of length 25 and 60 is zero, so the diagonal of the quadrilateral opposite this angle is a diameter of the circle. From the Pythagorean Theorem, or noticing the Pythagorean triple $(5, 12, 13)$, we find the diameter has length **65**. The moral here is that when given the side lengths of a cyclic quadrilateral, check to see if a diagonal is a diameter by seeing if the sides satisfy $a^2 + b^2 = c^2 + d^2 = x$. Make sure you see why this ensures that the quadrilateral has a pair of right interior angles.

63. If you don't remember the basics of transformational geometry, go back to Volume 1 and review. Let the angle of rotation be α. By definition, $\angle AOA' = \alpha$. From the principles of rotation, AB and its image $A'B'$ will intersect in an angle of α, as will AC and $A'C'$. Hence, $\angle AMA' = \angle AOA' = \angle ANA'$. From the first equality, M is on a circle with A, A', and O. From the second equality, N is on a circle with A, A', and O. Hence, the five points are all on one circle.

64. Hold on to your hat. From parallel lines, vertical angles, and angle bisectors,

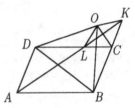

$$\begin{aligned}
\angle DLA &= \angle CLK \text{ (vertical angles)} \\
&= \angle KAB \text{ (since } DC \parallel AB) \\
&= \angle KAD \text{ (}AK \text{ bisects } \angle BAD) \\
&= \angle AKB \text{ (since } AD \parallel KB)
\end{aligned}$$

From these equalities triangles CLK, DLA, and ABK are isosceles, so $LC = CK$, $AD = DL$, and $DC = AB = BK$. Since we also have $OL = OC = OK$, $\triangle LCO \cong \triangle CKO$ by SSS congruency, so $\angle LCO = \angle CKO$. From SAS conguence, we have $\triangle DCO \cong \triangle BKO$. Therefore, $\angle CBO = \angle CDO$ and $DBCO$ is a cyclic quadrilateral.

65. Let Q be the center of square $ABCD$. Since $\angle APB + \angle AQB = 90° + 90° = 180°$, $APBQ$ is a cyclic quadrilateral. Thus,

$$\angle APQ = \angle ABQ = \angle BAQ = \angle QPB,$$

so Q lies on the angle bisector of $\angle APB$ (since $\angle APQ = \angle QPB$). As discussed in Volume 1, any line through the center of a square bisects the area of the square (try proving this yourself).

66. Let $EFGH$ be the quadrilateral formed by connecting the midpoints of the sides of $ABCD$, where E and F are the midpoints of AB and BC, respectively. Since $\triangle EBF \sim \triangle ABC$, $EF \parallel AC$. Similarly, we can show $GH \parallel AC \parallel EF$ and $EH \parallel BD \parallel FG$. Thus, $EFGH$ is a parallelogram. If $ABCD$ is orthodiagonal, $AC \perp BD$ implies $EF \perp FG$ and $EFGH$ is a rectangle and hence cyclic. For the 'only if' part, if $EFGH$ is a cyclic parallelogram, it must be a rectangle, as its opposite angles are equal and supplementary. Since $EFGH$ is a rectangle, $ABCD$ is orthodiagonal because the diagonals of $ABCD$ are parallel to the sides of $EFGH$ and are therefore perpendicular.

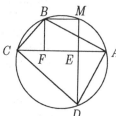

67. Since $\angle A + \angle C = 180°$, $ABCD$ is cyclic and BD is a diameter since $\angle BAD = 90°$. If we continue DE to meet the circle at M, we find that $EFBM$ is a rectangle (since $\angle DMB = 90°$, as it is inscribed in a semicircle). From the power of point E, we have $(EM)(ED) = (EC)(EA)$, so $EM = BF = \mathbf{21/5}$.

68. Since $AO \cdot CO = BO \cdot DO$, quadrilateral $ABCD$ is cyclic. Since $\triangle ABO \sim \triangle DCO$ and $\triangle BCO \sim \triangle ADO$, $CD = AB(OD/AO) = 9/2$ and $BC = AD/2$. From Ptolemy's Theorem,

$$(6)(9/2) + (AD)(AD/2) = (10)(11),$$

so $AD = \sqrt{\mathbf{166}}$.

69. Letting $AB = a$, $BC = b$, $CD = c$, and $DA = d$, we split the quadrilateral into two triangles with diagonal AC. Thus,

$$[ABCD] = \frac{1}{2}\left(ab\sin B + cd\sin D\right).$$

Squaring this we have

$$[ABCD]^2 = \frac{1}{4}\left(a^2b^2\sin^2 B + 2abcd\sin B \sin D + c^2d^2\sin^2 D\right).$$

Writing the first and last terms in terms of $\cos B$ and $\cos D$, we use the law of cosines and *lots* of algebra like that in our proof of Heron's formula to show the desired expression. If the quadrilateral is cyclic, $B + D = 180°$ and the second term in Brahmagupta's formula vanishes, leaving $[ABCD]^2 = (s-a)(s-b)(s-c)(s-d)$ for cyclic quadrilaterals.

Chapter 5

Conics and Other Curves

Solutions to Exercises

5-1 First we'll discuss the effects of varying a on the general equation $y - k = (1/4a)(x - h)^2$. First, positive a's correspond to upward opening parabolas and negative a's cause the parabola to open downward. As we increase a, $1/4a$ decreases, so larger changes must be made to x to affect y. Hence, increasing a causes the parabola to open wider. Similarly for the form $x - h = (1/4a)(y - k)^2$, negative a corresponds to leftward opening parabolas and positive a to rightward opening parabolas.

5-2 Since the axis divides the parabola in half, it must pass through the vertex. For upward or downward opening parabolas, the axis is vertical and hence has the equation $x = h$. For parabolas opening to the right or left, the equation is then $y = k$.

5-3 We'll just address the parabola $y - k = (1/4a)(x - h)^2$. The focus of this is $(h, k+a)$, so the line through the focus parallel to the directrix is $y = k + a$. To find the endpoints of the latus rectum, we let $y = k + a$ in our parabola equation, yielding $a = (1/4a)(x - h)^2$, or $x = h \pm 2a$. Hence, the endpoints of the latus rectum are $(h + 2a, k + a)$ and $(h - 2a, k + a)$, so the length of the segment is $4a$. We can use this to plot parabolas by plotting the vertex and focus, drawing the latus rectum, then drawing the curve through the endpoints of the latus rectum and the vertex.

5-4 The line is called the directrix because it determines which direction the parabola points. Pick a point as the focus, then use a few different lines (of all different slopes) as the directrix and you'll see this connection.

5-5 Completing the square, we have

$$y = (1/2)(x^2 + 6x) + 4$$

$$y + (1/2)(9) = (1/2)(x+3)^2 + 4$$
$$y = (1/2)(x+3)^2 - 1/2.$$

Hence, the parabola opens upward. The vertex is $(-3, -1/2)$, the focus is $(-3, -1/2+1/2) = (-3, 0)$ (since $1/4a = 1/2$, we find $a = 1/2$). The directrix is $y = -1/2 - 1/2 = -1$ and the length of the latus rectum is $4(1/2) = 2$.

5-6 Since the directrix is vertical and the focus is to the right of the directrix, the parabola points to the right. From the focus we have $k = 4$ and $h + a = 5/2$. From the directrix we find $h - a = 3/2$. Solving these we get $h = 2$ and $a = 1/2$. Hence, our parabola is $x - 2 = (1/2)(y - 4)^2$.

5-7 If $a = b$, we have $(x-h)^2 + (y-k)^2 = a^2$ and our ellipse is a circle, as the equation describes the set of points which are a away from (h, k). Thus, a circle is just an ellipse whose axes have the same length.

5-8 As c grows for a given a, the foci get further and further from the center and the ellipse appears more and more elongated. Hence, c/a measures how eccentric, or odd, the ellipse appears. In the case of a circle, $c = 0$ and the eccentricity of a circle, which has no elongation, is 0.

5-9 We segregate the x terms and y terms and complete the square:

$$3(x^2 - 2x) + 4(y^2 + 2y) = -3$$
$$3(x^2 - 2x + 1) + 4(y^2 + 2y + 1) = -3 + 3(1) + 4(1)$$
$$3(x - 1)^2 + 4(y + 1)^2 = 4.$$

Dividing by 4, we have

$$\frac{(x-1)^2}{4/3} + \frac{(y+1)^2}{1} = 1.$$

Since $4/3 > 1$, the major axis is parallel to the x axis. Thus, the center is $(\mathbf{1}, -\mathbf{1})$, $a = \sqrt{4/3} = 2\sqrt{3}/3$, and $b = 1$. Thus, $c = \sqrt{1/3} = \sqrt{3}/3$. The axes then have length $2a = \mathbf{4\sqrt{3}/3}$ and $2b = \mathbf{2}$. Finally, the foci have coordinates $(\mathbf{1 \pm \sqrt{3}/3, -1})$.

5-10 The only solution to the given equation is $(2, -1)$. Thus our 'ellipse' is actually only a point. If the number on the right is negative, there are no solutions since the sum of perfect squares is always nonnegative.

5-11 We'll consider the case where the major axis is parallel to the x axis:

$$\frac{(x-h)^2}{a^2} + \frac{(y-k)^2}{b^2} = 1.$$

Since the latus recti are segments on vertical lines through the foci, they have the equation $x = h \pm c$. We'll consider the line $x = h + c$. Substituting this in the above equation to find the intersection points, we have

$$\frac{c^2}{a^2} + \frac{(y-k)^2}{b^2} = 1.$$

Writing $c^2 = a^2 - b^2$, our equation becomes

$$\frac{(y-k)^2}{b^2} = \frac{b^2}{a^2}.$$

Solving for y, we find $y = k \pm (b^2/a)$. Hence, the distance between the endpoints of this latus rectum is $2b^2/a$. This also holds for the ellipse whose major axis is parallel to the y axis.

5-12 The center is the midpoint of the segment connecting the foci, so the center is $(-1, 1)$. Since the center is 4 away from each focus and the minor axis has length 4, we have $c = 4$ and $b = 2$, so $a^2 = c^2 + b^2 = 20$. Since the foci are on a horizontal line, the ellipse has major axis parallel to the x axis. Thus, our equation is

$$\frac{(x+1)^2}{20} + \frac{(y-1)^2}{4} = 1.$$

5-13 Letting $y - k = \pm\frac{b}{a}(x - h)$ in the hyperbola equation

$$\frac{(x-h)^2}{a^2} - \frac{(y-k)^2}{b^2} = 1,$$

we find $0 = 1$, which clearly can never be true. Hence, the lines $y - k = \pm\frac{b}{a}(x - h)$ never intersect the hyperbola. The lines are asymptotes because we can choose points arbitrarily close to this line which are on the hyperbola. (Why?)

5-14 By the same analysis as in the text, the center is (h, k), the vertices are a above and below the center (at $(h, k \pm a)$), the foci are $c = \sqrt{a^2 + b^2}$ above and below the center (at $(h, k \pm c)$), the transverse axis is again $2a$, the conjugate axis is $2b$, and finally, the asymptotes are $y - k = \pm\frac{a}{b}(x - h)$.

5-15 As we did with the ellipse, we'll consider the case where the transverse axis is parallel to the x axis:

$$\frac{(x-h)^2}{a^2} - \frac{(y-k)^2}{b^2} = 1.$$

As before, we consider the latus rectum on the line $x = h + c$. Substituting this in the above equation to find the intersection points, we have

$$\frac{c^2}{a^2} - \frac{(y-k)^2}{b^2} = 1.$$

Writing $c^2 = a^2 + b^2$, our equation becomes

$$\frac{(y-k)^2}{b^2} = \frac{b^2}{a^2}.$$

Solving for y, we find $y = k \pm (b^2/a)$. Hence, the distance between the endpoints of this latus rectum is $2b^2/a$.

5-16 First, no point on a coordinate axis can lie on $xy = c$ for nonzero c since if either x or y is zero then we cannot solve for the other. This alone does not mean the axes are asymptotes. We must show that the hyperbola comes arbitrarily close to the asymptotes. This is easily done by noting that we can choose arbitrarily small x and find y as c/x so that (x, y) is on the hyperbola. Hence we can find points on the hyperbola arbitrarily close to the y axis and similarly for the x axis.

5-17 The midpoint of the segment connecting the vertices is the center of the hyperbola, so the center is $(-2, -1)$. Since the vertices are on a vertical line, the hyperbola opens up and down. Since the vertices are $2\sqrt{2}$ from the center, $a = 2\sqrt{2}$. Since the conjugate axis has length 4, $b = 2$. Thus, our hyperbola is

$$\frac{(y+1)^2}{8} - \frac{(x+2)^2}{4} = 1.$$

5-18 For $(6, -6\sqrt{3})$ we have $r = \sqrt{36 + 108} = 12$, and $\theta = \tan^{-1}(-\sqrt{3})$. Since the point is in the fourth quadrant, we have $\theta = 300°$. Hence, the point is $(\mathbf{12, 300°})$. For the polar point $(-2, 405°)$ (remember, negative radii are perfectly ok), we have $x = r\cos\theta = (-2)\cos 405° = -\sqrt{2}$ and $y = (-2)\sin 405° = -\sqrt{2}$. Thus, our point is $(-\sqrt{2}, -\sqrt{2})$.

5-19 From $x = r\cos\theta$ and $y = r\sin\theta$, we have

$$\begin{aligned} 6(r\cos\theta)(r\sin\theta) &= 8 \\ 3r^2(2\cos\theta\sin\theta) &= 8 \\ 3r^2\sin 2\theta &= 8 \end{aligned}$$

as the polar equation.

5-20 For the first equation, we multiply by $\cos\theta$ and find $r\cos\theta = 4$, so $x = 4$ is the rectangular form. For the second, we multiply both sides by r to get r^2 on one side and $r\sin\theta = y$ on the other, resulting in $x^2 + y^2 = 3y$.

5-21 Horizontal lines are of the form $y = a$, which are $r\sin\theta = a$ in polar form and vertical lines are $x = b$, or $r\cos\theta = b$ in polar form. As discussed in Volume 1, lines through the origin are $\theta = c$, a constant.

5-22 Multiplying both sides by r to force r^2, $r\cos\theta$, and $r\sin\theta$ terms, we have

$$\begin{aligned} r^2 &= ar\sin\theta + br\cos\theta \\ x^2 + y^2 &= ay + bx. \end{aligned}$$

This rectangular form describes a circle.

   5-23   In our equations for (x, y) and (x', y') let $\theta = \alpha + \beta$, so that $x = r \cos \theta$, $y = r \sin \theta$, and $\beta = \theta - \alpha$. Thus, we can write

$$
\begin{aligned}
x' &= r \cos(\theta - \alpha) = r \cos \theta \cos \alpha + r \sin \theta \sin \alpha = x \cos \alpha + y \sin \alpha \\
y' &= r \sin(\theta - \alpha) = r \sin \theta \cos \alpha - r \cos \theta \sin \alpha = y \cos \alpha - x \sin \alpha.
\end{aligned}
$$

   5-24   Yes. Any circle, no matter how it is oriented, can be described as the set of points equidistant from a given point. As we saw in Volume 1, the distance formula yields the form of any circle and the form cannot include an xy term. Thus, any circle can be described without an xy term.

Solutions to Problems

70. Since the asymptotes of a hyperbola intersect at the center, we deduce that the center of the hyperbola is $(4, 1)$. Since the given vertex is to the right of the center, the hyperbola opens to the right and left. Since this vertex is 2 to the right of the center, we have $a = 2$. Returning to the our asymptote, since the slopes of these lines are $\pm \frac{3}{2}$, our value of b is 3. Hence, our hyperbola is

$$
\frac{(x - 4)^2}{4} - \frac{(y - 1)^2}{9} = 1.
$$

   71. If we instead return to our form of the parabola in the text, $y - k = (1/4a)(x - h)^2$, we immediately see $h = 4$ and $k = 2$ from the vertex. Hence, we have $y - 2 = (1/4a)(x - 4)^2$. Substituting the given point $(2, 0)$ in this equation for x and y (since the point is on the curve), we find $-2 = 1/a$, so $a = -1/2$. Thus, our parabola is

$$
y = \frac{1}{4(-1/2)}(x - 4)^2 + 2 = -\frac{x^2}{2} + 4x - 6.
$$

Our answer to the problem then is $(-1/2)(4)(-6) = \mathbf{12}$.

   72. Since the distance between the centers is $\sqrt{24^2 + 7^2} =$ 25, the circles clearly do not overlap. To fully contain the two circles, the third circle must have a diameter equal to the longest segment which can be drawn with endpoints on the 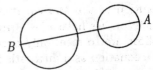 two circles. This segment is clearly the segment which passes through the two centers, as segment AB in the diagram. The length of AB is the distance between the two centers plus the two radii of the circles. (Make sure you see this.) Our desired radius is then $(25 + 3 + 4)/2 = \mathbf{16}$.

73. First, since $\sqrt{a^2 - b^2} = \sqrt{5}$ and the center of the ellipse is the origin, the points $(\pm\sqrt{5}, 0)$ are the foci of the ellipse. Hence, the two legs of the bug's path which together go from one focus to some point on the ellipse to the other focus have a total length equal to the major axis, or $2(3) = 6$. (This is from application of the constant sum of distances property of an ellipse.) The other leg of the bug's journey is just the distance between the foci, or $2\sqrt{5}$. Hence, the bug's total journey has length $\mathbf{6 + 2\sqrt{5}}$.

74. A line can intersect a hyperbola in 0, 1, or 2 points. Since we are given that the lines intersect the hyperbola, we can rule out 0. We may think that 1 is ruled out as well by the non-tangency condition, but that's not true. Consider a line parallel to one of the asymptotes. It will only meet the hyperbola in one point. If it met the hyperbola in two points, it must then also intersect the asymptote to which it is parallel, which is clearly a contradiction. Make sure you see this. Since each line intersects the hyperbola in 1 or 2 points, the possible numbers of intersections among the two lines are **2**, **3**, and **4**.

75. Let the x coordinate of A be k, so that $A = (k, -k^2/2)$. Hence, $B = (-k, -k^2/2)$ (why?) and the sides of the triangle have length $2k$. Using the distance formula we have $OA = AB$, so

$$\sqrt{k^2 + \frac{k^4}{4}} = 2k.$$

Squaring and rearranging, we find $k^4 - 12k^2 = k^2(k^2 - 12) = 0$, so $k = 2\sqrt{3}$. Hence, the sides of the triangle have length $2k = \mathbf{4\sqrt{3}}$.

76. Let the center of the base be the origin of a coordinate system. From the given information, the points $(12, 0)$, $(-12, 0)$, and $(8, 18)$ are all on the parabola. Since the center of the base is directly below the vertex, the x coordinate of the vertex is 0. Hence, we can describe our parabola as $y = cx^2 + k$ for some constants c and k. Using two of our given points on the parabola, we have

$$0 = c(12^2) + k$$
$$18 = c(8^2) + k.$$

Solving for c and k, we find $c = -9/40$ and $k = 162/5$. Thus, the vertex of the parabola is $(0, 32.4)$ and the desired height is **32.4**.

77. Any intersection of the given line and the ellipse will correspond to a simultaneous solution of the two equations describing the curves. Letting $y = mx + 1$ in the ellipse equation, we have $x^2 + 4(mx + 1)^2 = 1$, so $(4m^2 + 1)x^2 + 8mx + 3 = 0$. If the line and the ellipse are to meet only once, this equation must have only one solution. Hence, we view the equation as a quadratic in x and set the discriminant equal to 0, so

$$(8m)^2 - 4(4m^2 + 1)(3) = 0,$$

or $m^2 = \mathbf{3/4}$.

78. First we multiply by $\cos\theta$ to get rid of the $\sec\theta$, yielding

$$r\cos\theta = 2 + \cos^2\theta,$$

or $x = 2 + \cos^2\theta$. Multiplying both sides of this by r^2 (to turn the $\cos^2\theta$ into x^2), we have

$$
\begin{aligned}
xr^2 &= 2r^2 + r^2\cos^2\theta \\
x(x^2 + y^2) &= 2(x^2 + y^2) + x^2.
\end{aligned}
$$

Expanding this and rearranging, we have $x^3 + xy^2 - 3x^2 - 2y^2 = 0$.

79. Since F_1F_2 is a diameter of the circle, the triangle PF_1F_2 is a right triangle. Let x and y be the lengths of PF_1 and PF_2. Hence, $[PF_1F_2] = xy/2 = 26$ and $PF_1 + PF_2 = x + y = 15$ from the constant sum property of an ellipse (remember, P is on the ellipse and F_1 and F_2 are foci). The distance between the foci is the hypotenuse of our right triangle PF_1F_2 and hence is $\sqrt{x^2 + y^2}$. As discussed at length in Volume 1, we can find $x^2 + y^2$ as $x^2 + y^2 = (x + y)^2 - 2xy = 225 - 104 = 121$, so the desired distance is $\sqrt{121} = \mathbf{11}$.

80. Seeing distances and equations involved, we think to try analytic geometry. We let $A = (0, 1)$, $B = (0, 0)$, $C = (1, 0)$, and $D = (1, 1)$. Our condition $u^2 + v^2 = w^2$ then becomes

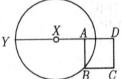

$$
\begin{aligned}
AP^2 + BP^2 &= CP^2 \\
x^2 + (y - 1)^2 + x^2 + y^2 &= (x - 1)^2 + y^2 \\
x^2 + 2x + (y - 1)^2 &= 1 \\
(x + 1)^2 + (y - 1)^2 &= 2.
\end{aligned}
$$

This describes a circle of radius $\sqrt{2}$ centered at $(-1, 1)$, or point X in the diagram. Any point on this circle can serve as P in the problem. The one furthest from D is found by drawing the line from D through the center of the circle meeting the circle again at Y as shown. Our desired distance is then $DX + XY = \mathbf{2 + \sqrt{2}}$.

81. Let the foci of the ellipse be X and Y and one point of tangency be P, where the circle has center X. One special property of an ellipse (and one of the reasons for the name foci for these special points) is that if we throw a ball from one focus and hit the ellipse, it will rebound directly to the other focus! Think about why this occurs. Hence, if we through a ball from X to P, it will rebound straight to Y. Since P is on the circle with X as its center, a ball thrown from X to P must go right back through X as well. The only way these can both be true is if X, Y, and P are all collinear, i.e. P is an endpoint of the major axis and the circle is 'fits' into the end of the ellipse. The point of tangency then is endpoint of the major axis. If we let C be the center of the ellipse, we then have $CP = 5$ and $CX = \sqrt{5^2 - 4^2} = 3$, so the radius of the resulting circle is $XP = \mathbf{2}$.

82. The given equations describe a hyperbola and a circle with the same center. Hence, we can take considerable advantage of the symmetry of the resulting figure. Let the points of intersection in order be A, B, C, and D, where A and B are one branch of the hyperbola and C and D are on the other. By symmetry, we must have $AB = CD$, $AD = BC$, and $AC = BD$. Hence, our quadrilateral $ABCD$ is a parallelogram with equal diagonals, which we know better as a **rectangle**. (By inspection of the equations, we can also find the solutions as $(3,4)$, $(4,3)$, $(-3,-4)$, $(-4,-3)$, but our intuitive approach is more interesting.)

83. Since the circle is tangent to both sides of the parabola, we deduce that its center is on the y axis. Thus, the circle can be described by $x^2 + (y - k)^2 = r^2$, where the center is $(0,k)$ and the radius is r. The points of intersection of this and the parabola $y = x^2$ are found by making this substitution in our circle equation, or

$$x^2 + (x^2 - k)^2 = r^2.$$

Writing this as a quadratic in x^2 and applying the quadratic formula, we have the equation $x^4 + (1 - 2k)x^2 + k^2 - r^2 = 0$, so

$$x^2 = \frac{2k - 1 \pm \sqrt{(2k - 1)^2 - 4(k^2 - r^2)}}{2}.$$

Since the points of tangency will clearly have the same y value and opposite x values, there can be only 1 distinct value for x^2. Hence, the discriminant above must be 0, leaving $x^2 = k - 1/2$. Since $y = x^2$, we have $y = k - 1/2$ as the y coordinate of the intersection point. Since the y coordinate of the center of the circle is k, the center is $k - (k - 1/2) = \mathbf{1/2}$ above the intersection point.

Chapter 6

Polynomials

Solutions to Exercises

6-1 To prove that these polynomials are unique, we show that if there is any pair of polynomials $\big(q'(x), r'(x)\big)$ which satisfy the conditions in the text for $q(x)$ and $r(x)$, then these must be equal to q and r. Thus, we have

$$f(x) = q(x)g(x) + r(x) = q'(x)g(x) + r'(x).$$

Rearranging this gives

$$\big(q(x) - q'(x)\big)g(x) = r'(x) - r(x).$$

Now, if $q(x) \neq q'(x)$, then the degree of the left-hand side of this equality is at least $\deg g$, while the degree of the right-hand side is at most $\deg r$. Since $\deg r < \deg g$, the degree of the left-hand side is always greater than that of the right-hand side, so the polynomials cannot be identical. Thus, we cannot have $q(x) \neq q'(x)$, so $q(x) = q'(x)$. This gives us

$$\big(q(x) - q'(x)\big)g(x) = (0)f(x) = 0 = r'(x) - r(x),$$

so $r(x) = r'(x)$ and the proof of uniqueness is complete.

6-2 Performing the synthetic division, we have

$$
\begin{array}{r|rrrrrr}
-3 & 1 & 3 & 2 & -1 & 1 & -7 \\
   &   & -3 & 0 & -6 & 21 & -66 \\
\hline
   & 1 & 0 & 2 & -7 & 22 & -73
\end{array}
$$

Hence, we find

$$\frac{x^5 + 3x^4 + 2x^3 - x^2 + x - 7}{x + 3} = x^4 + 2x^2 - 7x + 22 - \frac{73}{x + 3}.$$

6-3   Let $f(x)$ be the given polynomial. Since we clearly have $f(1) = 0$, we know $x = 1$ is a root. Performing synthetic division, we find that $f(x) = (x-1)(x^3 + 2x^2 + 4x + 21)$. Since the signs of the coefficients of the second factor are all positive, it has no positive roots. Thus we try $x = -1$, which fails, then $x = -3$ (skipping $x = -2$ because it's disallowed by the Rational Root Theorem). This works and we find $f(x) = (x-1)(x+3)(x^2 - x + 7)$. Hence, two of the roots are **1** and **−3**. The other two are the solutions of the quadratic $x^2 - x + 7 = 0$. We can't factor this, but from the quadratic formula, we find the roots $x = (1 \pm 3i\sqrt{3})/2$.

6-4   The other roots are simply $3 + i$ and $4 - \sqrt{2}$ as discussed in the text.

6-5   The first step is showing that our assertion is true for $n = 1$. This is quite simple, as we can only have $k = 1$. The assertion states that the sum of the roots of $a_1 x + a_0$ is $-a_0/a_1$. Since this is, in fact, the only root, it is indeed the sum of the roots.

Now we move to the inductive step. We assume that the assertion is true for $n = m$. Consider $f(x) = a_{m+1} x^{m+1} + \cdots + a_0$. We can factor this as

$$f(x) = a_{m+1}(x - r_{m+1})g(x)$$

where $g(x)$ is a degree m monic polynomial. As per our assertion, which we assume is true for all polynomials of degree m, we can write $g(x)$ in terms of its roots:

$$g(x) = x^m - (r_1 + \cdots + r_m)x^{m-1} + (r_1 r_2 + \cdots + r_{m-1} r_m)x^{m-2} + \cdots + (-1)^m r_1 r_2 \cdots r_m.$$

Thus, we can write $f(x)$ as

$$f(x) = a_{m+1}(x - r_{m+1})\big(x^m - (r_1 + \cdots + r_m)x^{m-1} + \cdots + (-1)^m r_1 r_2 r_3 \cdots r_m\big).$$

It is very important that you multiply this out for yourself and see that the product is indeed the expression we have below. Carry out the product by considering the coefficient of x^k in the product. It is the result of multiplying the coefficient of x^k in $g(x)$ by r_{n+1} and adding this to x times the coefficient of x^{k-1} of $g(x)$. Don't be intimidated by this product, it is very similar to multiplying out $(x+1)(x^3 + x^2 + x + 1)$. We find

$$f(x) = a_{m+1}\big(x^{m+1} - (r_1 + \cdots + r_{m+1})x^m + \cdots + (-1)^{m+1} r_1 r_2 r_3 \cdots r_{m+1}\big).$$

We see that $f(x)$ satisfies our assertion, so we have completed our induction. If you don't see that $f(x)$ satisfies the assertion, look at the coefficient of x^m. It is the negative of the sum of the roots of $f(x)$. Similarly, the coefficient of x^{m-1} is the 2nd symmetric sum of the roots and so on.

6-6   Factoring the polynomial will work, but it will take a while. Let's try to use the given information. Let the roots be a, b, and c, where $(a+b)/2 = c$ since one root is the average of the other two. From the given polynomial, $a + b + c = 27$, or $2c + c = 27$, so $c = 9$.

Then the other two roots are a and $18 - a$, and we can use the polynomial's constant term to write $a(18 - a)(9) = 720$, so $a = 8$ or 10. Either way, the three roots of the polynomial are 8, 9, and **10**.

6-7 The desired polynomial has roots which are reciprocals of the polynomial whose roots are $a + 3$, $b + 3$, and $c + 3$. This latter polynomial is

$$f(x - 3) = 3(x - 3)^3 - 14(x - 3)^2 + (x - 3) + 62 = 3x^3 - 41x^2 + 166x - 148.$$

(We could also use our synthetic division technique to determine this polynomial.) We find the polynomial whose roots are the reciprocals of those of $f(x - 3)$ by reversing the coefficients of $f(x - 3)$, finding

$$-148x^3 + 166x^2 - 41x + 3.$$

The sum of the roots of this polynomial is

$$\frac{1}{a + 3} + \frac{1}{b + 3} + \frac{1}{c + 3} = -\frac{166}{-148} = \frac{83}{74}.$$

6-8 If $n < k$, then several of the a_i in $a_n s_k + a_{n-1} s_{k-1} + \cdots + k a_{n-k}$ are 0 since $i < 0$. Eliminating these terms we are left with $a_n s_k + a_{n-1} s_{k-1} + \cdots + a_0 s_{k-n} = 0$.

6-9 Use Newton sums again:

$$2s_1 + 3 = 0, \quad s_1 = -\frac{3}{2};$$

$$2s_2 + 3s_1 + 2(1) = 0, \quad s_2 = \frac{5}{4};$$

$$2s_3 + 3s_2 + s_1 + 3(-4) = 0 \quad s_3 = \frac{39}{8}.$$

Solutions to Problems

84. Let $f(x) = x^{13} + 1$. The remainder is $f(1) = 2$.

85. First we use the Rational Root Theorem to decide what numbers could possibly be roots. After trying a few (usually start with the integers) using synthetic division, we finally find that $y = 3$ is a solution and

$$f(y) = 2y^4 - 9y^3 + 14y^2 + 6y - 63 = (y - 3)(2y^3 - 3y^2 + 5y + 21).$$

Now we go on trying to find the roots of $2y^3 - 3y^2 + 5y + 21$. Eventually you should find that $y = -3/2$ is a solution (you might have found that first) and that

$$f(y) = (y - 3)(y + 3/2)(2y^2 - 6y + 14),$$

so we can use the quadratic formula on the final quadratic to get the last two roots. Hence the roots are **3**, **-3/2**, and $(\mathbf{3 \pm i\sqrt{19}})/\mathbf{2}$.

86. Let $f(x) = x^3 + 3m^2x^2 + mx + 4$. The binomial $x + 2$ is a factor of this polynomial if and only if $f(-2) = 0$, so we have

$$-8 + 12m^2 - 2m + 4 = 0.$$

Solving this equation for m, we find that $x + 2$ is a factor of $f(x)$ if and only if $m = -1/2$ or $m = 2/3$.

87. The nth roots of 1 are solutions to the polynomial $x^n = 1$, or $x^n - 1 = 0$. The product of the roots of this polynomial is $(-1)^n(-1) = (-1)^{n+1}$.

88. Let the doubled roots be r and s. From the coefficient of x^3, we have $2r + 2s = 16$, or $r + s = 8$. From the coefficient of x^2 we find $r^2 + s^2 + 4rs = 94$. Since $p = -(2r^2s + 2rs^2) = -2rs(r + s)$ and $q = r^2s^2$, if we find rs and $r + s$, we find p and q. We already have $r + s$, and we can find rs by squaring $r + s = 8$ to get $r^2 + 2rs + s^2 = 64$. Subtracting this from $r^2 + s^2 + 4rs = 94$, we find $2rs = 30$, so $rs = 15$. Hence, $p = -30(8) = -240$ and $q = 15^2 = 225$, so $p + q = -\mathbf{15}$.

89. From our given information, we have

$$f(-7) = -a7^7 - b7^3 - c7 - 5 = 7,$$

so $a7^7 + b7^3 + c7 = -12$. Thus, $f(7) = a7^7 + b7^3 + c7 - 5 = -12 - 5 = -\mathbf{17}$.

90. Let the roots be r, s, and t. From the coefficient of x^2, we have $r + s + t = -[(-12)/4] = 3$. Since $r + s = 0$, we find $t = 3$. Hence, $c = rs + st + tr = rs + 3(r + s) = rs$ and $d = -rst = -3rs$. Thus, $d/c = -3rs/rs = -\mathbf{3}$.

91. There are a lot of really long ways to do this, but here we'll show you a clever method involving the understanding of polynomials. Let $f(x)$ be the given polynomial. Note that $f(1) = 1 + A + B + C + D$, so if we can find $f(1)$, we can find the answer. The two roots $3 \pm \sqrt{2}$ have sum 6 and product 7, so they're the roots of $x^2 - 6x + 7$. Similarly, $-3 \pm i\sqrt{2}$ are the roots of $x^2 + 6x + 11$, so $f(x) = (x^2 - 6x + 7)(x^2 + 6x + 11)$ and $f(1) = 2(18) = 36$. Since as we noted above we have $A + B + C + D = f(1) - 1$, our answer is **35**.

92. Since $P(x)$ has only terms of odd degree, it is an odd function. (Remember odd functions from Volume 1?) Thus, $P(-x) = -P(x)$. Since $P(3) = 6$, we have $P(-3) = -6$. Now we finish this as we did a similar example in the text:

$$P(x) = (x^2 - 9)g(x) + r(x).$$

Since $\deg r(x) < \deg(x^2 - 9)$, $r(x) = ax + b$, and putting 3 and -3 in the above equation for $P(x)$, we find $6 = 0 + 3a + b$ and $-6 = 0 - 3a + b$, so $b = 0$ and $a = 2$. The desired remainder is **$2x$**.

93. Note that for any even number, all the terms in the polynomial are even except the last term. Hence, since $p(0) = a_0$ is odd, $p(2N)$ is odd for all N. Similarly, all $p(2N + 1)$ have the same parity (meaning they're all odd or all even), so since $p(1)$ is odd, $p(2N+1)$ is odd for all N. Since for all integers n, $p(n)$ is odd, there are no integer roots of $p(x)$ (since 0 is even).

94. Since we have a quartic (degree four polynomial) divided by a cubic, the quotient must be a simple linear term like $x + a$. Multiplying this and the given cubic we have

$$(x + a)(x^3 + 3x^2 + 9x + 3) = x^4 + (3 + a)x^3 + (3a + 9)x^2 + (9a + 3)x + 3a.$$

Since this equals the given quartic, we have

$$x^4 + 4x^3 + 6px^2 + 4qx + r = x^4 + (3 + a)x^3 + (3a + 9)x^2 + (9a + 3)x + 3a.$$

Matching coefficients of x^3, we have $a = 1$. Matching coefficients of x^2, we have $6p = 12$, or $p = 2$. From x we get $q = 12/4 = 3$, and from the constants, $r = 3$. Hence, the answer is $(2 + 3)3 = \mathbf{15}$.

95. The desired expression is the sum of the squares of the reciprocals of the roots. We find the polynomial whose roots are the reciprocals of the roots of the original polynomial by reversing the order of the coefficients of the original polynomial, or

$$-7x^3 + 5x^2 - 6x + 1 = 0.$$

Our desired sum is the sum of the squares of the roots of this new polynomial. We use Newton's sums to get sums of powers of roots, so $a_3 s_1 + a_2 = 0$ gives $s_1 = 5/7$. The next one is $a_3 s_2 + a_2 s_1 + 2a_1 = 0$, so $-7s_2 + 25/7 - 12 = 0$, and $s_2 = \mathbf{-59/49}$.

96. We'll approach this in much the same way we proved that complex roots of polynomials with real coefficients always come in conjugate pairs. The given x is a solution to the polynomial, so we have

$$f(x) = c_4 x^4 + i c_3 x^3 + c_2 x^2 + i c_1 x + c_0 = 0.$$

Taking the conjugate of both sides, we have (remembering that $\overline{i} = -i$)

$$\begin{aligned}
0 &= \overline{c_4 x^4 + i c_3 x^3 + c_2 x^2 + i c_1 x + c_0} \\
&= \overline{c_4 x^4} + \overline{i c_3 x^3} + \overline{c_2 x^2} + \overline{i c_1 x} + \overline{c_0} \\
&= c_4 (\overline{x})^4 - i c_3 (\overline{x})^3 + c_2 (\overline{x})^2 - i c_1 \overline{x} + c_0
\end{aligned}$$

Make sure you recognize this last line as $f(-\overline{x})$; if you don't, try putting $-\overline{x}$ in the original polynomial. Hence, if x is a root, so is $-\overline{x}$, so $-(a - bi) = -a + \mathbf{b}i$ is a solution.

97. Let $f(x) = x^8$. Since $f(-1/2) = (-1/2)^8$, the remainder upon dividing $x + 1/2$ into $f(x)$ is $r_1 = (-1/2)^8 = (1/2)^8$, so we can write

$$f(x) = x^8 = (x + 1/2)q_1 + (1/2)^8.$$

Thus, .

$$
\begin{aligned}
(x + 1/2)q_1 &= x^8 - (1/2)^8 \\
&= [x^4 - (1/2)^4][x^4 + (1/2)^4] \\
&= [x^2 - (1/2)^2][x^2 + (1/2)^2][x^4 + (1/2)^4] \\
&= [x - 1/2][x + 1/2][x^2 + (1/2)^2][x^4 + (1/2)^4].
\end{aligned}
$$

Dividing by $x + 1/2$, we get

$$q_1(x) = [x - 1/2][x^2 + (1/2)^2][x^4 + (1/2)^4].$$

Thus, our remainder upon dividing $q_1(x)$ by $x + 1/2$ is $q_1(-1/2) = -1/16$.

98. This one's pretty tricky. We can rearrange the given equation as $(x + 1)(x + 4)(x + 2)(x + 3) + 1 = 0$, which has the advantage that the product of the first two terms has the same x coefficient as the product of the last two terms:

$$(x^2 + 5x + 4)(x^2 + 5x + 6) + 1 = 0$$

If we let t be the $x^2 + 5x$ common to our quadratics, we have $(t+4)(t+6)+1 = t^2+10t+25 = (t+5)^2 = 0$. Thus, $t = -5$ and solving $x^2 + 5x = -5$ gives the two roots $(-5 \pm \sqrt{5})/2$, both of which are double roots of the polynomial.

99. We can get the sum of all the a_i by just letting $x = 1$:

$$(1 + 1 + 1)^n = a_0 + a_1 + a_2 + \cdots + a_{2n}.$$

Now we need to get rid of the odd numbered terms. This suggests putting in $x = -1$, since then the odd numbered terms will be subtracted:

$$(1 - 1 + 1)^n = a_0 - a_1 + a_2 - a_3 + \cdots + a_{2n}.$$

Adding this to the first equality, we find

$$3^n + 1 = 2(a_0 + a_2 + a_4 + \cdots + a_{2n}).$$

Thus, the desired sum is $(3^n + 1)/2$. Remember the 'sticking numbers in' method for attacking polynomial problems. It is often very useful, especially when we are looking for the sum of coefficients of a polynomial, which is just the polynomial evaluated at $x = 1$.

100. As we've done many times before, we write

$$x^{203} - 1 = (x^4 - 1)g(x) + r(x),$$

where $\deg r(x) < 4$, so we can write $r(x) = ax^3 + bx^2 + cx + d$. We put in the roots of $x^4 - 1$ for x, making $(x^4 - 1)g(x) = 0$. These roots are 1, -1, i, and $-i$ (since $x^4 - 1 = (x^2 - 1)(x^2 + 1)$); trying each of these in turn, we have

$$
\begin{aligned}
0 &= a + b + c + d \\
-2 &= -a + b - c + d \\
-i - 1 &= -ai - b + ci + d \\
i - 1 &= ai - b - ci + d.
\end{aligned}
$$

If we add the first two equations, we get $b + d = -1$. Equating real parts of the last equation, we have $d - b = -1$. Adding these two gives $d = -1$, so $b = 0$. Similarly, subtracting the second equation from the first gives $a + c = 1$ and equating imaginary parts of the last equation gives $a - c = 1$. From these we find $a = 1$ and $c = 0$. Hence the remainder is $x^3 - 1$.

101. Seeing the expression $x^2 - 3x - 2$ in the first equation, we write $x^2 - 4x - 2 = 0$ as $x^2 - 3x - 2 = x$. If $x^2 - 3x - 2 = x$, we have

$$
\begin{aligned}
\left(x^2 - 3x - 2\right)^2 - 3(x^2 - 3x - 2) - 2 - x &= x^2 - 3x - 2 - x \\
&= x - x = 0,
\end{aligned}
$$

so all solutions to $x^2 - 3x - 2 = x$ are solutions to the given polynomial. Multiplying out the given polynomial, we find it is $x^4 - 6x^3 + 2x^2 + 20x + 8 = 0$. Since we know $x^2 - 4x - 2$ is one factor, we can write

$$
\begin{aligned}
x^4 - 6x^3 + 2x^2 + 20x + 8 &= (x^2 - 4x - 2)(x^2 + ax + b) \\
&= x^4 + (a - 4)x^3 + (b - 2 - 4a)x^2 - (4b + 2a)x - 2b.
\end{aligned}
$$

Matching coefficients of the polynomials, we find $a = -2$ and $b = -4$, so the solutions of the initial polynomial equation are the roots of $x^2 - 4x - 2$ and $x^2 - 2x - 4$, or $2 \pm \sqrt{6}$ and $1 \pm \sqrt{5}$.

102. Since P is a polynomial, it is either constant or it takes on infinitely many values. For the first case, we have $c = c^k$, so either $k = 1$ and c is arbitrary or $k > 1$ and $c = 0$ or 1. For non-constant $P(x)$, let $z = P(x)$. We then have $P(z) = z^k$ for infinitely many values of z. Hence the polynomial $P(z) - z^k$ has infinitely many roots but a finite degree, so the polynomial must be zero everywhere, or $P(z) - z^k = 0$, so that $P(x) = x^k$ is the only family of non-constant polynomials which solve the given equation.

103. From the coefficient of x^3, $a + b + c + d = 0$, so $a + b + c = -d$, and $(a + b + c)/d^2 = -1/d$. Proceeding similarly, the roots of the desired polynomial are $-1/a$, $-1/b$, $-1/c$, and $-1/d$.

The polynomial with roots $1/a$, $1/b$, $1/c$, and $1/d$ is found by reversing the coefficients of the original polynomial, to get $-3x^4 - bx^3 + 1 = 0$. The equation which has roots which are c times those of $f(x) = -3x^4 - bx^3 + 1$ is $f(x/c)$ (remember this from the chapter?). Hence, one polynomial with the given roots is $f(-x) = -3x^4 + bx^3 + 1$; we want the leading term to be 3, so we multiply by -1, giving $3x^4 - bx^3 - 1$.

104. Since $g(x)h(x) = f(x)$, we have, for all a_1, a_2, ..., a_n, $g(a_i)h(a_i) = f(a_i) = -1$. Since $g(a_i)$ and $h(a_i)$ are integers (why?), the two must be 1 and -1. Hence, $g(a_i)+h(a_i) = 0$ for each i, so that $q(x) = g(x) + h(x) = 0$ has n distinct roots. Since $g(x)h(x) = f(x)$, we have $\deg g(x)h(x) = \deg f(x) = n$. Because $g(x)$ and $h(x)$ are nonconstant, neither g nor h has degree larger than $n - 1$. Hence, $q(x) = g(x) + h(x)$ has no terms of x^n or higher degree. Since $\deg q(x) < n$, $q(x)$ has less than n factors and thus less than n roots. This is a contradiction to the above proof that $g(x) + h(x)$ has the n distinct a_i as roots. Hence, we cannot factor $f(x)$ as stated in the problem.

Chapter 7

Functions

Solutions to Exercises

7-1 We let the inverse function be $g(x)$, so that $f(g(x)) = \sqrt[3]{g(x)} = x$. Cubing both sides, we have $g(x) = x^3$.

7-2 We should have $f^0 \circ f^1(x) = f^1(x)$ if the composition exponents are to add properly. But $f^0 \circ f^1(x) = f^0(f^1(x))$; setting this equal to $f^1(x)$ yields $f^0(f^1(x)) = f^1(x)$. The only way this can be satisfied is if $f^0(x) = x$. This is *not* the same as $[f(x)]^0 = 1$.

7-3 For the first, assume there are two numbers x and y such that $f(x) = f(y)$, or $x^3 = y^3$, or $(x-y)(x^2 + xy + y^2) = 0$. The only way this can be solved is if $x = y$ or (using the quadratic formula) $x = -y(1 \pm \sqrt{3}\,i)/2$. Since the latter is ruled out because not both x and y can be real, we must have $x = y$. Thus $f(x) = x^3$ is $1:1$.

The second is not $1:1$ since, for example, $g(2) = g(-2) = 2$.

The third is not $1:1$ since, for example, $h(1) = h(1.5) = 1$.

The fourth is $1:1$ since if $j(x) = j(y)$, we have $x/2 = y/2$, or $x = y$.

7-4 With $f(x) = \sin x$ and $g(x) = \cos x$, we have $f(x+y) = \sin(x+y) = \sin x \cos y + \sin y \cos x = f(x)g(y) + f(y)g(x)$, so the first identity holds. We also have $[f(x)]^2 + [g(x)]^2 = \sin^2 x + \cos^2 x = 1$, so the second identity holds as well.

7-5 The first identity is $|xy| = |x||y|$. We look at three cases. If both x and y are positive, then xy is as well, so we have $|xy| = xy = |x||y|$. If exactly one of x and y is negative, then xy is negative, so we have $|xy| = -xy = |x||y|$. If both x and y are negative, then xy is positive, so we have $|xy| = xy = (-x)(-y) = |x||y|$. In all three cases the identity holds.

We can easily disprove the second identity by taking $x = 1$ and $y = -1$. This yields $f(x+y) = |x+y| = |1-1| = |0| = 0$ and $f(x) + f(y) = |x| + |y| = |1| + |-1| = 1 + 1 = 2$. The two are clearly not equal.

The third identity is false because $x = -1$ yields $f(f(x)) = |1| = 1 \neq -1$.

7-6

i. If n and x are integers, then nx and x are integers, so $\lfloor nx \rfloor = nx$ and $n\lfloor x \rfloor = nx$—the identity holds.

ii. Let $x = 1.5$ and $n = 2$. Then $\lfloor nx \rfloor = \lfloor 3 \rfloor = 3$ and $n\lfloor x \rfloor = 2\lfloor 1.5 \rfloor = 2(1) = 2$. The two are not equal, so the identity does not hold.

iii. This case allows the same values of n and x as the previous case, so the identity cannot hold in this case either.

7-7 $f(x) = x$ satisfies many, many identities; see how many you can come up with. A few are $f(x+y) = f(x) + f(y)$, $f(nx) = nf(x)$ for any n, $f(xy) = f(x)f(y)$, and $f(f(x)) = x$.

7-8 For $f(x) = cx$, we have $f(xy) = cxy$ and $xf(y) = xcy$. Since $cxy = xcy$, the identity holds for any c.

7-9 Substituting $y = 0$ yields $f(x) + f(x) = 2f(x) = 2x^2$. Thus $f(x) = x^2$ is the only possible solution. Trying this solution in the original equation, we have $f(x+y) + f(x-y) = 2x^2 + 2y^2$, not $2x^2 - 2y^2$. Thus our only candidate fails the test, and there are **no solutions**.

7-10

i. Let's start iterating the function. We have

$$f(x) = x + \frac{1}{x}$$

$$f(f(x)) = f(x) + \frac{1}{f(x)} = x + \frac{1}{x} + \frac{1}{x + \frac{1}{x}} = \frac{x^4 + 3x^2 + 1}{x^3 + x}.$$

This, it is fairly clear, is not going anywhere. (Not quite a proof.)

ii. We have

$$f(x) = \frac{x}{x-1}$$

$$f(f(x)) = \frac{\frac{x}{x-1}}{\frac{x}{x-1} - 1} = x.$$

Thus, $f(x) = x/(x-1)$ is cyclic and has order 2.

iii. We have

$$f(x) = \frac{1}{1+x}$$

$$f(f(x)) = \frac{1}{1+f(x)} = \frac{1}{1+\frac{1}{1+x}} = \frac{x+1}{x+2}$$

$$f(f(f(x))) = \frac{f(x)+1}{f(x)+2} = \frac{\frac{1}{1+x}+1}{\frac{1}{1+x}+2} = \frac{2+x}{3+2x}$$

and it is clear that this function is again not cyclic.

iv. We have

$$f(x) = 1-x$$
$$f(f(x)) = 1-(1-x) = x$$

and thus the function is cyclic and has order 2.

7-11 For $h(x) = x^2$, we get $f(x) = (x-1/2)^2 + x$. With this function f, we have

$$f((1+a)/2) = (a/2)^2 + (a/2+1)$$

and

$$f((1-a)/2) + a = (-a/2)^2 + (1-a/2) + a = (a/2)^2 + (a/2+1).$$

Thus, we have $f((1+a)/2) = f((1-a)/2)+a$, so $f(x)$ satisfies the given functional equation.

Solutions to Problems

105. Substituting $y = 2x$, we have $f(y) = 2/(2+y/2)$, so $2f(y) = 4/(2+y/2) = 8/(4+y)$. Thus $2f(x) = 8/(4+x)$.

106. We just write $f(g(x)) = f(2x) = 4/(2x-1)$ and $g(f(x)) = g(4/(x-1)) = 8/(x-1)$. Setting the two equal and solving the resulting linear equation, we find $x = 1/3$ as the only solution.

107. Let $a = 17/2$ and $x = 2$, so that $f(17) = 17f(2)/2 = 17(5)/2 = \mathbf{85/2}$.

108. Substituting in $y = 0$ yields $2f(x) = 2$, so the only possible candidate is $f(x) = 1$. Substituting this into the given functional equation yields $2 = y + 2$, which is not true for all y. Thus the given functional equation has **no solutions**.

109. Rearranging, we have $xf(x) = yf(y)$. If this is to hold for all x and y, we must have $xf(x) = c$ for some constant c. Thus $f(x) = c/x$, for constants c, are the only possible solutions. Substituting this into the equation, we find that $f(x) = c/x$ is a solution for any c.

110. To find $y = f^{-1}(-2)$, we write $-2 = f(y) = 1/(y+2)$, to get $y = -5/2$. We then have $g(f^{-1}(-2)) = g(-5/2) = \mathbf{3}$.

111. We write $y = f(x) = x/(1-x)$, so that $x = y/(1+y)$. Examining the answers, we see that $y/(1+y)$ can be rewritten as $-\mathbf{f(-y)}$.

112. Let's try them. For the first, the composition of $f(x) = ax + b$ and $g(x) = cx + d$ is $a(cx + d) + b = acx + (ad + b)$, which is clearly another function in the set. For the second, the composition of $f(x) = ax^2 + \cdots$ and $g(x) = bx^2 + \cdots$ is $a(bx^2 + \cdots)^2 + \cdots = ab^2x^4 + \cdots$, which is clearly not in the set. For the third, $f(g(x))$ is clearly a polynomial if f and g are both polynomials. For the fourth, $f(g(12)) = f(0)$, which is not necessarily 0, since 0 is not necessarily a root of f; thus 12 is not necessarily a root of $f \circ g$. Thus **two** of the given sets, the first and third, have the desired property.

113. Let $y = ax$; then $f(y) = f(ax) = \log_a x = \log_a(y/a) = \log_a y - 1$, or $f(x) = \log_a x - 1$.

114. We use the cyclic function $1/x$, substituting $x \to 1/x$ in the given equation to get the pair of equations

$$21f(x) - 7f\left(\frac{1}{x}\right) = 12x$$

$$21f\left(\frac{1}{x}\right) - 7f(x) = 12/x.$$

Adding three times the first equation to the second to eliminate $f(1/x)$, we have $56f(x) = 36x + 12/x$, or $f(x) = (9x + 3/x)/14$. Substituting this into the functional equation, we find that it is a solution; it is the only solution.

115. To find $f(1/2)$, we need to find x such that $g(x) = 1 - x^2 = 1/2$. Solving, we find $x = 1/\sqrt{2}$. Thus $f(1/2) = f(g(1/\sqrt{2})) = (1 - (1/\sqrt{2})^2)/(1/\sqrt{2})^2 = (1 - 1/2)/(1/2) = \mathbf{1}$.

116. From $f(x) = f(2a)^x$, we have $f(2a) = f(2a)^{2a}$. Dividing by $f(2a)$, we find $1 = f(2a)^{2a-1}$, or $2a - 1 = 0$, or $a = \mathbf{1/2}$.

117. Substituting $a = b = 0$ yields $f(0)^2 = f(0)$, so that $f(0)$ equals 0 or 1. Since $f(x) > 0$ for all x, only $f(0) = 1$ is allowed, so I is true.

Substituting $b = -a$, we have $f(a)f(-a) = f(a - a) = f(0) = 1$, so that $f(a) = 1/f(-a)$, and II is also true.

Substituting $b = 2a$, we have $f(a)f(2a) = f(3a)$, or $f(a)^3 = f(3a)$. We thus have $f(a) = \sqrt[3]{f(3a)}$, and III is true.

One solution to the given equation is $f(x) = 1$ for all x. (Do you see why?) In this case, even though $1 > 0$, we have $f(1) = f(0)$ rather than $f(1) > f(0)$. Thus IV is not always true.

In sum, **I, II, III** are the true statements.

118. We write $\sec^2 \theta = x/(x - 1)$, yielding $x = \sec^2 \theta/(\sec^2 \theta - 1) = \sec^2 \theta/\tan^2 \theta = 1/\sin^2 \theta$. Then $f(\sec^2 \theta) = f(x/(x - 1)) = 1/x = 1/(1/\sin^2 \theta) = \sin^2 \theta$.

119. For a number x to be in the domain of $g \circ f = g(f(x))$, x must first be in the domain of f, so that $x \geq -2$. Moreover, $f(x)$ must be in the domain of g, so that $f(x) < 5$, or $x^2 + x - 1 < 5$. We thus have $x^2 + x - 6 < 0$, which yields $(x + 3)(x - 2) < 0$. The solution to this inequality is $-3 < x < 2$. Finding all joint solutions of $x \geq -2$ and $-3 < x < 2$, we have $-2 \leq x < 2$ as the domain of $g \circ f$.

120. Setting $t = x$ yields $f(2x) - f(0) = 4x^2$. Substituting $x = y/2$, we then have $f(y) - f(0) = y^2$. Letting $f(0)$ be some arbitrary constant a, we have $f(x) = x^2 + a$. Testing this function, we find that it satisfies the given functional equation for any a.

121. Substituting in $x = 5$ yields $f(-4) - 4f(5) = 5$; substituting $x = -4$ yields $f(5) + 5f(-4) = 5$. Subtracting five times the first equation from the second equation yields $21f(5) = -20$, so that $f(5) = \mathbf{-20/21}$. (Note that this solution is possible because of the cyclic nature of the function $1 - x$. Can you use this to find $f(x)$ for all x?)

122. Substituting $x = a$ into the equation $f_b(x) = 2^a f_b(x - a)$, we have $f_b(a) = 2^a f_b(0) = 2^a b$. Thus $f_b(x) = 2^x b$, so $f_c(2x) = 2^{2x} c = (c/b^2)[f_b(x)]^2$.

123. We have

$$
\begin{aligned}
f\left(\frac{3x + x^3}{1 + 3x^2}\right) &= \log\left(\frac{1 + (3x + x^3)/(1 + 3x^2)}{1 - (3x + x^3)/(1 + 3x^2)}\right) \\
&= \log\left(\frac{(x^3 + 3x^2 + 3x + 1)/(1 + 3x^2)}{(-x^3 + 3x^2 - 3x + 1)/(1 + 3x^2)}\right) \\
&= \log\left(\frac{x^3 + 3x^2 + 3x + 1}{-x^3 + 3x^2 - 3x + 1}\right) \\
&= \log\left(\frac{1 + x}{1 - x}\right)^3 \\
&= 3\log\left(\frac{1 + x}{1 - x}\right) \\
&= \mathbf{3f(x)}.
\end{aligned}
$$

124. We have $f(4x) = 4x/(4x - 1)$. To express this as a function of $f(x)$, we solve $f(x) = x/(x - 1)$ for x, so $x = f(x)/(f(x) - 1)$. Then $f(4x) = 4[f(x)/(f(x) - 1)]/[4f(x)/(f(x) - 1) - 1] = \mathbf{4f(x)/(3f(x) + 1)}$.

125. We substitute $x = 2$ to get

$$f(2) + 2f(-1) = 2.$$

Seeing $f(-1)$ above, we substitute $x = -1$ to get

$$f(-1) + 2f(1/2) = -1,$$

and then take $x = 1/2$ to get

$$f(1/2) + 2f(2) = 1/2.$$

We can solve these three equations by subtracting twice the second equation from the first to get $f(2) - 4f(1/2) = 4$, then adding four times the third equation to get $9f(2) = 6$, or

$f(2) = \mathbf{2/3}$. (Again, this solution is possible because of a cyclic function. What is the cyclic function? Can you use it to solve for $f(x)$?)

126. Setting $t = 0$ we have $f(x) = f(x) + f(0) + 2\sqrt{f(x)}\sqrt{f(0)}$. This becomes $2\sqrt{f(x)}\sqrt{f(0)} = -f(0)$, so squaring yields $4f(x) = f(0)$ as the only solution. Letting $f(0) = a$, an arbitrary constant, we have $f(x) = a/4$. Is this a solution for any $a/4$? Substituting in the functional equation yields $a/4 = a/4 + a/4 + 2(a/4) = a$, so that $a = 0$. Thus the only solution is $f(x) = 0$.

127. Substituting $x = u - 1$ and $y = 1$ yields $f(u) - f(1) = (u - 1)/u$, or $f(u) = (u - 1)/u + f(1)$. These functions, for any constant $f(1) = c$, are the only candidates. Trying $f(u) = (u-1)/u + c$ in the functional equation, we have $f(x+y) - f(y) = (x + y - 1)/(x+y) + c - (y-1)/y - c = x/y(x+y)$. Thus the function given is a solution for any c.

128. We have $f(1985) = -1984 - 2f(1984)$, $f(1984) = 1983 - 2f(1983)$, $f(1983) = -1982 - 2f(1982),\ldots$, $f(2) = 1 - 2f(1)$, $f(1) = f(1986) = 1985 - 2f(1985)$. Adding these up, we have

$$f(1) + f(2) + \cdots + f(1985) = 1 - 2 + 3 - 4 + \cdots + 1985 - 2(f(1) + f(2) + \cdots + f(1985)).$$

Rearranging, we have

$$\begin{aligned} 3(f(1) + f(2) + \cdots + f(1985)) &= 1 - 2 + 3 - 4 + \cdots + 1985 \\ &= 1 + (3 - 2) + (5 - 4) + (7 - 6) + \cdots + (1985 - 1984) \\ &= 1 + 1984/2 = 993, \end{aligned}$$

so the desired sum is $993/3 = \mathbf{331}$.

129. Rearranging, we have $f(1-x) - (1-x) = f(x) - x$. Letting $f(y) - y = g(y)$, we have $g(1 - x) = g(x)$. We can write this as $g(1/2 - (x - 1/2)) = g(1/2 + (x - 1/2))$; this suggests writing $h(y) = g(1/2+y)$, so $h(y) = h(-y)$ and h is an even function. We claim that for *any* even function h, the corresponding function f is a solution. Starting from $h(x)$, we construct $g(x) = h(x - 1/2)$, and correspondingly $f(x) = g(x) + x = h(x-1/2) + x$. Substituting $f(x)$ into the functional equation, we have $f(1-x) = h(1/2 - x) + (1 - x) = h(x-1/2) + (1-x) = f(x) + 1 - 2x$ as long as h is even. Thus for any even h, $f(x) = h(x - 1/2) + x$ is a solution to the equation.

130. The given functional equation is

$$f(z) + f(\omega z + a) = g(z). \tag{1}$$

Recalling that $\omega^2 + \omega + 1 = 0$ for any third root of unity not equal to 1, we think to go for a cyclic function-type simplification. Thus we substitute $\omega z + a$ for z in the given equation to get

$$f(\omega z + a) + f(\omega^2 z + \omega a + a) = g(\omega z + a). \tag{2}$$

We then substitute $\omega z + a$ for z again in (2) to get

$$f(\omega^2 z + \omega a + a) + f(\omega^3 z + \omega^2 a + \omega a + a) = g(\omega^2 z + \omega a + a),$$

which because $\omega^2 + \omega + 1 = 0$ and $\omega^3 = 1$ becomes

$$f(\omega^2 z + \omega a + a) + f(z) = g(\omega^2 z + \omega a + a). \tag{3}$$

Equations (1), (2), and (3) are linear in terms of $f(z)$, $f(\omega z + a)$, and $f(\omega^2 z + \omega a + a)$. In fact, adding the three equations gives

$$f(z) + f(\omega z + a) + f(\omega^2 z + \omega a + a) = [g(z) + g(\omega z + a) + g(\omega^2 z + \omega a + a)]/2.$$

Subtracting (2) from this gives

$$f(z) = [g(z) - g(\omega z + a) + g(\omega^2 z + \omega a + a)]/2.$$

Since this equation specifies $f(z)$ specifically in terms of $g(z)$, this is the one and only one $f(z)$ which solves the given functional equation.

Chapter 8

Taking it to the Limit

Solutions to Exercises

8-2 As $n \to \infty$, the denominator of $\dfrac{1}{n^k}$ goes to ∞ for any $k > 0$. Since the numerator stays at 1, the fraction tends to 0. Thus $\lim\limits_{n \to \infty} \dfrac{1}{n^k} = 0$ for *any* positive k.

8-3 The upshot of our discussion in the text is that we need only consider the leading terms of each polynomial. We thus have

   i. $\lim\limits_{x \to \infty} \dfrac{2x^4}{4x^4} = \lim\limits_{x \to \infty} \dfrac{2}{4} = \dfrac{1}{2}.$

   ii. $\lim\limits_{x \to \infty} \dfrac{2x^3}{4x^4} = \lim\limits_{x \to \infty} \dfrac{2}{4x} = 0.$

  iii. $\lim\limits_{x \to \infty} \dfrac{2x^5}{4x^4} = \lim\limits_{x \to \infty} \dfrac{2x}{4} = \infty.$

8-4 The functional definition is that for some N, there exists no x such that $|f(x)| > |N|$. The sequence definition is that for some N there exists no n such that $|a_n| > |N|$.

8-5 Yes. Either the sequence/function's values exceed N for any finite N, or they don't. In the latter case the function is bounded, in the former case unbounded.

8-6 The "official" definition is rather tricky, but the essence of it is that no matter how small a neighborhood $(L - \epsilon, L + \epsilon)$ we take around the limit, for all sufficiently large x the function $f(x)$ will lie in the neighborhood.

8-7 If the degree of the top is less than or equal to the degree of the bottom, the rational function is convergent. If the degrees of the top and bottom are the same, the limit will be nonzero.

8-8 Using the calculator, we find $\sin(1/1000)/(1/1000) = .9999998$. It seems that the limit is tending to 1.

8-9 For $x < 0$, $|x| = -x$, so that

$$\lim_{x \to 0^-} \frac{x}{|x|} = \lim_{x \to 0^-} \frac{x}{-x} = \lim_{x \to 0^-} (-1) = -1;$$

for $x > 0$, $|x| = x$, so that

$$\lim_{x \to 0^+} \frac{x}{|x|} = \lim_{x \to 0^+} \frac{x}{x} = \lim_{x \to 0^+} (1) = 1.$$

Since the limits from the left and from the right are different, the overall limit does not exist.

8-10 It's more or less the same. In that case, though, we would have been looking at $\lim_{x \to \infty} \sin(1/x)/(1/x)$; there is no difference.

8-11 We have $(1 + 1/10)^{10} = 2.594$ and $(1 + 1/100)^{100} = 2.705$. It seems that the amount of interest is tending to a limit.

Solutions to Problems

131. We need to fill the hole at $x = 2$ by letting k be the limit as x tends to 2. We have

$$
\begin{aligned}
\lim_{x \to 2} \frac{\sqrt{2x + 5} - \sqrt{x + 7}}{x - 2} &= \lim_{x \to 2} \frac{(\sqrt{2x + 5} - \sqrt{x + 7})(\sqrt{2x + 5} + \sqrt{x + 7})}{(x - 2)(\sqrt{2x + 5} + \sqrt{x + 7})} \\
&= \lim_{x \to 2} \frac{x - 2}{(x - 2)(\sqrt{2x + 5} + \sqrt{x + 7})} \\
&= \lim_{x \to 2} \frac{1}{\sqrt{2x + 5} + \sqrt{x + 7}} = \frac{1}{6}.
\end{aligned}
$$

132.

   i. The denominator goes to ∞ as the numerator oscillates between -1 and 1, so the limit is **0**.

   ii. The top of the fraction can be factored as $(x + 2)(x^2 - 2x + 4)$. Dividing $x + 2$ out of the top and the bottom the limit becomes $\lim_{x \to -2} (x^2 - 2x + 4) = 4 + 4 + 4 = \mathbf{12}$.

   iii. The bottom factors into $(\sqrt{x} - 4)(\sqrt{x} + 4)$. Dividing the common factor of $\sqrt{x} - 4$ from the top and bottom leaves $\lim_{x \to 16} 1/(\sqrt{x} + 4) = \mathbf{1/8}$.

133. Dividing the polynomials, we find that

$$f(x) = \frac{x^2 - x - 2}{x + 2} = x - 3 + \frac{4}{x + 2}.$$

As $x \to \pm\infty$, the fraction vanishes, and the graph tends to the line equation $y = x - 3$.

134. We have

$$
\begin{aligned}
\lim_{x \to \infty} \left(\sqrt{4x^2 + 5x} - \sqrt{4x^2 + x}\right) &= \lim_{x \to \infty} \frac{\left(\sqrt{4x^2 + 5x} - \sqrt{4x^2 + x}\right)\left(\sqrt{4x^2 + 5x} + \sqrt{4x^2 + x}\right)}{\sqrt{4x^2 + 5x} + \sqrt{4x^2 + x}} \\
&= \lim_{x \to \infty} \frac{4x}{\sqrt{4x^2 + 5x} + \sqrt{4x^2 + x}} \\
&= \lim_{x \to \infty} \frac{4}{\sqrt{4 + 5/x} + \sqrt{4 + 1/x}} \\
&= \frac{4}{4} = 1.
\end{aligned}
$$

135. We have

$$\lim_{x \to 0} \sin^2 x/x = \left[\lim_{x \to 0} \sin x/x\right]\left[\lim_{x \to 0} \sin x\right] = (1)(0) = 0.$$

136. We have

$$\lim_{\theta \to 0} \theta \cot \theta = \left[\lim_{\theta \to 0} \theta/\sin\theta\right]\left[\lim_{\theta \to 0} \cos\theta\right] = \frac{1}{\lim\limits_{\theta \to 0} \sin\theta/\theta} \lim_{\theta \to 0} \cos\theta = 1.$$

137. We have

$$\lim_{x \to 0} \frac{1 - \cos x}{x} = \lim_{x \to 0} \frac{\sin^2 x}{x(1 + \cos x)} = \lim_{x \to 0} \frac{\sin^2 x}{x} \lim_{x \to 0} \frac{1}{(1 + \cos x)} = (0)(1) = 0,$$

as desired.

138. Dividing the polynomials, we have

$$\frac{x^3}{x^2 - 1} = x + \frac{x}{x^2 - 1}.$$

As $x \to \pm\infty$ the function tends to the slant asymptote $y = x$; as $x \to \pm 1$ the function diverges, so we have the vertical asymptotes $x = 1$ and $x = -1$.

139. Dividing the top and bottom by x, we have $\lim\limits_{x \to \infty} 6/\sqrt{9 + 17/x}$; thus the limit is $6/3 = 2$.

140. Dividing the top and bottom by x we have

$$\lim_{x \to \infty} \frac{\sqrt{3 + 17/x}}{1} = \sqrt{3}.$$

Chapter 9

Complex Numbers

Solutions to Exercises

9-1   The complex number $\frac{1}{2} + \frac{3}{2}i$ corresponds to the point $(\frac{1}{2}, \frac{3}{2})$ in the plane and $-\frac{7}{3} + \sqrt{2}\,i$ corresponds to $(-\frac{7}{3}, \sqrt{2})$.

9-2   We can quickly analyze the graphs of each case by noting $\operatorname{Re}(z) = x$ and $\operatorname{Im}(z) = y$, so that $\operatorname{Re}(z) = 1$ corresponds to the vertical line $x = 1$, $\operatorname{Re}(z) + \operatorname{Im}(z) = 1$ to the line $x + y = 1$, and $\operatorname{Im}(z) < 1$ to $y < 1$ (or the half-plane below $y = 1$).

9-3   First, z corresponds to $(3, 2)$. Since $\overline{z}$ corresponds to $(3, -2)$, it is the reflection of z in the x axis. (This is always true of a complex number and its conjugate.) We find z^2 is represented by the point $(5, 12)$ and $z - 1$ by $(2, 2)$, so that $z - 1$ is a translation 1 unit to the left of z.

9-4   We graph these polar representations of complex numbers just as we would polar coordinates on the real Cartesian plane. The first point is in the first quadrant, while the second is on the negative x axis (at $(-3, 0)$ to be exact).

9-5   The curve $r = 1$ represents all points which are 1 away from the origin; thus, the curve is a circle with radius 1 centered at the origin. As discussed in Volume 1 and in our section on polar coordinates, $\theta = \pi/3$ describes a line through the origin.

9-6   Applying the properties discussed in the chapter, we have

$$
\begin{aligned}
|(12 + 5i)(7 - 24i)| &= |12 + 5i|\,|7 - 24i| \\
&= \sqrt{144 + 25}\,\sqrt{49 + 576} \\
&= \mathbf{325}.
\end{aligned}
$$

9-7 Let $w = 5$ and $z = -5$. Then $|w + z| = |w| + |z|$ gives $0 = 10$, which is clearly false.

9-8 If $z = cw$ and w has the polar form (r, θ), then $z = (cr, \theta)$ (why?), so that the equality condition in polar form is that z and w have the same angle θ in polar form.

9-9 Since $|-w| = |w|$, we can replace w by $-w$ in the inequality $|z + w| \le |z| + |w|$ to yield $|z - w| \le |z| + |-w| = |z| + |w|$, as desired.

9-10 Since i has the polar representation $(1, \pi/2)$, multiplying the complex number z by i leaves the magnitude unchanged but adds $\pi/2$ to the angle of z. This corresponds to a 90° counterclockwise rotation about the origin.

9-11 Are you convinced?

9-12 Since the polar form of i is $(1, \pi/2)$, then $i^n = (1, \pi/2)^n = (1^n, n\pi/2) = (1, n\pi/2)$.

9-13 Let the reciprocal be $w = (r, \phi)$. Since $zw = 1 = (1, 0)$, we have $zw = (1 \cdot r, \theta + \phi) = (1, 0)$. Hence, $r = 1$ and $\phi = -\theta$ and the reciprocal of z is $(1, -\theta)$. Thus, $1/z$ is the reflection of z in the x axis. Does this make sense? What is the relationship between z and $1/z$ for points not on the unit circle? (It isn't a simple reflection!)

9-14 Since $w = \frac{\sqrt{2}}{2} + i\frac{\sqrt{2}}{2}$ is on the unit circle, the powers of w are all on the unit circle (since the magnitude of w is 1, all powers of w have magnitude 1). Since $w = (1, 45°)$, there are 8 distinct powers of w, because $w^9 = (1, 405°) = (1, 45°)$ brings us back to w and we start all over. (The same holds for the negative powers, except these powers proceed clockwise around the circle rather than counterclockwise.) For $z = \frac{1}{2} + i\frac{1}{2}$, the magnitude is less than 1, so the positive powers get closer and closer to 0, while the negative powers get larger and larger. Again, the positive powers go counterclockwise (from 45° to 90° to 135°, etc.) and the negative clockwise.

9-15 First we write $-4\sqrt{2} + 4\sqrt{2}\,i$ in polar form, as $z = (8, 135°)$. To raise z to the 3/4 power, we first cube it then take the fourth root. Hence we have

$$
\begin{aligned}
z^{3/4} &= [(8, 135°)^3]^{1/4} \\
&= (512, 405°)^{1/4} \\
&= (512, 45°)^{1/4} \\
&= (512^{1/4}, \frac{45°}{4} + \frac{360°k}{4}),
\end{aligned}
$$

where k takes the values 0, 1, 2, 3. Simplifying $\sqrt[4]{512}$ as $4\sqrt[4]{2}$, we have the following as our four values (in polar form) of $(-4\sqrt{2} + 4\sqrt{2}\,i)^{3/4}$:

$$
(4\sqrt[4]{2}, \frac{45°}{4}), \quad (4\sqrt[4]{2}, \frac{405°}{4}), \quad (4\sqrt[4]{2}, \frac{765°}{4}), \quad (4\sqrt[4]{2}, \frac{1125°}{4}).
$$

9-16 For $\sin^2 x + \cos^2 x$, we evaluate the two squares as

$$
\sin^2 x = \left(\frac{e^{ix} - e^{-ix}}{2i}\right)^2 = \frac{e^{2ix} - 2e^0 + e^{-2ix}}{-4} = \frac{-e^{2ix} - e^{-2ix} + 2}{4}
$$

and

$$\cos^2 x = \left(\frac{e^{ix} + e^{-ix}}{2} \right)^2 = \frac{e^{2ix} + 2e^0 + e^{-2ix}}{4} = \frac{e^{2ix} + e^{-2ix} + 2}{4}.$$

Adding these expressions for $\cos^2 x$ and $\sin^2 x$ clearly gives $\sin^2 x + \cos^2 x = 1$. For $\sin 2x = 2 \sin x \cos x$ we multiply our expressions for $\sin x$ and $\cos x$:

$$\sin x \cos x = \frac{e^{ix} - e^{-ix}}{2i} \cdot \frac{e^{ix} + e^{-ix}}{2} = \frac{e^{2ix} - e^{-2ix}}{4i} = \frac{1}{2} \cdot \frac{e^{2ix} - e^{-2ix}}{2i}.$$

This final expression equals $\frac{1}{2} \sin 2x$, proving the assertion. (If you don't see that the last expression above equals $\frac{1}{2} \sin 2x$, try putting $2x$ in our formula for $\sin x$.)

    9-17 Using our formulas for the hyperbolic sine and cosine, we have

$$\cosh^2 x - \sinh^2 x = \frac{e^{2x} + 2 + e^{-2x}}{4} - \frac{e^{2x} - 2 + e^{-2x}}{4} = \frac{e^{2x} + 2 + e^{-2x} - e^{2x} + 2 - e^{-2x}}{4} = 1.$$

Try to show that $\sinh 2x = 2 \sinh x \cosh x$ and $\cosh 2x = \cosh^2 x + \sinh^2 x$.

    9-18 We can equate the imaginary parts of the expression for $\cos 3\theta + i \sin 3\theta$ in the previous example, yielding

$$\begin{aligned} \sin 3\theta &= 3 \cos^2 \theta \sin \theta - \sin^3 \theta \\ &= 3(1 - \sin^2 \theta) \sin \theta - \sin^3 \theta \\ &= -4 \sin^3 \theta + 3 \sin \theta. \end{aligned}$$

    9-19 Since $e^{in\theta} = \cos n\theta + i \sin n\theta$, the sum on the right is clearly the imaginary part of the sum on the left. This enables us to write the unwieldy sum $\sum\limits_{n=1}^{j} k \sin n\theta$ in terms of the geometric series $\sum\limits_{n=1}^{j} k e^{in\theta}$, which is much easier to evaluate.

    9-20 The cube roots of unity are $e^0 = 1$, $e^{2i\pi/3} = -1/2 + i\sqrt{3}/2$, and $e^{4i\pi/3} = -1/2 - i\sqrt{3}/2$. The fourth roots of unity are $e^0 = 1$, $e^{i\pi/2} = i$, $e^{i\pi} = -1$, and $e^{3i\pi/2} = -i$.

    9-21 If -1 is an nth root of 1, then the point -1 must be on the regular polygon formed by the nth roots. Since there are the same number of vertices of this polygon above the x axis as below, and there are two vertices on the axis (if there's a vertex at $(-1, 0)$), there must be an even number of vertices of the polygon. Hence -1 is an nth root of unity if and only if n is even.

    9-22 Since $5(2\pi)/17 > \pi/2 > 4(2\pi)/17$ and $9(2\pi)/17 > \pi > 8(2\pi)/17$, the roots $e^{2\pi ki/17}$ are in the second quadrant for $k = 5, 6, 7,$ and, 8, so there are 4 roots in the second quadrant.

Solutions to Problems

141. Applying our properties from the chapter we have

$$\left| \frac{7 - 24i}{4 + 3i} \right| = \frac{|7 - 24i|}{|4 + 3i|} = \frac{\sqrt{49 + 576}}{\sqrt{16 + 9}} = \mathbf{5}.$$

142. We could multiply out the products or use polar form, but here we'll use clever algebraic notation because we notice that $2 - 2i$ is twice the conjugate of $i + 1$:

$$
\begin{aligned}
(1 + i)^4 (2 - 2i)^3 &= (i + 1)^4 (2^3)(1 - i)^3 \\
&= 8(1 + i)[(1 + i)(1 - i)]^3 \\
&= 8(1 + i)(2)^3 = \mathbf{64 + 64i}.
\end{aligned}
$$

Try using polar form to complete this problem.

143. As mentioned in the text, the product of the nth roots of 1 are the solutions of the polynomial equation $x^n - 1 = 0$. From our discussion in the chapter on polynomials, the product of the roots of this equation is $(-1)^n(-1) = (-1)^{n+1}$.

144. Let $w = 2 + i$. We evaluate $f(w)$, $f^2(w)$, $f^3(w)$, and look for a pattern. We find $f(2 + i) = (3 + i)/(1 + i) = 2 - i$ and $f^2(2 + i) = f(2 - i) = 2 + i$. Thus, we see that $f^{2n}(2 + i) = 2 + i$ and $f^{2n+1}(2 + i) = 2 - i$, so the answer to our problem is $\mathbf{2 - i}$.

145. Since the cube of the number $z = (r, \theta)$ is $(r^3, 3\theta)$, z^3 will be real if and only if $3\theta = n\pi$. Since 2 and K are positive, the point representing $2 + Ki$ is in the first quadrant. Hence, $0 \le \theta \le 90°$ for $2 + Ki$. Thus, we must have $3\theta = 180°$, so $\theta = 60°$. Since there is only one K such that $(2 + Ki)$ has the polar representation $(r, 60°)$, only **1** K that satisfies the problem.

146. The slope of the line through two points is the ratio of the difference in y coordinates to the difference in x coordinates. Since the difference in y coordinates of the points w and z in the complex plane is the difference of the imaginary parts of the numbers and the difference in the x coordinates is the difference in real parts of w and z, the slope between the points which represent w and z is $\operatorname{Im}(z - w)/\operatorname{Re}(z - w)$.

147. Let $F = z = (r, \theta)$. Hence, we have $1/z = (1/r, -\theta)$. Since F is outside the unit circle, $r > 1$, so that $1/r < 1$. Thus, the reciprocal of z is inside the circle. Since the angle of $1/z$ is $-\theta$, it is on the opposite side of the x axis from z. The only point which satisfies these restrictions is point C.

148. To find one sixth root of -64, we write -64 as $64e^{i\pi}$. Hence, one sixth root of -64 is $64^{1/6}e^{i\pi/6} = 2e^{i\pi/6}$. The other roots have the same magnitude, 2, but different angles (which differ from $\pi/6$ by multiples of $2\pi/6 = \pi/3$). Since we only want the roots with positive x, we only want the roots with angle between $-\pi/2$ and $\pi/2$, exclusive. These roots are $2e^{\pi/6}$ and $2e^{-\pi/6}$. Their product then is $2 \cdot 2e^{\pi/6 - \pi/6} = 4e^0 = \mathbf{4}$.

149. Letting $z = x + yi$ and writing the given equation in terms of x and y we have $\sqrt{x^2 + y^2} = y + 1$. Squaring both sides, we have $x^2 + y^2 = y^2 + 2y + 1$. Rearranging, we find $x^2 - 2y - 1 = 0$, which is a **parabola**.

150. From DeMoivre's Theorem, we have

$$(\cos\theta + i\sin\theta)^5 = \cos 5\theta + i\sin 5\theta.$$

To find $\cos 5\theta$, we equate the real part on the right to that on the left, so we find

$$
\begin{aligned}
\cos 5\theta &= \cos^5\theta + \binom{5}{2}i^2\cos^3\theta\sin^2\theta + \binom{5}{4}i^4\cos\theta\sin^4\theta \\
&= \cos^5\theta - 10\cos^3\theta(1 - \cos^2\theta) + 5\cos\theta(1 - \cos^2\theta)^2 \\
&= 16\cos^5\theta - 20\cos^3\theta + 5\cos\theta.
\end{aligned}
$$

151. Let $w = \cos 12° + i\sin 12°$ and $z = \cos 48° + i\sin 48°$. Point A represents w and B represents z. Point $w + z$ is found by copying $\overrightarrow{OB}$ starting from A. (Why? Compare this to adding $4 + 2i$ and $3 + 4i$.) This gives us point C. Since $|z| = |w| = 1$, we have $OA = OB = BC = CA$ and $OACB$ is a parallelogram. Since $\angle BOA = 48° - 12° = 36°$, 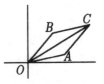 $\angle COA = 36°/2 = 18°$. Thus, CO makes an angle of $18° + 12° = 30°$ with the real axis and hence has polar representation $(r, 30°)$ for some r. Thus, $(w+z)^6 = (r^6, 6\cdot 30°) = (r^6, 180°)$ and $(w+z)^6 = -r^6$. Hence, $(w+z)^6$ has no imaginary part and the answer to our problem is **0**.

152. We can solve the given equation for x by first multiplying by x then using the quadratic formula. Our equation becomes $x^2 - 2x\cos\theta + 1 = 0$. Applying the quadratic formula we have

$$x = \frac{2\cos\theta \pm \sqrt{4\cos^2\theta - 4}}{2} = \cos\theta \pm \sqrt{\cos^2\theta - 1} = \cos\theta \pm \sqrt{-\sin^2\theta} = \cos\theta \pm i\sin\theta.$$

Hence, $x = \cos\theta \pm i\sin\theta = e^{\pm i\theta}$. Thus we find $x^n = [e^{\pm i\theta}]^n = e^{\pm in\theta}$ and $1/x^n = 1/e^{\pm in\theta} = e^{-\pm in\theta}$. Thus,

$$x^n + \frac{1}{x^n} = e^{\pm in\theta} + e^{-\pm in\theta} = 2\cos n\theta.$$

Make sure you see why $\cos n\theta = (e^{in\theta} + e^{-in\theta})/2$.

153. The given sum looks very formidable; however, note that $\cos n\theta = \text{Re}(e^{in\theta})$. Thus, we can write our sum, which we'll call S, as

$$S = \text{Re}\left(\sum_{n=0}^{\infty}\frac{e^{in\theta}}{2^n}\right) = \text{Re}\left(\sum_{n=0}^{\infty}\left(\frac{e^{i\theta}}{2}\right)^n\right).$$

The last sum is a geometric series with first term 1 and ratio $e^{i\theta}/2$. Hence, S becomes

$$S = \text{Re}\left(\frac{1}{1 - e^{i\theta}/2}\right) = \text{Re}\left(\frac{1}{1 - \frac{1}{2}\cos\theta - \frac{i}{2}\sin\theta}\right).$$

To determine the real part of S, we must rationalize the denominator by multiplying top and bottom by $1 - \frac{1}{2}\cos\theta + \frac{i}{2}\sin\theta$, yielding

$$S = \text{Re}\left(\frac{1 - \frac{1}{2}\cos\theta + \frac{i}{2}\sin\theta}{(1 - \frac{1}{2}\cos\theta)^2 + \frac{1}{4}\sin^2\theta}\right) = \frac{1 - \frac{1}{2}\cos\theta}{(1 - \frac{1}{2}\cos\theta)^2 + \frac{1}{4}\sin^2\theta}.$$

Since $\cos\theta = 1/5$, we have $\sin^2\theta = 1 - 1/25 = 24/25$ and

$$S = \frac{1 - 1/10}{(9/10)^2 + (1/4)(24/25)} = \frac{6}{7}.$$

154. Since z is a root of the polynomial, we have

$$z^n + a_{n-1}z^{n-1} + \cdots + a_1 z + a_0 = 0.$$

To get a z^{n+1} term, we multiply the given equation by $(z - 1)$, giving

$$(z - 1)(z^n + a_{n-1}z^{n-1} + \cdots + a_1 z + a_0) = 0$$
$$z^{n+1} + (a_{n-1} - 1)z^n + (a_{n-2} - a_{n-1})z^{n-1} + \cdots + (a_0 - a_1)z - a_0 = 0.$$

We solve this equation for z^{n+1} since we wish to prove that $z^{n+1} = 1$. This yields

$$z^{n+1} = (1 - a_{n-1})z^n + (a_{n-1} - a_{n-2})z^{n-1} + \cdots + (a_1 - a_0)z + a_0.$$

We can now apply the Triangle Inequality to this relation, noting that each of the coefficients on the right side are positive:

$$|z^{n+1}| \leq |(1 - a_{n-1})z^n| + |(a_{n-1} - a_{n-2})z^{n-1}| + \cdots + |(a_1 - a_0)z| + |a_0|$$
$$|z|^{n+1} \leq (1 - a_{n-1})|z^n| + (a_{n-1} - a_{n-2})|z^{n-1}| + \cdots + (a_1 - a_0)|z| + a_0$$
$$|z|^{n+1} \leq (1 - a_{n-1})|z|^n + (a_{n-1} - a_{n-2})|z|^{n-1} + \cdots + (a_1 - a_0)|z| + a_0.$$

Since we are given $|z| \geq 1$, we have $|z|^i \geq |z|^j$ for all $i \geq j$. (Make sure you see why.) Hence, each of the powers on the left side are less than or equal to $|z|^n$, so we can write

$$|z|^{n+1} \leq (1 - a_{n-1})|z|^n + (a_{n-1} - a_{n-2})|z|^n + \cdots + (a_1 - a_0)|z|^n + a_0|z|^n = |z|^n.$$

Make sure you understand why the sum equals $|z|^n$. Thus, we have $|z|^{n+1} \leq |z|^n$ and $|z| \geq 1$, which can only be true if $|z| = 1$. Now let's return to our expression of the Triangle Inequality,

$$|z|^{n+1} \leq (1 - a_{n-1})|z^n| + (a_{n-1} - a_{n-2})|z^{n-1}| + \cdots + (a_1 - a_0)|z| + a_0.$$

For $|z| = 1$, this inequality becomes and equality. The Triangle Inequality can only be an equality if each of the terms $(1 - a_{n-1})z^n$, $(a_{n-1} - a_{n-2})z^{n-1}, \ldots$, a_0 have the same angle when written in polar form. Since the last term, a_0, is real, all the terms must be real. From the equation

$$z^{n+1} = (1 - a_{n-1})z^n + (a_{n-1} - a_{n-2})z^{n-1} + \cdots + (a_1 - a_0)z + a_0,$$

we see that since each term on the right is real and positive (why positive?), z^{n+1} is real and positive. Thus, $|z|^{n+1} = 1$ implies $z^{n+1} = 1$.

Chapter 10

Vectors and Matrices

Solutions to Exercises

10-1 For Property 2, we know that $\vec{v} \cdot \vec{w} = \|\vec{v}\| \|\vec{w}\| \cos \theta$, where θ is the angle between $\vec{v}$ and $\vec{w}$. Assuming $\|\vec{v}\|$ and $\|\vec{w}\|$ are not zero, the only way this dot product can be zero is if $\cos \theta = 0$; this happens only when $\theta = \pi/2$ or $3\pi/2$, and in both of these cases $\vec{v}$ and $\vec{w}$ are perpendicular.

Property 3 is immediate: $(c\vec{v}) \cdot \vec{w} = \|c\vec{v}\| \|\vec{w}\| \cos \theta = c\|\vec{v}\| \|\vec{w}\| \cos \theta = c\vec{v} \cdot \vec{w}$.

10-2 The tail is at $(0,0)$, while the head is at $(2,3)$; thus the Pythagorean Theorem gives the length as $\sqrt{2^2 + 3^2} = \sqrt{13}$. (Make sure you can write down a formula for the length of an arbitrary vector $(x \quad y)$.)

10-3 The dot product of the two is $(1)(-6) + (17)(1) + (-3)(5) + (2)(2) = -6 + 17 - 15 + 4 = 0$, so the two are perpendicular.

10-4 To find the top entry in the product vector, we go along the top row of the given matrix and down the given vector, to get $(2)(1) + (-4)(-1) = 6$. To get the bottom entry, we go along the bottom row of the given matrix and down the given vector, to get $(-6)(1) + (8)(-1) = -14$. thus the product vector is $\begin{pmatrix} 6 \\ -14 \end{pmatrix}$.

10-5

i. Let the general vector be $\begin{pmatrix} x \\ y \end{pmatrix}$; then transforming by $\begin{pmatrix} 1 & 0 \\ 0 & -1 \end{pmatrix}$ yields $\begin{pmatrix} 1 & 0 \\ 0 & -1 \end{pmatrix} \begin{pmatrix} x \\ y \end{pmatrix} = \begin{pmatrix} x \\ -y \end{pmatrix}$. The matrix reflects the vector across the x axis.

ii. The general matrix $\begin{pmatrix} a & b \\ c & d \end{pmatrix}$ takes the general vector $\begin{pmatrix} x \\ y \end{pmatrix}$ to $\begin{pmatrix} ax + by \\ cx + dy \end{pmatrix}$. For this to equal the vector we started with, or $\begin{pmatrix} x \\ y \end{pmatrix}$, we must have $b = c = 0$, $a = d = 1$. Thus the identity matrix is $\begin{pmatrix} 1 & 0 \\ 0 & 1 \end{pmatrix}$.

iii. A 3D vector looks like $\begin{pmatrix} x \\ y \\ z \end{pmatrix}$, and is transformed by a matrix as:

$$\begin{pmatrix} a & b & c \\ d & e & f \\ g & h & i \end{pmatrix} \begin{pmatrix} x \\ y \\ z \end{pmatrix} = \begin{pmatrix} ax + by + cz \\ dx + ey + fz \\ gx + hy + iz \end{pmatrix}.$$

You should easily be able to write down the 3D identity matrix, as well as matrices which reflect in the xy, yz, and xz planes.

10-6   We let $\vec{v} = \begin{pmatrix} v_1 \\ v_2 \end{pmatrix}$ and $\vec{w} = \begin{pmatrix} w_1 \\ w_2 \end{pmatrix}$. Then

$$\begin{aligned} \underline{A}(\vec{v} + \vec{w}) &= \begin{pmatrix} a & b \\ c & d \end{pmatrix} \begin{pmatrix} v_1 + w_1 \\ v_2 + w_2 \end{pmatrix} = \begin{pmatrix} av_1 + aw_1 + bv_2 + bw_2 \\ cv_1 + cw_1 + dv_2 + dw_2 \end{pmatrix} \\ &= \begin{pmatrix} av_1 + bv_2 \\ cv_1 + dv_2 \end{pmatrix} + \begin{pmatrix} aw_1 + bw_2 \\ cw_1 + dw_2 \end{pmatrix} = \underline{A}\vec{v} + \underline{A}\vec{w}, \end{aligned}$$

which is the first requirement of linearity, and

$$\underline{A}(r\vec{v}) = \begin{pmatrix} a & b \\ c & d \end{pmatrix} \begin{pmatrix} rv_1 \\ rv_2 \end{pmatrix} = \begin{pmatrix} arv_1 + brv_2 \\ crv_1 + drv_2 \end{pmatrix} = r \begin{pmatrix} av_1 + bv_2 \\ cv_1 + dv_2 \end{pmatrix} = r\underline{A}\vec{v},$$

which is the second.

10-7   First we do the multiplication inside the brackets. For the top entry we get $(3)(1) + (-4)(1) = -1$, and for the bottom entry we get $(5)(1) + (-6)(1) = -1$. Thus the first multiplication yields $\begin{pmatrix} -1 \\ -1 \end{pmatrix}$, and our original product simplifies to

$$\begin{pmatrix} -1 & 2 \\ 3 & -4 \end{pmatrix} \begin{pmatrix} -1 \\ -1 \end{pmatrix}.$$

To execute this multiplication we do the same thing. The top entry is $(-1)(-1) + (2)(-1) = -1$, while the second is $(3)(-1) + (-4)(-1) = 1$. Thus the overall product is $\begin{pmatrix} -1 \\ 1 \end{pmatrix}$.

10-8 We stated in the text that

$$\begin{pmatrix} a & b \\ c & d \end{pmatrix} \begin{pmatrix} e & f \\ g & h \end{pmatrix} = \begin{pmatrix} ae + bg & af + bh \\ ce + dg & cf + dh \end{pmatrix}.$$

Considering only the first columns of the second multiplied matrix and the product matrix, our multiplication looks like

$$\begin{pmatrix} a & b \\ c & d \end{pmatrix} \begin{pmatrix} e \\ g \end{pmatrix} = \begin{pmatrix} ae + bg \\ ce + dg \end{pmatrix},$$

which is a normal matrix multiplication of a vector. Similarly, considering only the second columns yields

$$\begin{pmatrix} a & b \\ c & d \end{pmatrix} \begin{pmatrix} f \\ h \end{pmatrix} = \begin{pmatrix} af + bh \\ cf + dh \end{pmatrix},$$

which is again simple matrix-vector multiplication. If you ever forget how to do matrix multiplication, just do it column-by-column like this and you're home free.

10-9 Comparing the form of the product matrix, $\begin{pmatrix} 0 & 1 \\ -1 & 0 \end{pmatrix}$, to the general rotation matrix, $\begin{pmatrix} \cos\theta & -\sin\theta \\ \sin\theta & \cos\theta \end{pmatrix}$, we see that this product matrix corresponds to a rotation by 270°. This is exactly what we would expect, since performing a 90° rotation then a 180° rotation should yield a $90° + 180° = 270°$ rotation!

10-10 We evaluate each entry of the product $\begin{pmatrix} 2 & -3 \\ -4 & 5 \end{pmatrix} \begin{pmatrix} 1 & 1 \\ 2 & 3 \end{pmatrix}$ separately. To get the *upper left* entry, we go across the *upper* row of the first matrix and down the *left* column of the second, to get $(2)(1) + (-3)(2) = -4$. (Make sure you see how the terms in this sum correspond to the entries of the matrices.) To get the *upper right* entry, we go across the *upper* row of the first matrix and down the *left* column of the second, to get $(2)(1)+(-3)(3) = -7$. To get the *lower left* entry of the product, we go across the *lower* row of the first matrix and down the *left* column of the second, to get $(-4)(1) + (5)(2) = 6$. To get the *lower right* entry of the product, we go across the *lower* row of the first matrix and down the *right* column of the second, to get $(-4)(1) + (5)(3) = 11$. Thus the final product is $\begin{pmatrix} -4 & -7 \\ 6 & 11 \end{pmatrix}$.

Matrix multiplication takes some getting used to. Practice until you can do it without too much thought, as it is an essential tool.

10-11 Geomtrically, the equivalent is a reflection through the origin. In matrices, we multiply the matrix for reflection through the y axis, $\begin{pmatrix} -1 & 0 \\ 0 & 1 \end{pmatrix}$, by the matrix for reflection through the x axis, $\begin{pmatrix} 1 & 0 \\ 0 & -1 \end{pmatrix}$, to get $\begin{pmatrix} -1 & 0 \\ 0 & 1 \end{pmatrix} \begin{pmatrix} 1 & 0 \\ 0 & -1 \end{pmatrix} = \begin{pmatrix} -1 & 0 \\ 0 & -1 \end{pmatrix}$. This corresponds exactly to the reflection through the origin which we got geometrically. (Why?)

10-12   We have $\begin{pmatrix} 1 & 1 \\ 1 & 0 \end{pmatrix} \begin{pmatrix} 1 & 1 \\ 0 & 1 \end{pmatrix} = \begin{pmatrix} 1 & 2 \\ 1 & 1 \end{pmatrix}$, while $\begin{pmatrix} 1 & 1 \\ 0 & 1 \end{pmatrix} \begin{pmatrix} 1 & 1 \\ 1 & 0 \end{pmatrix} = \begin{pmatrix} 2 & 1 \\ 1 & 0 \end{pmatrix}$.

10-13   Using the form of the rotation matrix, we get $A = \begin{pmatrix} 1/2 & -\sqrt{3}/2 \\ \sqrt{3}/2 & 1/2 \end{pmatrix}$. Since A^6 corresponds to a rotation by $60° \times 6 = 360°$, which is the same as a rotation by $0°$, A^6 must be the identity matrix $\begin{pmatrix} 1 & 0 \\ 0 & 1 \end{pmatrix}$.

10-14   In exactly the same way as we found the 2×2 identity, the 3×3 identity is

$$\begin{pmatrix} 1 & 0 & 0 \\ 0 & 1 & 0 \\ 0 & 0 & 1 \end{pmatrix}.$$

10-15

i. Rotation by an angle θ about the x axis leaves the x-coordinates of all points the same, while transforming the y- and z-coodinates according to

$$\begin{pmatrix} y \\ z \end{pmatrix} \Longrightarrow \begin{pmatrix} \cos\theta & -\sin\theta \\ \sin\theta & \cos\theta \end{pmatrix} \begin{pmatrix} y \\ z \end{pmatrix}.$$

The 3D matrix accomplishing the rotation is thus

$$\begin{pmatrix} 1 & 0 & 0 \\ 0 & \cos\theta & -\sin\theta \\ 0 & \sin\theta & \cos\theta \end{pmatrix}.$$

(Verify for yourself that this matrix leaves the x-coordinate alone and performs the desired transformation to the y- and z-coordinates.)

ii. To squash any 3D vector to $\vec{0}$, we need the matrix

$$\begin{pmatrix} 0 & 0 & 0 \\ 0 & 0 & 0 \\ 0 & 0 & 0 \end{pmatrix}.$$

iii. Reflection in the xy plane leaves the x- and y-coordinates of a point alone but changes the z-coordinate to $-z$. Thus the matrix we want is

$$\begin{pmatrix} 1 & 0 & 0 \\ 0 & 1 & 0 \\ 0 & 0 & -1 \end{pmatrix}.$$

10-16 The 3×3 case you can do for yourself. For the 2×4 and 4×3 case, let's multiply

$$\begin{pmatrix} 1 & -2 & -3 & 4 \\ 5 & -6 & -7 & 8 \end{pmatrix} \begin{pmatrix} 9 & 10 & 11 \\ 12 & 13 & 14 \\ 15 & 16 & 17 \\ 18 & 19 & 20 \end{pmatrix}.$$

The product matrix is

$$\begin{pmatrix} (1)(9) + (-2)(12) + (-3)(15) + (4)(18) \\ (5)(9) + (-6)(12) + (-7)(15) + (8)(18) \end{pmatrix}$$

$$(1)(10) + (-2)(13) + (-3)(16) + (4)(19)$$
$$(5)(10) + (-6)(13) + (-7)(16) + (8)(19)$$

$$\begin{pmatrix} (1)(11) + (-2)(14) + (-3)(17) + (4)(20) \\ (5)(11) + (-6)(14) + (-7)(17) + (8)(20) \end{pmatrix},$$

where we have staggered the entries of the 2×3 matrix to make them fit on the page. Make sure you understand how these terms come about by going across rows and down columns. From a 2×4 and a 4×3 matrix, we get a product which is 2×3.

For the third case, let's multiply $(\, a \quad b \quad c \,)$ by $\begin{pmatrix} x \\ y \\ z \end{pmatrix}$. We get $(\, ax + by + cz \,)$, a 1×1 matrix which corresponds the the dot product of the two matrices if they are taken as vectors!

10-17 The two do indeed agree.

10-18 We can write $a_{ij} = j - i$, which sums up the entire matrix in a single equation.

Solutions to Problems

155. Recalling that the 2D rotation matrix is $\begin{pmatrix} \cos\theta & -\sin\theta \\ \sin\theta & \cos\theta \end{pmatrix}$, we simply substitute in $\theta = 45°$ to get $\begin{pmatrix} \sqrt{2}/2 & -\sqrt{2}/2 \\ \sqrt{2}/2 & \sqrt{2}/2 \end{pmatrix}$.

156. Since a rotation by x and then by y is the same as a rotation by $x + y$, we have

$$\begin{pmatrix} \cos x & -\sin x \\ \sin x & \cos x \end{pmatrix} \begin{pmatrix} \cos y & -\sin y \\ \sin y & \cos y \end{pmatrix} = \begin{pmatrix} \cos(x+y) & -\sin(x+y) \\ \sin(x+y) & \cos(x+y) \end{pmatrix}.$$

Multiplying the matrices, we have

$$\begin{pmatrix} \cos x \cos y - \sin x \sin y & -\cos x \sin y - \sin x \cos y \\ +\cos x \sin y + \sin x \cos y & \cos x \cos y - \sin x \sin y \end{pmatrix} = \begin{pmatrix} \cos(x+y) & -\sin(x+y) \\ \sin(x+y) & \cos(x+y) \end{pmatrix},$$

and by comparing the matrices on the two sides of this equation we have the desired identities.

157. The product is

$$\begin{pmatrix} (2)(-2) + (1)(4) + (9)(3) & (2)(11) + (1)(4) + (9)(-2) & (2)(-1) + (1)(-3) + (9)(1) \\ (-6)(-2) + (0)(4) + (-3)(3) & (-6)(11) + (0)(4) + (-3)(-2) & (-6)(-1) + (0)(-3) + (-3)(1) \\ (1)(-2) + (3)(4) + (2)(3) & (1)(11) + (3)(4) + (2)(-2) & (1)(-1) + (3)(-3) + (2)(1) \end{pmatrix}$$

$$= \begin{pmatrix} 27 & 8 & 4 \\ 3 & -60 & 3 \\ 16 & 19 & -8 \end{pmatrix}.$$

158. Since $PQRS$ is a parallelogram with P and R diagonally opposite, $\overrightarrow{PQ} = \overrightarrow{SR}$. If $S = (s_1, s_2)$, we thus have $(4 \quad -3) = (9 - s_1 \quad 1 - s_2)$, which yields $s_1 = 5$ and $s_2 = 4$. Thus the coordinates of S are $(5, 4)$.

159. We have

$$\cos \theta = \frac{(3 \quad 4 \quad 5) \cdot (-1 \quad 4 \quad 3)}{\|(3 \quad 4 \quad 5)\| \|(-1 \quad 4 \quad 3)\|} = \frac{28}{10\sqrt{13}} = \frac{14\sqrt{13}}{65}.$$

160. To multiply a 2×3 and a 4×2 matrix, we have to put the 4×2 first and the 2×3 second. The dimension of the product is a 4×3 matrix, so has **12** elements.

161. Let $B = \begin{pmatrix} x & y \\ z & w \end{pmatrix}$. Then $AB = BA$ becomes

$$\begin{pmatrix} 15x + 2z & 15y + 2w \\ 6x + 7z & 6y + 7w \end{pmatrix} = \begin{pmatrix} 15x + 6y & 2x + 7y \\ 15z + 6w & 2z + 7w \end{pmatrix},$$

which results in the four equations $15x+2z = 15x+6y$, $15y+2w = 2x+7y$, $6x+7z = 15z+6w$, and $6y + 7w = 2z + 7w$. The first and last equations yield $z = 3y$; plugging this into the second and third equations gives $2x - 2w = 8y = 8z/3$ for each. From this last equation, z must be divisible by 3 if x and w are both integers. Trying $z = 3$ as the smallest such z, we get $y = 1$ and $x - w = 4$. The smallest positive integers x and w satisfying this equation are $x = 5$ and $y = 1$. The sum of the entries of the matrix is $x + y + z + w = 1 + 1 + 5 + 3 = \mathbf{10}$.

162. We multiply the vector by the matrix to get

$$\begin{pmatrix} 1 & 4 & 1 \\ -2 & 0 & 0 \\ 3 & 2 & -3 \end{pmatrix} \begin{pmatrix} 3 \\ 1 \\ 2 \end{pmatrix} = \begin{pmatrix} \mathbf{9} \\ \mathbf{-6} \\ \mathbf{5} \end{pmatrix}.$$

163. The given sum can be thought of as the dot product of the vectors $(\,2 \quad 3 \quad 6\,)$ and $(\,\sin x \cos y \quad \sin x \sin y \quad \cos x\,)$. The maximum value of this dot product is the product of the lengths of the two vectors, $\sqrt{4 + 9 + 36} = \sqrt{49} = 7$ and

$$\sqrt{\sin^2 x \cos^2 y + \sin^2 x \sin^2 y + \cos^2 x} = \sqrt{\sin^2 x + \cos^2 x} = 1,$$

or **7**. This maximum is attained when the two vectors are parallel. The minimum, attained when the two vectors point in opposite directions, is the negative of the product of the lengths, or **−7**.

Chapter 11

Cross Products and Determinants

Solutions to Exercises

11-1   The area of the *triangle* so spanned is $\frac{1}{2}\|\vec{v}\|\|\vec{w}\|\sin\theta$. The area of the parallelogram spanned by the vectors is twice this, or $\|\vec{v}\|\|\vec{w}\|\sin\theta$.

11-2   Let $\vec{v}$ and $\vec{w}$ both have length 1, so that the area of the parallelogram spanned is just $\sin\theta$, where θ is the angle between $\vec{v}$ and $\vec{w}$ and ranges between 0 and 2π. The cross product points straight up and has length $\sin\theta$. For $\theta = 0$, $\sin\theta = 0$, so the head of the cross product is at the origin. As θ increases, the head rises straight up until, for $\theta = \pi/2$, it is at height 1. As θ continues to increase, the head swings back down to 0, until for $\theta = \pi$ it is at the origin again. As θ increases to $3\pi/2$, the head drops to a depth of -1 below the xy plane, then it swings back up to 0 as θ gets up to 2π.

11-3   Point the index finger of your right hand directly away from you and your middle finger toward the left. Your thumb, the cross product, then points up. Now, *without changing the position of your fingers*, point your middle finger away from you and your index finger to the left. (This will take some twisting of your arm.) If you're doing it the way we intended, your thumb points straight down. This illustrates the fact that $\vec{v}\times\vec{w} = -\vec{w}\times\vec{v}$.

11-4   All we have to do is show that the dot products of the defined vector with $\vec{v}$ and $\vec{w}$ are 0. Since $\vec{v} = (\,x_1 \quad y_1 \quad z_1\,)$ and $\vec{w} = (\,x_2 \quad y_2 \quad z_2\,)$, these dot products are

$$x_1(y_1z_2 - y_2z_1) + y_1(z_1x_2 - z_2x_1) + z_1(x_1y_2 - x_2y_1)$$

and

$$x_2(y_1z_2 - y_2z_1) + y_2(z_1x_2 - z_2x_1) + z_2(x_1y_2 - x_2y_1),$$

both of which simplify to 0.

11-5 Letting the two 2D vectors be $(\begin{array}{ccc} x_1 & y_1 & 0 \end{array})$ and $(\begin{array}{ccc} x_2 & y_2 & 0 \end{array})$, with $z_1 = z_2 = 0$, the formula in the text gives the cross product as

$$(\begin{array}{ccc} 0 & 0 & x_1 y_2 - x_2 y_1 \end{array}),$$

which is indeed straight up or straight down.

11-6 The cross product of $\vec{v}$ and $\vec{w}$ in this notation is $(\begin{array}{ccc} 0 & 0 & v_1 w_2 - w_1 v_2 \end{array})$. The area of the parallelogram spanned is the length of the cross product vector, or $|v_1 w_2 - w_1 v_2|$.

11-7 When we multiply everything out, the term we're interested is actually the two terms

$$v_1 w_2 \underline{A\vec{i}} \times \underline{A\vec{j}} + w_1 v_2 \underline{A\vec{j}} \times \underline{A\vec{i}}.$$

To put them together, we have to use $\underline{A\vec{j}} \times \underline{A\vec{i}} = -\underline{A\vec{i}} \times \underline{A\vec{j}}$, which is the source of the $-$ sign.

11-8 This can be seen in many ways. The simplest is that the area of the parallelogram spanned by $\vec{v}$ and itself is zero.

11-9 Multiplying the vectors for each vertex of the rectangle by the given matrix, we find that the image under transformation has vertices $(13, 7.5)$, $(12, 7)$, $(19, 11.5)$, and $(18, 11)$. This is not a rectangle, though it is a parallelogram defined by the vectors $(\begin{array}{cc} 1 & .5 \end{array})$ and $(\begin{array}{cc} 7 & 4.5 \end{array})$. Evaluating the cross product of these vectors, we get 1 as the area of the parallelogram, so since the original rectangle has area 2, the parallelogram's area has changed by a factor of **0.5**. We didn't actually have to compute this cross product, though—the area is multiplied by the absolute value of the determinant, or $|-.5| = .5$.

11-10 The determinant of the matrix is 11, so the area of the image of the circle is 11 times the original area, or $11(4\pi) = \mathbf{44\pi}$.

11-11 The individual determinants are 13, 2, and -8, so the determinant of the product is $(13)(2)(-8) = \mathbf{-208}$.

11-12 Let's use our shorthand on a generic determmant:

$$\begin{vmatrix} a_{11} & a_{12} & a_{13} \\ a_{21} & a_{22} & a_{23} \\ a_{31} & a_{32} & a_{33} \end{vmatrix} \begin{matrix} a_{11} & a_{12} \\ a_{21} & a_{22} \\ a_{31} & a_{32} \end{matrix}$$

$$\rightarrow a_{11}a_{22}a_{33} + a_{12}a_{23}a_{31} + a_{13}a_{21}a_{32} - a_{31}a_{22}a_{13} - a_{32}a_{23}a_{11} - a_{33}a_{21}a_{12}$$

This last expression is exactly the one we used in the text, so our shorthand gives the correct answer.

11-13 Since one element from each row and column appears in each three-term product in the expression for the 3×3 determinant, each three-term product is multiplied by c. Thus the entire expression is multiplied by c.

11-14 Since every term in the expression for the determinant is multiplied by c, each three-term product is multiplied by c^3. Thus the entire expression is multiplied by c^3, and the determinant of $\underline{B}$ is $c^3|\underline{A}|$.

11-15 Each 2×2 determinant is preceded by a term a_{ij}; the sign of the term is given by $(-1)^{i+j}$.

11-16 For example, in the 4×4 case it looks like

$$\begin{pmatrix} 1 & -1 & 1 & -1 \\ -1 & 1 & -1 & 1 \\ 1 & -1 & 1 & -1 \\ -1 & 1 & -1 & 1 \end{pmatrix}.$$

The checkerboard pattern is the same for any matrix.

11-17 Expanding across the first column of $\left| \begin{pmatrix} a_{11} & a_{12} \\ a_{21} & a_{22} \end{pmatrix} \right|$, we have $a_{11}|(a_{22})| - a_{12}|(a_{21})| = a_{11}a_{22} - a_{12}a_{21}$. This is the correct form of the determinant.

11-18 Let's do the determinant

$$\begin{vmatrix} 3 & -2 & 11 \\ 0 & -5 & 2 \\ 7 & 7 & -4 \end{vmatrix}.$$

Expanding by minors down the first column, we have

$$3 \begin{vmatrix} -5 & 2 \\ 7 & -4 \end{vmatrix} - 0 \begin{vmatrix} -2 & 11 \\ 7 & -4 \end{vmatrix} + 7 \begin{vmatrix} -2 & 11 \\ -5 & 2 \end{vmatrix}.$$

(Make sure you see how we got this expression.) Evaluating the individual determinants, the overall determinant becomes $3(6) + 7(51) = \mathbf{375}$. You can confirm for yourself that the shortcut method gives the same result.

11-19 Expanding by minors across the first row, the determinant becomes

$$a_{11} \begin{pmatrix} a_{22} & 0 & \cdots & 0 \\ 0 & a_{33} & \cdots & 0 \\ \vdots & \vdots & \ddots & \vdots \\ 0 & 0 & \cdots & a_{nn} \end{pmatrix}.$$

Expanding the remaining determinant by minors, we have

$$a_{11}a_{22} \begin{pmatrix} a_{33} & 0 & \cdots & 0 \\ 0 & a_{44} & \cdots & 0 \\ \vdots & \vdots & \ddots & \vdots \\ 0 & 0 & \cdots & a_{nn} \end{pmatrix},$$

and so on until the overall determinant is $a_{11}a_{22}\cdots a_{nn}$.

11-20 Expanding by minors across the first row, the determinant becomes

$$a_{11}\begin{pmatrix} a_{22} & 0 & \cdots & 0 \\ a_{32} & a_{33} & \cdots & 0 \\ \vdots & \vdots & \ddots & \vdots \\ a_{n2} & a_{n3} & \cdots & a_{nn} \end{pmatrix}.$$

Expanding the remaining determinant by minors, we have

$$a_{11}a_{22}\begin{pmatrix} a_{33} & 0 & \cdots & 0 \\ a_{43} & a_{44} & \cdots & 0 \\ \vdots & \vdots & \ddots & \vdots \\ a_{n3} & a_{n4} & \cdots & a_{nn} \end{pmatrix},$$

and so on until the overall determinant is $a_{11}a_{22}\cdots a_{nn}$.

11-21 Expanding by minors along the row or column which is all zeros, the determinant is $0(\text{something}) + 0(\text{something}) + \cdots = 0$.

11-22 Subtracting the first row from all the others yields

$$\begin{vmatrix} 17 & 23 & 23 & 23 \\ 0 & -6 & 0 & 0 \\ 0 & -6 & -6 & 0 \\ 0 & -6 & -6 & -6 \end{vmatrix}.$$

Expanding by minors down the first column then gives

$$17\begin{vmatrix} -6 & 0 & 0 \\ -6 & -6 & 0 \\ -6 & -6 & -6 \end{vmatrix}.$$

Since the new determinant is triangular, the result is the product of the diagonal elements, or $(-6)(-6)(-6) = -216$. Hence the original determinant is $17(-216) = -\mathbf{3672}$.

11-23 Subtracting one identical row or column from the other yields a matrix with one row or column which is all zeros. We have seen already that the determinant of such a matrix is 0.

11-24 Let the elements in one row of an $n \times n$ matrix be multiplied by c . If the elements of that row were $a_{i1}, a_{i2}, \ldots, a_{i3}$ and have corresponding minors $A_{i1}, A_{i2}, \ldots, A_{i3}$. The determinant of the matrix before multiplying the row by c is

$$(-1)^{i+1}a_{i1}A_{i1} + (-1)^{i+2}a_{i2}A_{i2} + \cdots + (-1)^{i+n}a_{in}A_{in},$$

and after multiplying by c the determinant is

$$(-1)^{i+1}ca_{i1}A_{i1} + (-1)^{i+2}ca_{i2}A_{i2} + \cdots + (-1)^{i+n}ca_{in}A_{in}.$$

Clearly this is c times the original determinant.

For the case of multiplying all the elements by c we do it one row at a time. If the original determinant was D, then after multiplying one row c the determinant is cD, after multiplying a second row by c it's c^2D, by repeating our original argument, and so on. After multiplying all n rows by c the determinant is c^nD.

11-25 Expanding the given form by minors, we find that the determinant is $x_0(y_1z_2 - y_2z_1) + y_0(z_1x_2 - z_2x_1) + z_0(x_1y_2 - x_2y_1)$. This is the dot product of the vectors $(\begin{matrix} x_0 & y_0 & z_0 \end{matrix})$ and $(\begin{matrix} y_1z_2 - y_2z_1 & z_1x_2 - z_2x_1 & x_1y_2 - x_2y_1 \end{matrix})$. But the second vector is the cross product of $(\begin{matrix} x_1 & y_1 & z_1 \end{matrix})$ and $(\begin{matrix} x_2 & y_2 & z_2 \end{matrix})$, so the given determinant is $(\begin{matrix} x_0 & y_0 & z_0 \end{matrix}) \cdot ((\begin{matrix} x_1 & y_1 & z_1 \end{matrix}) \times (\begin{matrix} x_2 & y_2 & z_2 \end{matrix}))$, as desired.

11-26 If we substitute $(\begin{matrix} x_1 & y_1 & z_1 \end{matrix})$ or $(\begin{matrix} x_2 & y_2 & z_2 \end{matrix})$ for $(\begin{matrix} x_0 & y_0 & z_0 \end{matrix})$ in the determinant of the previous exercise, we get a determinant with two identical rows. Since we earlier proved that such a determinant is 0, the given cross product is perpendicular to both $(\begin{matrix} x_1 & y_1 & z_1 \end{matrix})$ and $(\begin{matrix} x_2 & y_2 & z_2 \end{matrix})$.

11-27 A matrix with determinant 0 takes any finite volume to 0. To invert such a matrix, another matrix would have to take the volume 0 image back to the finite original volume, which is impossible. Thus a determinant-0 matrix cannot have an inverse.

11-28 We start with the matrix $\begin{pmatrix} a & b \\ c & d \end{pmatrix}$. First we evaluate the determinant, $ad - bc$. Second we replace each entry with its minor, to get $\begin{pmatrix} d & c \\ b & a \end{pmatrix}$. Third we append the checkerboard of signs, to get $\begin{pmatrix} d & -c \\ -b & a \end{pmatrix}$. Fourth, and finally, we transpose the matrix and divide by the determinant, to get $\dfrac{1}{ad - bc}\begin{pmatrix} d & -b \\ -c & a \end{pmatrix}$. This is exactly the form we got in the text.

11-29 The determinant is 1. Replacing each term by its minor, we get

$$\begin{pmatrix} 1 & 0 & \cdots & 0 \\ 0 & 1 & \cdots & 0 \\ \vdots & \vdots & \ddots & \vdots \\ 0 & 0 & \cdots & 1 \end{pmatrix}.$$

Appending the checkerboard of signs leaves this matrix unchanged, since all the nonzero terms get a $+$; dividing by the determinant also leaves it unchanged, since the determinant is 1. Thus none of the steps changes the matrix, so the result is again the identity matrix. This is what we would expect, since the identity times itself is the identity.

11-30   We'll use the matrix

$$\begin{pmatrix} 4 & 3 & 2 \\ -3 & 2 & -1 \\ 2 & 5 & 2 \end{pmatrix}.$$

The determinant is 10. Replacing each term by its minor yields

$$\begin{pmatrix} 9 & -4 & -19 \\ -4 & 4 & 14 \\ -7 & 2 & 17 \end{pmatrix},$$

and appending the checkerboard of signs makes this

$$\begin{pmatrix} 9 & 4 & -19 \\ 4 & 4 & -14 \\ -7 & -2 & 17 \end{pmatrix}.$$

Dividing through by the determinant and transposing, the inverse is thus

$$\frac{1}{10} \begin{pmatrix} 9 & 4 & -7 \\ 4 & 4 & -2 \\ -19 & -14 & 17 \end{pmatrix}.$$

If we multiply this by the original matrix we get the identity matrix, as desired. (Try it.)

Solutions to Problems

164. The entries of A are 2, 3, 5, and 7. The determinant is $ad - bc$, where a through d are the entries in any order. To maximize this determinant, we let $a = 5$, $d = 7$, $b = 2$, and $c = 3$; then the determinant is $(7)(5) - (2)(3) = \mathbf{29}$.

165. We do some row operations to simplify the matrix, adding the third row to the first to get

$$\begin{vmatrix} 6 & 9 & 1 & 0 \\ -3 & -2 & 2 & 3 \\ 2 & 5 & 4 & -2 \\ 3 & -3 & -2 & 0 \end{vmatrix},$$

then adding 3/2 times the third row to the second to get

$$\begin{vmatrix} 6 & 9 & 1 & 0 \\ 0 & 11/2 & 8 & 0 \\ 2 & 5 & 4 & -2 \\ 3 & -3 & -2 & 0 \end{vmatrix}.$$

Expanding by minors down the last column, our determinant is then

$$-(-2)\begin{vmatrix} 6 & 9 & 1 \\ 0 & 11/2 & 8 \\ 3 & -3 & -2 \end{vmatrix},$$

which by adding -2 times the third row to the first becomes

$$2\begin{vmatrix} 0 & 15 & 5 \\ 0 & 11/2 & 8 \\ 3 & -3 & -2 \end{vmatrix}.$$

Expanding by minors down the first column now gives

$$6\begin{vmatrix} 15 & 5 \\ 11/2 & 8 \end{vmatrix} = 6[(15)(8) - 5(11/2)] = 6(185/2) = \mathbf{555}.$$

166. There will be no inverse exactly when the determinant is zero. We use our shorthand method to find the determinant, writing

$$\begin{vmatrix} 1 & 4 & c \\ 2 & -1 & 7 \\ 3 & -2 & 11 \end{vmatrix}\begin{matrix} 1 & 4 \\ 2 & -1 \\ 3 & -2 \end{matrix},$$

The down diagonals yield $(1)(-1)(11) = -11$, $(4)(7)(3) = 84$, and $(c)(2)(-2) = -4c$. The up diagonals yield $-(3)(-1)(c) = 3c$, $-(-2)(7)(1) = 14$, and $-(11)(2)(4) = -88$. Adding these six terms together yields $-c - 1$ as the determinant, so the determinant is zero when $c = \mathbf{-1}$.

167. We recall that the determinant of a product is the product of the determinants. The determinant of A is $(2)(4) - (1)(3) = 5$, of B is $(2)(4) - (3)(5) = -7$, and of C is $(2)(1) - (1)(6) = -4$. The product is $(5)(-7)(-4) = \mathbf{140}$.

168. We subtract the first row from the second and third rows to get

$$\begin{vmatrix} a & 1 & 1 & 1 \\ 1-a & a-1 & 0 & 0 \\ 1-a & 0 & a-1 & 0 \\ 1 & 1 & 1 & a \end{vmatrix},$$

then we subtract a times the first row from the last row to get

$$\begin{vmatrix} a & 1 & 1 & 1 \\ 1-a & a-1 & 0 & 0 \\ 1-a & 0 & a-1 & 0 \\ 1-a^2 & 1-a & 1-a & 0 \end{vmatrix}.$$

Expanding by minors down the fourth column then yields

$$-\begin{vmatrix} 1-a & a-1 & 0 \\ 1-a & 0 & a-1 \\ 1-a^2 & 1-a & 1-a \end{vmatrix}.$$

Factoring $a - 1$ from each entry, we get $(a - 1)^3$ in front, since the matrix is 3×3. Thus our determinant becomes

$$-(a-1)^3 \begin{vmatrix} -1 & 1 & 0 \\ -1 & 0 & 1 \\ -1-a & -1 & -1 \end{vmatrix}.$$

Using the shorthand methods on the determinant which remains, we get $0 + (-1 - a) + 0 - 0 - 1 - 1 = -a - 3$. Thus the original determinant is $-(a-1)^3(-a-3) = (a-1)^3(a+3)$.

169. Since the matrix is 2×2, factoring a 4 out of every term brings a $4^2 = 16$ out front. Thus $\begin{vmatrix} 4W & 4X \\ 4Y & 4Z \end{vmatrix} = 16 \begin{vmatrix} W & X \\ Y & Z \end{vmatrix} = 16(4) = \mathbf{64}$.

170. Subtracting the first row from all the rest yields

$$\begin{vmatrix} 3 & 1 & 1 & 1 & 1 & 1 \\ 0 & 2 & 0 & 0 & 0 & 0 \\ 0 & 2 & 2 & 0 & 0 & 0 \\ 0 & 2 & 2 & 2 & 0 & 0 \\ 0 & 2 & 2 & 2 & 2 & 0 \\ 0 & 2 & 2 & 2 & 2 & 2 \end{vmatrix},$$

then expanding by minors down the first column gives

$$3 \begin{vmatrix} 2 & 0 & 0 & 0 & 0 \\ 2 & 2 & 0 & 0 & 0 \\ 2 & 2 & 2 & 0 & 0 \\ 2 & 2 & 2 & 2 & 0 \\ 2 & 2 & 2 & 2 & 2 \end{vmatrix}.$$

Since the remaining determinant is triangular, its determinant is equal to the product of the diagonal elements, or $2^5 = 32$. Hence the original determinant is $3(32) = \mathbf{96}$.

171. To find A^{-1}, we first divide by the determinant, 2, then replace every element by its minor, to get $\frac{1}{2} \begin{pmatrix} 1 & -1 \\ -2 & 4 \end{pmatrix}$, then transpose the result, to get $A^{-1} = \frac{1}{2} \begin{pmatrix} 1 & -2 \\ -1 & 4 \end{pmatrix}$. To find A^{-2}, we square this to get $\frac{1}{4} \begin{pmatrix} 1 & -2 \\ -1 & 4 \end{pmatrix} \begin{pmatrix} 1 & -2 \\ -1 & 4 \end{pmatrix} = \frac{1}{4} \begin{pmatrix} 3 & -10 \\ -5 & 18 \end{pmatrix} = \begin{pmatrix} 3/4 & -5/2 \\ -5/4 & 9/2 \end{pmatrix}$.

172. We will create a determinant equation which is satisfied only when (x, y) is on the circle:

$$\begin{vmatrix} x^2 + y^2 & x & y & 1 \\ 10 & -3 & 1 & 1 \\ 20 & 2 & 4 & 1 \\ 29 & 5 & -2 & 1 \end{vmatrix} = 0.$$

Why does this have the desired property? Substituting in $(x, y) = (-3, 1)$, $(2, 4)$, and $(5, -2)$, you can see that in each case the determinant is zero because it has a repeated row. Since expanding the determinant will give the equation of a circle (do you see why?) which is satisfied by the given three points, this is the unique circle passing through the three points.

Similar techniques to this one can be used to write the equations of lines, planes, and conic sections. Though this method is not too generally useful, you should play with the determinants until you can put the desired equations in determinant form.

Chapter 12

Analytical Techniques

Solutions to Exercises

12-1 From the discussion in the chapter, we have

$$\tan\theta = \frac{2/3 - 1/3}{1 + (2/3)(1/3)} = \frac{3}{11}.$$

The answer is not $3/11$, however, since the problem asks for the tangent of the *obtuse* angle. Hence, we require the negative value, $-3/11$ (which we could have found from using $1/3$ as m_2 rather than $2/3$).

12-2 First we recognize the equation as the description of a hyperbola. With a bit of algebra, we write the equation as

$$\frac{(y-2)^2}{9} - \frac{(x-4)^2}{4} = 1.$$

Now recall that $\sec^2\theta - \tan^2\theta = 1$. Comparing this to the form of our hyperbola, we want

$$\frac{(y-2)^2}{9} = \sec^2\theta \quad \text{and} \quad \frac{(x-4)^2}{4} = \tan^2\theta,$$

so $y = 2 + 3\sec\theta$ and $x = 4 + 2\tan\theta$ is our parametric representation.

12-3 Since we know that $\sin^2\theta + \cos^2\theta = 1$, we write the first equation as $x = (1 - \cos^2\theta)/\cos\theta$. Since $y = \cos\theta$, we have

$$x = \frac{1 - y^2}{y},$$

which is the equation of the curve in rectangular coordinates.

12-4 As discussed in the text, the dot product $\overrightarrow{WZ} \cdot \vec{n}$ is the product of the length of the projection of $\overrightarrow{WZ}$ onto $\vec{n}$ and the length of $\vec{n}$ itself. Since we are only interested in the length of the projection, we must divide $\overrightarrow{WZ} \cdot \vec{n}$ by $\|\vec{n}\|$.

12-5 As in the example in the text, we consider our points in the plane as points in the space with $z = 0$. Let $\vec{a} = (\ x_2 - x_1 \quad y_2 - y_1 \quad 0\ )$ and $\vec{b} = (\ x_3 - x_1 \quad y_3 - y_1 \quad 0\ )$. The area of the triangle is $\|\vec{a} \times \vec{b}\|/2$. We find that

$$\vec{a} \times \vec{b} = (\ 0 \quad 0 \quad x_1 y_2 + x_2 y_3 + x_3 y_1 - x_1 y_3 - x_2 y_1 - x_3 y_2\ ).$$

The area of the triangle is half the magnitude of this vector, or

$$\text{Area} = |(x_1 y_2 + x_2 y_3 + x_3 y_1 - x_1 y_3 - x_2 y_1 - x_3 y_2)/2|.$$

Evaluating the determinant expression in the problem, we get the same expression as above, so the determinant in the problem does indeed give the area.

12-6 The previous exercise virtually proves the assertion for a triangle. For induction, suppose that the process works for n points. If we tack on an $n + 1$th vertex, we just add another triangle as shown in the diagram. Let A through E be the original n points and X be our added point. The area of $ABCDEX$ is $[ABCDE] + [AEX]$. Since $ABCDE$ has n vertices, our process works for finding $[ABCDE]$, so we write

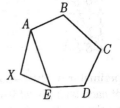

$$
\begin{array}{cccc}
 & x_1 & y_1 & \\
 & x_2 & y_2 & \\
x_2 y_1 & x_3 & y_3 & x_1 y_2 \\
\vdots & \vdots & \vdots & \vdots \\
x_{n-1} y_{n-2} & x_n & y_n & x_{n-2} y_{n-1} \\
x_n y_{n-1} & x_1 & y_1 & x_{n-1} y_n \\
x_1 y_n & & & x_n y_1
\end{array}
$$

and let K_r be the sum of the right column and K_l be the sum of the left. Then we have $[ABCDE] = |(K_r - K_l)/2|$. For the triangle AEX, we note that point A is (x_1, y_1), E is (x_n, y_n), and X is (x_{n+1}, y_{n+1}), so we find $[AEX]$ by writing

$$
\begin{array}{cccc}
 & x_1 & y_1 & \\
 & x_n & y_n & \\
x_n y_1 & x_{n+1} & y_{n+1} & x_1 y_n \\
x_{n+1} y_n & x_1 & y_1 & x_n y_{n+1} \\
x_1 y_{n+1} & & & x_{n+1} y_1
\end{array}
$$

and letting L_r be the sum on the right and L_l be the sum on the left. Then $[AEX] = |(L_r - L_l)/2|$. If we write all the vertices of $ABCDEX$ as the problem suggests, we have

$$
\begin{array}{cccc}
 & x_1 & y_1 & \\
 & x_2 & y_2 & \\
x_2 y_1 & x_3 & y_3 & x_1 y_2 \\
\vdots & \vdots & \vdots & \vdots \\
x_n y_{n-1} & x_{n+1} & y_{n+1} & x_{n-1} y_n \\
x_{n+1} y_n & x_1 & y_1 & x_n y_{n+1} \\
x_1 y_{n+1} & & & x_{n+1} y_1
\end{array}
$$

and we let M_r be the sum of the terms on the right and M_l be the sum of those on the left. By direct comparison we find that the terms occurring in $K_r - K_l + L_r - L_l$ are exactly those which occur in $M_r - M_l$. Hence, $|(M_r - M_l)/2|$ represents the sum of the area of $ABCDE$ and our new triangle and thus our induction is complete. Note that our induction is not completely 100% rigorous, but it should give you a pretty good idea how it goes.

12-7 Instead of dealing directly with right triangle ABC, we complete the rectangle $ABCD$ and view $\triangle ABC$ as half this rectangle. Notice that $\triangle ACD$ is just the rotation of $\triangle ABC$ about the center of $ABCD$. Clearly, $\triangle ABC$ and $\triangle ACD$ have the same number of interior points $I_\triangle$ and the same number of boundary points. We'll divide the boundary points of the triangles into those inside the rectangle (the points on AC) and those on the perimeter of the rectangle. The latter is simple; there are $a + b + 1$ points on the perimeter of each triangle which are also on the perimeter of the rectangle. For the former, we let $B_\triangle$ be the number of lattice points on AC (besides A and C). Since the area of $\triangle ABC$ is $ab/2$, to prove Pick's Theorem we must show that

$$ab/2 = I_\triangle + \frac{B_\triangle + a + b + 1}{2} - 1$$

To prove this, we apply Pick's Theorem to $ABCD$. Since all the interior points of $ABCD$ are either interior points of one triangle or the other (but not both) or on segment AC, we have

$$ab = (2I_\triangle + B_\triangle) + \frac{2a + 2b}{2} - 1$$

Dividing this by 2 we have

$$\frac{ab}{2} = I_\triangle + \frac{B + a + b}{2} - \frac{1}{2},$$

which is equivalent to our desired expression. Hence we have proven that Pick's Theorem indeed holds for right triangles whose sides are parallel to the coordinate axes.

12-8 Number the vertices of polygon P from 1 to n. We divide the polygon into $n - 2$ triangles by drawing segments from vertex 1 to the vertices 3 through $n - 1$. Now let I_p

and B_p be the number of interior points and boundary points of the polygon and $I_\triangle$ be the number of points inside any of the triangles. If we apply Pick's Theorem to the triangles and add the results we will get the area A of the polygon. Each interior point of the polygon is either an interior point of one triangle or a boundary point of two triangles. Hence in summing the Pick's Theorem results from the triangles, each interior point of the polygon is included exactly once. The boundary points of P are boundary points of the triangles. Let the number of the boundary points of P which are not vertices of P be B_*; hence $B_p = B_* + n$. Each of the members of B_* is included once with weight 1/2 in the triangle Pick's Theorem results because each one is on exactly one triangle. The vertices are another matter. Vertex 1 appears in all $n - 2$ triangles, vertices 2 and $n - 1$ are only on 1, and the other $n - 3$ are on 2 triangles each. Summing these we have $(n-2)+1+1+2(n-3) = 3n-6$, each with weight 1/2. Since we are adding $n - 2$ Pick's Theorem equations to get the area A of the polygon, we have $n - 2$ '-1's, so our result is

$$
\begin{aligned}
A &= I_p + \frac{B_*}{2} + \frac{3n-6}{2} - (n-2) \\
&= I_p + \frac{B_p - n}{2} + \frac{3n-6}{2} - \frac{2n-4}{2} \\
&= I_p + B_p - 1,
\end{aligned}
$$

which proves Pick's Theorem for our polygon.

    12-9   Order the points A, B, and C from least to greatest y coordinate and from least to greatest x coordinate. Hence there are 4 points which have the largest or smallest of one of these coordinates. Since there are only 3 distinct points, one point must be on an extreme in both lists. This point is our corner as point B in the proof. The rectangle is then easily constructed by drawing the appropriate lines from B. (Make sure you see this.)

    12-10   We can extend our argument to non-convex polygons by noting that we can chop any non-convex region into convex pieces. If we apply Pick's Theorem to each piece then sum the results we will prove Pick's Theorem for the non-convex region.

    12-11   The vector from the first point to the second is $(\,2-1 \quad 3-(-1) \quad 1-3\,) = (\,1 \quad 4 \quad -2\,) = \vec{v}$, so to get a point on the line we can add any multiple of $\vec{v}$ to $(1, -1, 3)$. Thus, our parametric representation is

$$
\begin{aligned}
x &= 1+t \\
y &= -1 + 4t \\
z &= 3 - 2t.
\end{aligned}
$$

    12-12   First we find two vectors in the given plane. Letting the points in the order of the problem be P, Q, and R, we have the vectors $\overrightarrow{PQ} = (\,-1 \quad -5 \quad 0\,)$ and $\overrightarrow{PR} = (\,-2 \quad -4 \quad 1\,)$. Thus, the vector $\overrightarrow{PQ} \times \overrightarrow{PR} = (\,-5 \quad 1 \quad -6\,)$ is normal to the plane. Hence, for any point $S = (x, y, z)$ in the plane the vector $\overrightarrow{PS}$ is normal to $(-5 \quad 1 \quad -6)$, so

$$(x - 1 \quad y - 2 \quad z - 1) \cdot (-5 \quad 1 \quad -6) = 0.$$

Thus, our plane is $5x - y + 6z - 9 = 0$.

12-13 First, just like the vector $(A \quad B)$ is normal to the line $Ax + By + C = 0$, the vector $\vec{n} = (A \quad B \quad C)$ is normal to the plane $Ax + By + Cz + D = 0$. From here we proceed just as we did in finding the distance from a point to a line. Let $P = (x_1, y_1, z_1)$ be a point in the plane and point Q be the given (x_0, y_0, z_0). Our desired distance then is the length of the projection of $\overrightarrow{PQ} = (x_0 - x_1 \quad y_0 - y_1 \quad z_0 - z_1)$ onto the normal vector through P. As before, we use the dot product to find this length as

$$\begin{aligned} D &= \frac{|\overrightarrow{PQ} \cdot \vec{n}|}{\|\vec{n}\|} = \frac{|A(x_0 - x_1) + B(y_0 - y_1) + C(z_0 - z_1)|}{\sqrt{A^2 + B^2 + C^2}} \\ &= \frac{|Ax_0 + By_0 + Cz_0 - (Ax_1 + By_1 + Cz_1)|}{\sqrt{A^2 + B^2 + C^2}} \\ &= \frac{|Ax_0 + By_0 + Cz_0 + D|}{\sqrt{A^2 + B^2 + C^2}}, \end{aligned}$$

where we have used the fact that (x_1, y_1, z_1) is on the plane so that $Ax_1 + By_1 + Cz_1 = -D$. If you don't quite follow this, compare it to the example in the book where we find the distance from a point to a line.

12-14 Since $\vec{a} \times \vec{b}$ is normal to plane OAB, it is in the same direction as $\vec{n}$. Hence, we can write $\vec{a} \times \vec{b} = \|\vec{a} \times \vec{b}\|\vec{n}$ since the cross product has magnitude $\|\vec{a} \times \vec{b}\|$ and direction $\vec{n}$. Thus, we can write

$$\vec{c} \cdot (\vec{a} \times \vec{b}) = \vec{c} \cdot (\|\vec{a} \times \vec{b}\|\vec{n}) = \|\vec{a} \times \vec{b}\|(\vec{c} \cdot \vec{n}).$$

12-15 Regardless of the order of the vectors in the product, the box product still has magnitude equal to the volume of the parallelepiped spanned by the three vectors. This parallelepiped is the same for any ordering of the vectors, so the volume remains the same as does the magnitude of the box product.

12-16 Let the vectors be $\vec{u}$, $\vec{v}$, and $\vec{w}$. Since

$$\vec{v} \times \vec{w} = \begin{vmatrix} \vec{i} & \vec{j} & \vec{k} \\ x_2 & y_2 & z_2 \\ x_3 & y_3 & z_3 \end{vmatrix},$$

to find $\vec{u} \cdot (\vec{v} \times \vec{w})$, we multiply the first term of $\vec{u}$ by the coefficient of $\vec{i}$ in the cross product, the second term of $\vec{u}$ by the coefficient of $\vec{j}$, and the third term of $\vec{u}$ by the coefficient of $\vec{k}$, then add the three results. This procedure is exactly the same as substituting the components of $\vec{u}$ for the $\vec{i}$, $\vec{j}$, and $\vec{k}$ in the above cross product. (Make sure you see why!) Our box product then is

$$\vec{u} \cdot (\vec{v} \times \vec{w}) = \begin{vmatrix} x_1 & y_1 & z_1 \\ x_2 & y_2 & z_2 \\ x_3 & y_3 & z_3 \end{vmatrix}.$$

For a tetrahedron, we choose the first point to be the origin; hence, the vectors which form the tetrahedron are $(x_2 - x_1 \quad y_2 - y_1 \quad z_2 - z_1)$, $(x_3 - x_1 \quad y_3 - y_1 \quad z_3 - z_1)$, and $(x_4 - x_1 \quad y_4 - y_1 \quad z_4 - z_1)$. The volume is the absolute value of 1/6 of the box product of these, or

$$V = \left| \frac{1}{6} \begin{vmatrix} x_2 - x_1 & y_2 - y_1 & z_2 - z_1 \\ x_3 - x_1 & y_3 - y_1 & z_3 - z_1 \\ x_4 - x_1 & y_4 - y_1 & z_4 - z_1 \end{vmatrix} \right|.$$

12-17 The z coordinate is easy; it's just $z = -4$. As for x and y, we convert the $(3, 120°)$ from polar to rectangular coordinates as $x = r \cos \theta = -3/2$ and $y = r \sin \theta = 3\sqrt{3}/2$. Hence our point is $(-3/2, 3\sqrt{3}/2, -4)$.

12-18 The equation for a cylinder in rectangular coordinates is $x^2 + y^2 = k^2$ for some constant k. Letting $x = r \cos \theta$ and $y = r \sin \theta$, we have $x^2 + y^2 = r^2(\cos^2 \theta + \sin^2 \theta) = r^2 = k^2$ as our equation in cylindrical coordinates. If we take the square root, we find that the equation for a cylinder in cylindrical coordinates is just $r = k$. Does this make sense? A cylinder is the set of points k away from the z axis, so the radius is constant while z and θ are unrestricted.

12-19 Using our values for x, y, and z, we have

$$\begin{aligned} x^2 + y^2 + z^2 &= \rho^2 \cos^2 \theta \sin^2 \phi + \rho^2 \sin^2 \theta \sin^2 \phi + \rho^2 \cos^2 \phi \\ &= \rho^2 \sin^2 \phi (\cos^2 \theta + \sin^2 \theta) + \rho^2 \cos^2 \phi \\ &= \rho^2 \sin^2 \phi + \rho^2 \cos^2 \phi \\ &= \rho^2, \end{aligned}$$

as desired.

12-20 Every point on the sphere is a constant distance k from the origin, no matter what ϕ and θ are. Since this distance from a point to the origin in polar coordinates is simply ρ, our equation for a sphere centered at the origin is $\rho = k$.

12-21 We've already addressed the curve $\rho = \rho_1$ (it's a sphere), so we move on to $\theta = \theta_1$. For this surface, ρ and ϕ can take any value and the resulting graph is a plane perpendicular to the xy plane which makes an angle of θ with the positive x axis. Similarly, if we let ϕ be constant and ρ and θ vary, we trace out a cone, since varying θ from 0 to 2π while keeping ϕ and ρ constant makes circles. Varying ρ varies the radius, ultimately forming a cone.

12-22 The equation $x^2 + y^2 = r^2$ in the (x, y) plane describes a circle; hence, for $x^2 + y^2 = z^2$ at each value of z we have a circle. Thus, every cross-section of the graph is a circle; however, the graph is not a cylinder, because the radii of these circles are not all the same. In fact, at $z = z_1$, the radius is z_1 and the distance from the center of the circle to the origin (which is clearly on the graph) is also z_1. From this we see that the graph is **a cone**, since the ratio of the radius of any of the cross-sectional circles to the distance (i.e. the height of the cone) from the center of the circle to vertex (the origin) is constant. If you don't quite buy this, try graphing the equation or writing the equation in cylindrical coordinates.

12-23 Since $\overrightarrow{AB} = \vec{B} - \vec{A}$ and likewise for $\overrightarrow{BC}$, we can write

$$\overrightarrow{AB} + \overrightarrow{BC} = \vec{B} - \vec{A} + \vec{C} - \vec{B} = \vec{C} - \vec{A} = \overrightarrow{AC}.$$

12-24 Again we write $\overrightarrow{AB} = \vec{B} - \vec{A}$ and likewise for $\overrightarrow{AC}$ and we find

$$\overrightarrow{AB} - \overrightarrow{AC} = \vec{B} - \vec{A} - (\vec{C} - \vec{A}) = \vec{B} - \vec{C} = \overrightarrow{CB}.$$

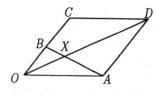

12-25 Let O be the origin. If we extend the line past X to the point D such that OA is the side of a parallelogram with sides parallel to OA and OB as shown, we have $\triangle XBO \sim \triangle XAD$. Hence, $AD/BO = AX/BX = 2$ and $OX/XD = 1/2$. Thus, we have $OC = 2OB$. Hence, $\vec{C} = 2\vec{B}$ and $\vec{D} = 2\vec{B} + \overrightarrow{CD} = 2\vec{B} + \vec{A}$ since $\vec{A}$ and $\overrightarrow{CD}$ have the same direction and magnitude. Since $OX/XD = 1/2$, we find $OX/OD = 1/3$ and $\vec{X} = \vec{D}/3 = (2\vec{B} + \vec{A})/3$. Can you extend this argument to show that if point X is on AB such that $AX = c(BX)$, then $\vec{X} = (c\vec{B} + \vec{A})/(c + 1)$. Is this still true if c is a fraction? An irrational number?

12-26 Let D and E be the feet of the angle bisectors drawn from A and B, respectively. Since I is on both AD and BE, we can write

$$\vec{I} - \vec{A} = k_1(\vec{D} - \vec{A})$$
$$\vec{I} - \vec{B} = k_2(\vec{E} - \vec{B}).$$

Using the example in the text to find $\vec{D}$ and $\vec{E}$, we have

$$\vec{I} = k_1\left(\frac{b\vec{B} + c\vec{C}}{b + c} - \vec{A}\right) + \vec{A}$$

$$\vec{I} = k_2\left(\frac{a\vec{A} + c\vec{C}}{a + c} - \vec{B}\right) + \vec{B}.$$

Equating coefficients of $\vec{C}$ and $\vec{B}$, we find

$$\frac{k_1 c}{b+c} = \frac{k_2 c}{a+c} \quad \text{and} \quad 1 - k_2 = \frac{k_1 b}{b+c}.$$

Solving for k_2 we find $k_2 = (a+c)/(a+b+c)$, so using the second equation for $\vec{I}$ above, we find

$$\vec{I} = \frac{a\vec{A} + b\vec{B} + c\vec{C}}{a+b+c}.$$

    12-27   Just as in the prior example, we apply the law of cosines to find

$$(\vec{A} - \vec{C}) \cdot (\vec{A} - \vec{C}) = \|\vec{A}\|^2 + \|\vec{C}\|^2 - 2\|\vec{A}\|\|\vec{C}\| \cos \angle AOC.$$

Comparing this to the given equation, we have $\cos \angle AOC = 1/2$, so that $\angle AOC = 60°$.

    12-28   The lines defined as AG in the previous example are the altitudes of regular tetrahedron $ABCD$; hence, all that we have proved for those segments is also true for the altitudes of a regular tetrahedron.

    12-29   In the prior example, we have $\vec{X} - \vec{A} = (3/4)(\vec{G} - \vec{A})$, so that $AX = 3GX$. Segment XG is the radius of the inscribed sphere since XG is perpendicular to BCD and the perpendicular segments from X to the centers of each of the other 3 faces have the same length. Similarly, $AX = BX = CX = DX$ and the sphere with center X and radius AX is circumscribed about the tetrahedron. Since $AX/AG = 3/4$ and $XG/AG = 1/4$, the circumradius and inradius are 3/4 and 1/4, respectively, of the altitude length.

    12-30   Let AG be the altitude from A to G, the centroid of $\triangle BCD$. We find AG by considering right triangle AGB. We know hypotenuse AB has length 6. The altitudes of equilateral triangle BCD (and hence the medians) have length $3\sqrt{3}$. Since BG is 2/3 the median from B, it has length $(2/3)(3\sqrt{3}) = 2\sqrt{3}$. Thus, from $\triangle AGB$, we have $AG = 2\sqrt{6}$. From the prior exercise, the inradius is $(1/4)(2\sqrt{6}) = \sqrt{6}/2$ and the circumradius is $3\sqrt{6}/2$. Since the area of $\triangle BCD$ is $9\sqrt{3}$, the volume of $ABCD$ is $(AG)[BCD]/3 = \mathbf{18\sqrt{2}}$.

Solutions to Problems

173. This is exactly like an example in the text. Our vectors spanning the tetrahedron are $\overrightarrow{AB}$, $\overrightarrow{AC}$, and $\overrightarrow{AD}$, or $(3 \quad 3 \quad -2)$, $(1 \quad 0 \quad -1)$, and $(2 \quad 4 \quad -2)$. Finding our volume as in the example, we have

$$V = \left| \frac{1}{6} \begin{vmatrix} 3 & 3 & -2 \\ 1 & 0 & -1 \\ 2 & 4 & -2 \end{vmatrix} \right| = \frac{4}{6} = \frac{2}{3}.$$

174. Solving the first equation for 2^p, we have $2^p = x - 1$. We can write the second equation if terms of 2^p as $y = 1 + 1/2^p$. Hence, we have $y = 1 + 1/(x - 1) = x/(x-1)$.

175. As you should have determined in an exercise in the chapter, the graph of $x^2 + y^2 = z^2$ represents a cone. Bounding this by $z \leq 6$, we find that the cone has height 6 and radius 6, so the volume is $6(6^2)\pi/3 = 72\pi$.

176. Projecting P onto the x axis, y axis, and z axis, we find points X, Y, and Z, respectizely. Hence, we have $\cos\theta_1 = ZO/OP$, $\cos\theta_2 = XO/OP$, and $\cos\theta_3 = YO/OP$. Since $OP^2 = XO^2 + YO^2 + ZO^2$, we have

$$\cos^2\theta_1 + \cos^2\theta_2 + \cos^2\theta_3 = 1.$$

From this we solve for $\cos\theta_3$ as $\sqrt{1 - R^2 - S^2}$.

177. The line is in the direction from the first point to the second, or $(-3 \quad -3 \quad -6)$. Hence the line goes through the point $(1, 2, 3)$ and in the direction $(-3 \quad -3 \quad -6)$, so the line is

$$(1, 2, 3) + t(-3, -3, -6) = 0,$$

just as in the text. Thus, our parametric equations describing the line are

$$\begin{aligned} x &= 1 - 3t \\ y &= 2 - 3t \\ z &= 3 - 6t. \end{aligned}$$

178. Set up a coordinate system with $B = (0, 0, 0)$, $A = (v, 0, 0)$, and $C = (0, w, 0)$. Let $D = (a, b, c)$. Since $\angle BAD = \pi/2$, point D is in the plane perpendicular to line BA. This plane is described by $x = v$, so we have $a = v$. Since $\angle BCD = \pi/2$, we have $b = w$. (Make sure you see both of these.) Applying the Pythagorean Theorem to $\triangle CDA$, we find

$$v^2 + w^2 = CA^2 = CD^2 + DA^2 = v^2 + c^2 + w^2 + c^2,$$

so $c = 0$, and point D is in the xy plane along with the other three points.

179. First we observe that since $\overrightarrow{BP}$ and $\overrightarrow{AP}$ are in opposite directions and $AP = k(BP)$, we have $k\overrightarrow{BP} + \overrightarrow{AP} = 0$ and likewise $k\overrightarrow{RD} + \overrightarrow{RC} = 0$. We know that $\overrightarrow{BP} + \overrightarrow{PR} + \overrightarrow{RD} = \overrightarrow{BD}$ and $\overrightarrow{AP} + \overrightarrow{PR} + \overrightarrow{RC} = \overrightarrow{AC}$. Hence, we have

$$\begin{aligned} \overrightarrow{PR} &= \frac{(k+1)\overrightarrow{PR} + k\overrightarrow{BP} + \overrightarrow{AP} + k\overrightarrow{RD} + \overrightarrow{RC}}{k+1} \\ &= \frac{k(\overrightarrow{BP} + \overrightarrow{PR} + \overrightarrow{RD}) + \overrightarrow{AP} + \overrightarrow{PR} + \overrightarrow{RC}}{k+1} \\ &= \frac{k\overrightarrow{BD} + \overrightarrow{AC}}{k+1}. \end{aligned}$$

Similarly we find

$$\overrightarrow{QS} = \frac{-k\overrightarrow{AC} + \overrightarrow{BD}}{k+1}.$$

We can find the area of $PQRS$ as $\|\overrightarrow{PR} \times \overrightarrow{QS}\|/2$, since the area of a quadrilateral is half the product of its diagonals times the sine of the angle between them. Make sure you see this. Hence, we have

$$[PQRS] = \frac{1}{2} \left\| \left(\frac{k\overrightarrow{BD} + \overrightarrow{AC}}{k+1} \right) \times \left(\frac{-k\overrightarrow{AC} + \overrightarrow{BD}}{k+1} \right) \right\|$$

$$= \left\| -\frac{k^2}{2(k+1)^2} \overrightarrow{BD} \times \overrightarrow{AC} + \frac{1}{2(k+1)^2} \overrightarrow{AC} \times \overrightarrow{BD} \right\|,$$

since $\overrightarrow{AC} \times \overrightarrow{AC} = \overrightarrow{BD} \times \overrightarrow{BD} = 0$. Because $\overrightarrow{BD} \times \overrightarrow{AC} = -\overrightarrow{AC} \times \overrightarrow{BD}$, we then have

$$[PQRS] = \frac{k^2+1}{(k+1)^2} \cdot \frac{1}{2} \cdot \|\overrightarrow{AC} \times \overrightarrow{BD}\| = \frac{k^2+1}{(k+1)^2} \cdot [ABCD].$$

Thus, we have $[PQRS]/[ABCD] = (k^2+1)/(k+1)^2$. Setting this equal to 0.52 from the information in the problem, we have the quadratic (after a bit of algebra) $6k^2 - 13k + 6 = 0$. Factoring, we have the values $k = \mathbf{2/3}$ and $k = \mathbf{3/2}$.

180. We have a sphere and a point on the sphere, so we can try analytic geometry. Let the corner of the room be the origin and the radius of the sphere be r. The floor then is the xy plane and the walls are the yz plane and the xz plane. Since the center of the sphere is r away from the floor and the walls, the center is (r, r, r). Hence, the equation describing the sphere is

$$(x - r)^2 + (y - r)^2 + (z - r)^2 = r^2.$$

Fortunately, we are told that the point $(5, 5, 10)$ is on the sphere. Putting this point in our equation, we have

$$(5 - r)^2 + (5 - r)^2 + (10 - r)^2 = 3r^2 - 40r + 150 = r^2.$$

Thus, $r^2 - 20r + 75 = (r - 5)(r - 15) = 0$ and the radius of the sphere is 5 or 15. These two radii account for the two spheres in the problem. Hence the diameters are 10 and 30 and our desired sum is **40**.

181. Since $\triangle ABC$ is an isosceles right triangle, we can describe the vertices A, B, and C as $(k, 0)$, $(-k, 0)$, and $(0, k)$, respectively. (Why?) Since point P is on AB, it is on the y axis and we can describe it by $(p, 0)$. Hence, we have $2CP^2 = 2(\sqrt{p^2 + k^2})^2 = 2p^2 + 2k^2$. Similarly, we find

$$AP^2 + BP^2 = (\sqrt{(k-p)^2})^2 + (\sqrt{(-k-p)^2})^2 = k^2 - 2kp + p^2 + k^2 + 2kp + p^2.$$

Thus, we have $AP^2 + BP^2 = 2p^2 + 2k^2 = 2CP^2$.

182. Let $a = x + y$. Thus, we have $|a + z| + |a - z| \leq 8$. Since $|b| + |c| \geq b + c$ for all b and c, we have $8 \geq |a + z| + |a - z| \geq 2a$. Thus, we have $a = x + y \leq 4$. Similarly, we have $8 \geq |a + z| + |a - z| \geq a + z - (a - z) = 2z$. Thus we have $z \leq 4$ as well. Our region then becomes $0 \leq x + y \leq 4$, $0 \leq z \leq 4$. Thus, we have a right prism whose base is a right triangle (bounded by the line $x + y = 4$ and the x, y axes) and whose height is 4. The vertices of our triangle are $(0, 0)$, $(4, 0)$, and $(0, 4)$. Hence the area of the triangle is $4(4)/2 = 8$ and our volume is (base area)(height)$= (8)(4) = \mathbf{32}$.

183. Since we have a line perpendicular to a plane, the fact that $\vec{a} \cdot \vec{b} = 0$ if and only if $\vec{a} \perp \vec{b}$ is useful. Let the three edges of the rectangular box be described by $\vec{x} = \overrightarrow{AD}$, $\vec{y} = \overrightarrow{AB}$, and $\vec{z} = \overrightarrow{AA_1}$. Since C_1 is across the box from A, we have $\overrightarrow{AC_1} = \overrightarrow{AD} + \overrightarrow{DC} + \overrightarrow{CC_1} = \vec{x} + \vec{y} + \vec{z}$ (since $\overrightarrow{DC} = \overrightarrow{AB}$ and $\overrightarrow{AA_1} = \overrightarrow{CC_1}$). Furthermore, we find $\overrightarrow{A_1D} = \overrightarrow{AD} - \overrightarrow{AA_1} = \vec{x} - \vec{z}$ and $\overrightarrow{A_1B} = \overrightarrow{AB} - \overrightarrow{AA_1} = \vec{y} - \vec{z}$. Since the edges of a rectangular box are perpendicular, we have $\vec{x} \cdot \vec{y} = \vec{y} \cdot \vec{z} = \vec{z} \cdot \vec{x} = 0$. Similarly, AC_1 being perpendicular to A_1BD gives us $AC_1 \perp A_1D$ and $AC_1 \perp A_1B$. From the first we have

$$
\begin{aligned}
0 &= (\vec{x} + \vec{y} + \vec{z}) \cdot (\vec{x} - \vec{z}) \\
&= \vec{x} \cdot \vec{x} + \vec{y} \cdot \vec{x} - \vec{y} \cdot \vec{z} - \vec{z} \cdot \vec{z} \\
&= \|\vec{x}\| - \|\vec{z}\|,
\end{aligned}
$$

so that $\|\vec{x}\| = \|\vec{z}\|$. Similarly from $AC_1 \perp A_1B$ we find $\|\vec{y}\| = \|\vec{z}\|$. Thus, the lengths of the three different edges of the box are all equal, so the box is a cube.

184. Recalling our work in the chapter with tetrahedrons, we decide to try vectors! Let the origin be the centroid of $ABCD$. Hence, we have $\vec{A} + \vec{B} + \vec{C} + \vec{D} = 0$ and we wish to show $\vec{E} + \vec{F} + \vec{G} + \vec{H} = 0$. Subtracting these, we find that we can also prove the problem by showing

$$
\overrightarrow{AE} + \overrightarrow{BF} + \overrightarrow{CG} + \overrightarrow{DH} = 0.
$$

Since $\overrightarrow{BD} \times \overrightarrow{CD}$ is normal to BCD, it is parallel to $\overrightarrow{AE}$ (since AE is on the altitude from A to BCD). Hence, we write

$$
\overrightarrow{BD} \times \overrightarrow{CD} = (\vec{D} - \vec{B}) \times (\vec{D} - \vec{C}) = \vec{B} \times \vec{C} + \vec{C} \times \vec{D} + \vec{D} \times \vec{B}.
$$

Since $\|\overrightarrow{BD} \times \overrightarrow{CD}\| = 2[BCD]$, $h_a[BCD]/3 = V$, and $\|\overrightarrow{AE}\| = k/h_a$ (given), we have

$$
\|\overrightarrow{AE}\| = \frac{k}{h_a} = \frac{k[BCD]}{3V} = \frac{k\|\overrightarrow{BD} \times \overrightarrow{CD}\|}{6V}.
$$

Since $\overrightarrow{AE}$ and $\overrightarrow{BD} \times \overrightarrow{CD}$ are in the same direction, we have

$$
\overrightarrow{AE} = \frac{k}{6V} \left(\vec{B} \times \vec{C} + \vec{C} \times \vec{D} + \vec{D} \times \vec{B} \right).
$$

We find similar expressions for $\overrightarrow{BF}$, $\overrightarrow{CG}$, and $\overrightarrow{DH}$. Putting them all together, we find

$$\frac{6V}{k}\left(\overrightarrow{AE} + \overrightarrow{BF} + \overrightarrow{CG} + \overrightarrow{DH}\right) =$$

$$\left(\vec{B} \times \vec{C} + \vec{C} \times \vec{D} + \vec{D} \times \vec{B}\right) + \left(\vec{A} \times \vec{D} + \vec{D} \times \vec{C} + \vec{C} \times \vec{A}\right) +$$

$$\left(\vec{A} \times \vec{B} + \vec{B} \times \vec{D} + \vec{D} \times \vec{B}\right) + \left(\vec{A} \times \vec{C} + \vec{C} \times \vec{B} + \vec{B} \times \vec{A}\right) = 0$$

as a consequence of repeated application of $\vec{x} \times \vec{y} = -\vec{y} \times \vec{x}$. Hence $\overrightarrow{AE} + \overrightarrow{BF} + \overrightarrow{CG} + \overrightarrow{DH} = 0$, so $\vec{E} + \vec{F} + \vec{G} + \vec{H} = 0$, and the centroid of $EFGH$ is also O.

Chapter 13

Equations and Expressions

Solutions to Exercises

13-1 What did you learn?

13-2 Let $y = 1$; from the repeated equation $-3y - z = -1$ we find $z = -2$ and using these we find $(x, y, z) = (\mathbf{7}, \mathbf{1}, -\mathbf{2})$. Similarly, we can pick $y = 0$ to get the solution $(-\mathbf{1}, \mathbf{0}, \mathbf{1})$, and so on.

13-3 Eliminating x from the first two equations would leave

$$\begin{aligned} x + y + 3z &= 2 \\ -3y - z &= -1 \\ -3y - z &= 0. \end{aligned}$$

Since no solution satisfies the last two equations simultaneously, there are no solutions to this system.

13-4 Eliminating the x's is easier than eliminating the z's.

13-5 First we set up our matrix:

$$\begin{pmatrix} 4 & 2 & 1 & 3 \\ 2 & -3 & 1 & 6 \\ 1 & -3 & 2 & 6 \end{pmatrix}.$$

Multiplying the third row by 4 and subtracting the first row leaves

$$\begin{pmatrix} 4 & 2 & 1 & 3 \\ 2 & -3 & 1 & 6 \\ 0 & -14 & 7 & 21 \end{pmatrix}.$$

Multiplying the second row by 2 and subtracting the first row from it leaves

$$\begin{pmatrix} 4 & 2 & 1 & 3 \\ 0 & -8 & 1 & 9 \\ 0 & -14 & 7 & 21 \end{pmatrix}.$$

Finally, we multiply the last row by 4 and subtract 7 times the second row from the result (to make the second element in the last row 0) to get

$$\begin{pmatrix} 4 & 2 & 1 & 3 \\ 0 & -8 & 1 & 9 \\ 0 & 0 & 21 & 21 \end{pmatrix}.$$

Writing this in equation form we have

$$\begin{aligned} 4x + 2y + z &= 3 \\ -8y + z &= 9 \\ 21z &= 21. \end{aligned}$$

From these we quickly find $(x, y, z) = (1, -1, 1)$.

13-6   Just like our other examples in the text, we add the equations since the terms on the left are patterned, giving

$$3w + 3x + 3y + 3z = 102.$$

Hence, $w + x + y + z = 34$. Since $w + x + y = 20$, we have $34 = w + x + y + z = 20 + z$, so $z = 14$. Similarly, we use $w + x + z = 22$ to get $y = 12$ and the other two equations to get $(w, x, y, z) = (-2, 10, 12, 14)$.

13-7   Buoyed by our previous success with addition, let's try adding them:

$$xy + yz + zx = 12\sqrt{6} + 54\sqrt{2} + 48\sqrt{3}.$$

Not too helpful. How else can we combine the three equations to get a nice symmetric equation? Try multiplication:

$$(xy)(yz)(zx) = (12\sqrt{6})(54\sqrt{2})(48\sqrt{3}) = 12 \cdot 54 \cdot 48 \cdot 6.$$

Hence, $(xyz)^2 = 12 \cdot 54 \cdot 48 \cdot 6$, or $xyz = \sqrt{12 \cdot 54 \cdot 48 \cdot 6} = 432$. Since $xy = 12\sqrt{6}$, we can divide this equation into the one for xyz, or

$$\frac{xyz}{xy} = \frac{432}{12\sqrt{6}},$$

so $z = 6\sqrt{6}$. We can do the same to get x and y and we find $(x, y, z) = (4\sqrt{2}, 3\sqrt{3}, 6\sqrt{6})$. Our bag of tricks is apparently not limited to addition!

13-8 For the factorization of $a^n - b^n$, consider the sum

$$a^{n-1} + a^{n-2}b + \cdots + ab^{n-2} + b^{n-1}.$$

This is an n term geometric series with first term a^{n-1} and common ratio b/a. From our discussion of geometric series in Volume 1, we have

$$a^{n-1} + a^{n-2}b + \cdots + ab^{n-2} + b^{n-1} = \frac{a^{n-1} - a^{n-1}\left(\frac{b}{a}\right)^n}{1 - \frac{b}{a}} = \frac{a^n - b^n}{a - b}.$$

Multiplying by $a - b$ gives the desired factorization. The factorization of $a^{2n+1} + b^{2n+1}$ is similarly proved by viewing

$$a^{2n} - a^{2n-1}b + \cdots - ab^{2n-1} + b^{2n}$$

as a $2n + 1$ term geometric series with first term a^{2n} and common ratio $-b/a$.

13-9 Write the product as

$$(a + b + c + d)(a + b + c + d)(a + b + c + d).$$

The resulting terms are of the form a^3, a^2b, or abc. All the cubed terms can occur in only one way. The terms with one squared and one linear variable, such as a^2b, can each occur in 3 ways since the linear term (b for a^2b) can be taken from each of the three terms and the squared term from the other two for a total of three ways to get a^2b. If you don't see this, write the product as $(a_1 + b_1 + c_1 + d_1)(a_2 + b_2 + c_2 + d_2)(a_3 + b_3 + c_3 + d_3)$ and note that the three a^2b terms are $a_1a_2b_3$, $a_1a_3b_2$, and $a_2a_3b_1$. Now we move to the terms like abc. The a can be selected in 3 ways and the b can be chosen in 2 ways from the remaining two terms, and the c can be picked in only one. Hence, abc occurs six times (try finding them all in our above subscripted product). Hence, our desired expansion is

$$a^3 + b^3 + c^3 + d^3$$
$$+ 3(a^2b + b^2a + a^2c + c^2a + a^2d + d^2a + b^2c + c^2b + b^2d + d^2b + c^2d + d^2c)$$
$$+ 6(abc + abd + acd + bcd).$$

13-10 The common denominator is $w^2x^2y^2z^2$ and our desired fraction is

$$\frac{w^2yz + wx^2z + wxy^2 + xyz^2}{w^2x^2y^2z^2}.$$

13-11 Writing the desired expression with a common denominator, we have

$$\frac{1}{xy} + \frac{1}{yz} + \frac{1}{zx} = \frac{z + x + y}{xyz} = \frac{6}{2} = \mathbf{3}.$$

13-12   We can permute the three solutions among the labels x, y, and z in $3! = \mathbf{6}$ ways. The solutions are $(5, 6, -4)$; $(6, 5, -4)$; $(5, -4, 6)$; $(6, -4, 5)$; $(-4, 5, 6)$; and $(-4, 6, 5)$.

13-13   Writing the expression with the common denominator $(a - b)(a - c)(b - c)$ we have

$$\frac{(b + c)(b - c) - (c + a)(a - c) + (a + b)(a - b)}{(a - b)(a - c)(b - c)} = \frac{b^2 - c^2 + c^2 - a^2 + a^2 - b^2}{(a - b)(a - c)(b - c)} = 0,$$

as desired. Remember that sometimes the algebra is simple enough to use instead of our clever polynomial approach.

Solutions to Problems

185. Factoring $a^3 - b^3$ as a difference of cubes, we find $(a - b)(a^2 + ab + b^2) = 19x^3$. Since $a - b = x$, we find $a^2 + ab + b^2 = 19x^2$. Letting $b = a - x$, we can substitute for b and find $a^2 + a(a - x) + (a - x)^2 = 19x^2$, or $a^2 - ax - 6x^2 = 0$. Factoring this gives $(a - 3x)(a + 2x) = 0$, so $a = \mathbf{3x}$ or $a = \mathbf{-2x}$.

186. Seeing the pattern in the vairables, we add the equations, yielding

$$(x + y + y + z + z + x)(x + y + z) = 66 + 77 + 99.$$

Simplifying the equation, we have $2(x + y + z)^2 = 242$, so $x + y + z = \pm 11$. Trying the positive result, we write $x + y + z = 11$ and we can write the equations as

$$
\begin{aligned}
11(x + y) &= 66 \\
11(y + z) &= 99 \\
11(z + x) &= 77.
\end{aligned}
$$

From the first equation we find $x + y = 6$. Since we know $x + y + z = 11$, we have $6 + z = 11$, or $z = 5$. Similarly, we use the second equation to get x and the last to get y. We find that $(x, y, z) = (\mathbf{2, 4, 5})$. Trying the negative solution for $(x + y + z)$, we find (in the same way as above) the solution $(\mathbf{-2, -4, -5})$.

187. Seeing the expressions $a^2 + b^2 + c^2$ and $ab + bc + ca$, we are reminded of our expression

$$(a + b + c)^2 = (a^2 + b^2 + c^2) + 2(ab + bc + ca).$$

Since all perfect squares are nonnegative, we can write

$$(a^2 + b^2 + c^2) + 2(ab + bc + ca) \geq 0,$$

or $ab + bc + ca \geq -(a^2 + b^2 + c^2)/2$. Since $a^2 + b^2 + c^2 = 1$, the minimum value of $ab + bc + ca$ is $\mathbf{-1/2}$.

188. Since 2^{22} isn't a perfect cube, we can't use those factorizations. We don't have a difference of squares, either, so we 'force' the presence of a perfect square by introducing a $2(2^{11})$ term:

$$2^{22} + 1 = 2^{22} + 2(2^{11}) + 1 - 2(2^{11}).$$

Since $2^{22} + 2(2^{11}) + 1 = (2^{11} + 1)^2$, we have

$$(2^{11} + 1)^2 - 2^{12} = (2^{11} + 1 - 2^6)(2^{11} + 1 + 2^6),$$

where we have factored as a difference of squares. We can easily evaluate these factors as 1985 and 2113. Testing these, we find 2113 is prime but 1985 factors into $(5)(397)$, so $2^{22} + 1 = \mathbf{(2113)(5)(397)}$.

189. Letting x, y, z, and w be the numbers, the given information is

$$w + \frac{x + y + z}{3} = 29$$

$$x + \frac{w + y + z}{3} = 23$$

$$y + \frac{w + x + z}{3} = 21$$

$$z + \frac{w + x + y}{3} = 17.$$

Seeing the pattern on the left, we add the equations to find $2(w + x + y + z) = 90$, or $w + x + y + z = 45$. Using this and the first equation, we have $x + y + z = 45 - w$, so $w + (x + y + z)/3 = w + (45 - w)/3 = 2w/3 + 15 = 29$, and $w = 21$. Continuing in this manner for each of the other equations, we find that $(w, x, y, z) = \mathbf{(21, 12, 9, 3)}$.

190. Writing the second term with a common denominator (xyz) and doing the same for the fourth, our product is

$$\left(\frac{1}{x + y + z}\right)\left(\frac{zy + xz + yx}{xyz}\right)\left(\frac{1}{xy + yz + zx}\right)\left(\frac{z + x + y}{xyz}\right).$$

Cancelling the common terms $(x+y+z)$ and $(xy+yz+zx)$, the product is merely $\mathbf{1/x^2 y^2 z^2}$.

191. First we can evaluate the last term $\sqrt{3 - 2\sqrt{2}}$ as $\sqrt{(-1 + \sqrt{2})^2} = -1 + \sqrt{2}$. We can evaluate the numerator of the first expression in exactly the same way we evaluated similar expressions in the chapter. We write $z = \sqrt{\sqrt{5} + 2} + \sqrt{\sqrt{5} - 2}$. Squaring both sides of this, we have $z^2 = \sqrt{5} + 2 + 2\sqrt{5 - 4} + \sqrt{5} - 2 = 2\sqrt{5} + 2$. Hence, $z = \sqrt{2\sqrt{5} + 2}$ (since we want the positive value of z). Thus, our first term in the desired expression is

$$\frac{\sqrt{\sqrt{5} + 2} + \sqrt{\sqrt{5} - 2}}{\sqrt{\sqrt{5} + 1}} = \frac{\sqrt{2\sqrt{5} + 2}}{\sqrt{\sqrt{5} + 1}} = \frac{\sqrt{2}\sqrt{\sqrt{5} + 1}}{\sqrt{\sqrt{5} + 1}} = \sqrt{2}.$$

The answer is $\sqrt{2} - (-1 + \sqrt{2}) = \mathbf{1}$.

192. Seeing equations near to those in the relationship between roots and coefficients of a polynomial, we look for a way to manipulate the given equations into this form. The first equation is for $x + y - z$, so we let $w = -z$ and the equations become

$$
\begin{aligned}
x + y + w &= 0 \\
-wx - xy - yw &= 27 \\
-xyw &= 54.
\end{aligned}
$$

Rewriting the last two equations as $wx + xy + yw = -27$ and $xyw = -54$, we let x, y and w be the roots of a polynomial, which is then $t^3 - 27t + 54 = 0$. Factoring, we find $t^3 - 27t + 54 = (t - 3)^2(t + 6) = 0$, so the solutions for t are 3, 3, and -6. Letting each of the variables (x, y, and w) in turn take the value -6 and the other two variables equal 3, we find the solutions (remember $z = -w$) $(x, y, z) = (\mathbf{-6, 3, -3})$, $(\mathbf{3, -6, -3})$, and $(\mathbf{3, 3, 6})$.

193. The system has no solution if

$$
\begin{vmatrix} n & 1 & 0 \\ 0 & n & 1 \\ 1 & 0 & n \end{vmatrix} = 0,
$$

or $n^3 + 1 = 0$. Hence, if $n = \mathbf{-1}$ we cannot find a unique solution. To show that this is a 'no solution' situation rather than infinitely many solutions, let $n = -1$ and add the three equations to get $0 = 3$.

194. Number the vertices from 1 to 20; let V_i be the number at vertex i. Let S be the common sum shared by all of the faces. For each face, we can write a sum of 5 V_i's which equals S. We have 12 such equations, and each V_i occurs in three of them (since each vertex is a vertex of three faces). If we add the 12 equations, we get

$$
3 \sum_{i=1}^{20} V_i = 12S,
$$

where the summation is a result of each V_i occurring in 3 of the twelve equations. Since

$$
\sum_{i=1}^{20} V_i = 1 + 2 + \cdots + 20 = 210,
$$

we have $12S = 630$. Thus, $S = 52.5$; however S must be an integer since it is a sum of the five integers at each vertex. Hence, we have a contradiction, so we cannot number the vertices as described.

195. As discussed in the chapter, to show that two cubic polynomials are identical, we need only show that they are the same at four points. Let $f(x) = a_1(x + 1)^3 + a_2(x + 2)^3 +$

$a_3(x+3)^3 + a_4(x+4)^3$ and $g(x) = (2x+1)^3$. Seeing the coefficients in the linear equations given, we see that $f(0) = 1$ from the first linear equation. Similarly we see $f(1) = 27$, $f(2) = 125$ and $f(3) = 343$. Since $g(0) = 1$, $g(1) = 27$, $g(2) = 125$, and $g(3) = 343$, $g(x)$ and $f(x)$ are cubic polynomials which agree at four points and thus are the same polynomial. Matching the coefficient of x^3 of $f(x)$ and $g(x)$ gives $a_1 + a_2 + a_3 + a_4 = 8$ and $f(-5) = g(-5)$ gives us $64a_1 + 27a_2 + 8a_3 + a_4 = 729$.

196. Let x, y, and z be the lengths of the edges of the solid. Hence, $xy = 135$, $yz = 30$, and $xz = 50$. Since we seek xyz, we take the product of the three equations to find $(xyz)^2 = 135 \cdot 30 \cdot 50$, so $xyz = \mathbf{450}$.

197. Putting all expressions on one side of the equal sign and writing them with the common denominator $(a-b)(b-c)(c-a)$, we find that we must show that

$$\frac{-bc(b+c)(b-c) - ca(c+a)(c-a) - ab(a+b)(a-b) - (a+b+c)(a-b)(b-c)(c-a)}{(a-b)(b-c)(c-a)}$$

equals zero. Thus, we let

$$f(c) = -bc(b+c)(b-c) - ca(c+a)(c-a) - ab(a+b)(a-b) - (a+b+c)(a-b)(b-c)(c-a).$$

Since $f(c)$ is a cubic equation in c, we can show that $f(c) = 0$ (and hence the identity holds) by showing that $f(c)$ has four distinct roots. Looking at each of the terms, we decide to try the roots 0, a, b, and $-a - b$:

$$
\begin{aligned}
f(0) &= 0 - 0 - ab(a+b)(a-b) - (a+b)(a-b)(b)(-a) = 0; \\
f(a) &= -ba(b+a)(b-a) - 0 - ab(a+b)(a-b) - 0 = 0; \\
f(b) &= 0 - ba(b+a)(b-a) - ab(a+b)(a-b) - 0 = 0; \\
f(-a-b) &= -b(-a-b)(-a)(2b+a) - (-a-b)(a)(-b)(-2a-b) - ab(a+b)(a-b) - 0 \\
&= [(a+b)(ab)][-(a+2b) + (2a+b)] - ab(a+b)(a-b) = 0.
\end{aligned}
$$

Thus, we have found four roots to a cubic. These four are all distinct unless $-a - b = 0$. We can treat that case separately (and swiftly), just using direct algebra on the original identity. Thus, $f(c) \equiv 0$ for all c and we have proven the identity.

198. Recognizing $-y^2 - z^2 + 2yz$ as $-(y-z)^2$, we can write the given expression as

$$x^2 - (y-z)^2 + x + y - z.$$

Now we factor as the difference of squares to find

$$(x - y + z)(x + y - z) + x + y - z = (x - y + z + 1)(x + y - z)$$

as our desired factorization.

199. We can compare the fractions better if the numerators or denominators are the same. We can simplify the numerators easily. For example,

$$\frac{a+b-c}{c} = \frac{a+b}{c} - 1.$$

If we do this then add one to all the resulting terms in the equation we find

$$\frac{a+b}{c} = \frac{a+c}{b} = \frac{b+c}{a}.$$

We can now make the numerators the same by adding 1 to all parts of the equation, yielding

$$\frac{a+b+c}{c} = \frac{a+b+c}{b} = \frac{a+b+c}{a}.$$

Hence, either the denominators are all the same ($a = b = c$), from which the desired expression equals $(2a)(2a)(2a)/a^3 = \mathbf{8}$, or the numerators are all 0 ($a+b+c = 0$). For this case, $(a+b)(b+c)(c+a)/abc = (-c)(-a)(-b)/abc = \mathbf{-1}$.

200. Generally, equations are easiest to attack if all the variables are on one side. Hence, we divide by the $(a+b)$ or the ab terms. Trying the former isn't promising (try and see), but the latter yields

$$
\begin{aligned}
1 &= 2(1/b + 1/a) \\
1 &= 3(1/c + 1/b) \\
1 &= 4(1/a + 1/c).
\end{aligned}
$$

We see now that dividing each equation by the coefficient of the reciprocals gives a nice patterned system. We then add the equations to get $2(1/a + 1/b + 1/c) = 1/2 + 1/3 + 1/4$, so $1/a + 1/b + 1/c = 13/24$. We combine this with the first equation above to get $1 = 2(13/24 - 1/c)$, so $c = 24$. Similarly, $a = 24/5$ and $b = 24/7$, and $5a + 7b + 9c = \mathbf{264}$.

201. Seeing the cubes, we cube both sides, yielding

$$
\begin{aligned}
(x+9) - 3\sqrt[3]{(x+9)^2(x-9)} + 3\sqrt[3]{(x+9)(x-9)^2} - (x-9) &= 27 \\
-3\sqrt[3]{(x+9)(x-9)}(\sqrt[3]{x+9} - \sqrt[3]{x-9}) &= 9 \\
-3\sqrt[3]{x^2 - 81}(3) &= 9.
\end{aligned}
$$

Dividing by 9 and cubing to find x^2, we get $x^2 = \mathbf{80}$.

202. Recognizing expressions as squares of binomials, we write

$$\frac{a^2 + b^2 - c^2 + 2ab}{a^2 + c^2 - b^2 + 2ac} = \frac{(a+b)^2 - c^2}{(a+c)^2 - b^2}.$$

Factoring these as the difference of squares, we have

$$\frac{(a+b+c)(a+b-c)}{(a+c+b)(a+c-b)} = \frac{a+b-c}{a-b+c}.$$

203. Seeing the cube roots, we think of cubing. Let

$$x = \sqrt[3]{5+2\sqrt{13}} + \sqrt[3]{5-2\sqrt{13}}$$

and cube this to get

$$x^3 = 10 + 3\sqrt[3]{5+2\sqrt{13}}\sqrt[3]{5-2\sqrt{13}}\left(\sqrt[3]{5+2\sqrt{13}} + \sqrt[3]{5-2\sqrt{13}}\right)$$

$$x^3 = 10 + 3\sqrt[3]{25-52}\,(x),$$

so we have $x^3 + 9x - 10 = 0$. Factoring, we get $(x-1)(x^2+x+10) = 0$. Since the quadratic has no real roots, the only solution is $x = \mathbf{1}$.

204. We see lots of nice symmetric expressions. Recall that

$$(x+y+z)^3 = x^3 + y^3 + z^3 + 3(xy^2 + x^2y + yx^2 + y^2z + zx^2 + z^2x) + 6xyz,$$

so $(x+y+z)^3 = 4 + 3(12) + 24 = 64$ and $x+y+z = 4$. Since

$$(x+y+z)(xy+yz+zx) = xy^2 + x^2y + yx^2 + y^2z + zx^2 + z^2x + 3xyz,$$

we find $4(xy+yz+zx) = 24$, so $xy+yz+zx = \mathbf{6}$.

205. We write $g(x^{12}) = g(x)h(x) + r(x)$. Since $\deg r(x) < \deg g(x)$, $\deg r(x) < 5$. Like other similar problems, we find the roots of $g(x)$ and use these in the initial equation above. Since $(x-1)g(x) = x^6 - 1$, the roots of $g(x)$ are the five sixth roots of unity besides 1. Hence each solution α_i of $g(x)$ satisfies $\alpha_i^6 = 1$, so $g(\alpha_i^{12}) = g(1) = 6$. Since $g(\alpha_i) = 0$ for each of the five α_i, the initial equation evaluated at these 5 points gives $r(\alpha_i) = 6$ for each α_i. Hence the polynomial $r(x) - 6$ has 5 distinct roots. Since the degree of $r(x) - 6$ is at most 4, $r(x) - 6$ must therefore be everywhere 0. Hence, $r(x) = 6$ at all points x and the remainder is $\mathbf{6}$.

206. Since $(\sqrt[6]{x})^2 = \sqrt[3]{x}$, we can combine the first and third equations as

$$16 + \sqrt[3]{y} + \sqrt[3]{z} = \left(4 + \sqrt[6]{y} + \sqrt[6]{z}\right)^2,$$

from which we find (after a bit of algebra)

$$4\sqrt[6]{y} + 4\sqrt[6]{z} + \sqrt[6]{yz} = 0.$$

Since y and z are positive, this equation can never be satisfied, and there are **no solutions** to this system.

207. Since the equation is a quadratic in a (or in b), we can apply the quadratic formula to find

$$a = \frac{-4 \pm \sqrt{16 + 16b^2 + 16b}}{8} = \frac{-1 \pm \sqrt{1 + b + b^2}}{2}.$$

Since $b^2 < b^2 + b + 1 < (b+1)^2$, the quantity $b^2 + b + 1$ cannot be the perfect square of an integer for any positive integer b. Hence if b is an integer, a cannot be.

208. From the given equation, we know that $x + 2$ divides $x^2 + 3$. We wish to find a linear factor, or better yet, a constant term, which $x + 2$ divides. Since $x + 2$ divides $x^2 + 3$, it also divides $x^2 + 3 - x(x + 2) = 2x - 3$. Similarly we can knock off the x by noting that $x + 2$ divides $2x - 3 - 2(x + 2) = -7$. Hence, $x + 2$ equals either 1 or 7 (since we want positive integer solutions). The first gives a negative solution for x, but for $x + 2 = 7$ we have $x = 5$, from which $y = 4$. Our only solution is $(x, y) = (\mathbf{5}, \mathbf{4})$.

209. Let $A = bc - a^2$, $B = ca - b^2$, and $C = ab - c^2$. We can link the given expression in the equality to the desired expression by noting that

$$\left(\frac{1}{A} + \frac{1}{B} + \frac{1}{C}\right)\left(\frac{a}{A} + \frac{b}{B} + \frac{c}{C}\right) = \frac{a}{A^2} + \frac{b}{B^2} + \frac{c}{C^2} + \frac{b+c}{BC} + \frac{c+a}{AC} + \frac{a+b}{AB}$$

$$= \frac{a}{A^2} + \frac{b}{B^2} + \frac{c}{C^2} + \frac{(b+c)A + (c+a)B + (a+b)C}{ABC}.$$

Since direct algebra reveals $(b + c)A + (c + a)B + (a + b)C = 0$, if $(1/A + 1/B + 1/C) = 0$, we must have $(a/A^2 + b/B^2 + c/C^2) = 0$.

Chapter 14

Inequalities

Solutions to Exercises

14-1 The given expression is the perfect square of $(2x - 3y)$. Since $(2x - 3y)^2 \geq 0$, we have the desired inequality.

14-2 Since the less than side is a perfect square, we can write $(xy + 1)^2 \geq 0$. Make sure you see why this is *not* useful: the $(xy + 1)^2$ in the problem is on the less than side, not the greater than side. Let's try multiplying out the two sides instead:

$$x^2y^2 + x^2 + y^2 + 1 \geq x^2y^2 + 2xy + 1.$$

Rearranging this we have $x^2 - 2xy + y^2 \geq 0$. Since this expression is $(x - y)^2$, we have the desired inequality. Make sure you see that all of our steps are reversible.

14-3 To determine when equality holds, we examine the equality conditions on our three uses of AM-GM. From $(x^2 + y^2)/2 \geq xy$, we have the condition $x = y$. From the other two we find $y = z$ and $z = x$. Hence, in order for equality to hold, we must have $x = y = z$.

14-4 By the AM-GM Inequality, we have

$$\frac{\frac{a}{b} + \frac{b}{a}}{2} \geq \sqrt{\left(\frac{a}{b}\right)\left(\frac{b}{a}\right)}.$$

The right hand side is 1, so we have $\frac{a}{b} + \frac{b}{a} \geq 2$. From the equality condition for AM-GM, this sum equals 2 when $a/b = b/a$, or $a = b$ (since they are both positive).

14-5 Since the square of a real number is nonnegative, any sum of squares is nonnegative as well. Hence, we have

$$(a_1x + b_1)^2 + (a_2x + b_2)^2 + (a_3x + b_3)^2 + \cdots + (a_nx + b_n)^2 \geq 0.$$

We can write the left side as a quadratic expression by grouping x^2 and x terms. This gives us

$$\left(\sum_{i=1}^{n} a_i^2\right) x^2 + \left(2\sum_{i=1}^{n} a_i b_i\right) x + \sum_{i=1}^{n} b_i^2 \geq 0.$$

Since this quadratic is always greater than or equal to zero, it must have 1 or 0 real roots. If a quadratic has two roots, it must at some point cross the x axis and therefore be negative. Since the quadratic has no more than 1 real root, its discriminant must be 0 or negative; thus, we have

$$\left(2\sum_{i=1}^{n} a_i b_i\right)^2 - 4\left(\sum_{i=1}^{n} a_i^2\right)\left(\sum_{i=1}^{n} b_i^2\right) \leq 0.$$

A simple rearrangement of this yields Cauchy's inequality. The equality condition follows from noting that the original quadratic can equal 0 if and only if all n squares equal 0 for the same x, so $a_i x' + b_i = 0$ for all i for some specific x'. Thus, b_i/a_i must be constant is the equality condition.

14-6 This is an example where assuming $x = y = z$ will send us down the wrong path. Since we're maximizing, we want xyz on the smaller side. Using AM-GM on the three quantities in the sum, we find

$$\frac{2x + y + z}{3} \geq \sqrt[3]{2xyz}.$$

Cubing both sides we find $xyz \leq 32$. The equality, or maximum value, is obtained when $2x = y = z$ (the equality condition of AM-GM), or $2x + y + z = y + y + y = 12$. Hence, we have equality when $y = z = 4$ and $x = 2$. The maximum value is then **32**.

14-7 No. We can only use 'without loss of generality' when the objects of interest are indistinct. When we have $x + y = 4$, x and y are virtually indistinct, as exchanging them results in *exactly* the same equation. Unfortunately, when $2x + y = 4$, reversing x and y changes the problem to $x + 2y = 4$, which is different from the original. We cannot proceed 'without loss of generality;' we must find another way.

14-8 This statement follows immediately from the equality condition of AM-GM applied to the prior example, from which $a = b = c$ and $\triangle ABC$ is equilateral.

14-9 Using summations to denote the sums we have

$$\sqrt[m]{\frac{\sum_{i=1}^{k} a_i^m}{k}} \geq \sqrt[n]{\frac{\sum_{i=1}^{k} a_i^n}{k}}.$$

14-10 For $n = 1$, there is no root and the resulting expression is the Arithmetic Mean. For $m = 2$ we have the root mean square, so if $m = 2$ and $n = 1$ the Power Mean Inequality is RMS $\geq$ AM.

Solutions to Problems

210. Since $(x + y)^2 = x^2 + y^2 + 2xy = 1 + 2xy$, our problem is maximizing xy. From the Trivial Inequality, $(x^2 + y^2)/2 \geq \sqrt{x^2 y^2} = xy$. Thus, $xy \leq 1/2$. Since the maximum value of xy is $1/2$, the maximum of $(x + y)^2$ is $1 + 2(1/2) = \mathbf{2}$. This is attained when $x = y = \pm\sqrt{2}/2$.

211. Let x and y equal some very big number, say n, and let $z = 1/n^2$. Thus, $xyz = (n)(n)(1/n^2) = 1$ as required, but the three sums in question are $2n$, $n + 1/n^2$ and $n + 1/n^2$. All three of these are at least as large as n. Since we can make n as large as we want, $\min\{x + y, x + z, y + z\}$ has no maximum.

212. As an example in the text, we showed that the given expression is greater than or equal to one by using Cauchy's Inequality. From the equality condition for Cauchy's Inequality, we have

$$\frac{(\cos^3 \alpha)/\cos \beta}{\cos \alpha \cos \beta} = \frac{(\sin^3 \alpha)/\sin \beta}{\sin \alpha \sin \beta},$$

from which we find $\tan^2 \alpha = \tan^2 \beta$. Since α and β are both first quadrant angles, this implies $\alpha = \beta$.

213. From AM-GM, we have

$$\frac{A + 2B + 3C + 4D}{4} \geq \sqrt[4]{(A)(2B)(3C)(4D)},$$

so $\sqrt[4]{24ABCD} \leq 2$. Finally, $ABCD \leq 16/24$, so that the maximum value of the product is $\mathbf{2/3}$.

214. Without loss of generality, let $x \leq y \leq z$. Then, the largest of the three sums in question is $y + z$. We can relate the given product to a sum with AM-GM, so $(x + y + z) \geq 3\sqrt[3]{xyz} = 3$. Since x is the smallest of the three numbers, $x \leq 1$ (if $x > 1$, then $xyz > 1$, a contradiction). Hence, $y + z \geq 3 - x \geq 2$. Thus, the minimum value of $y + z$ is 2 and this is attained when $x = y = z = 1$.

215. Without loss of generality, let $x \leq y \leq z$. Hence, the smallest of the desired products is xy and our problem is to maximize this product. Since $x + y = 3 - z$, we have

$$\sqrt{xy} \leq \frac{x + y}{2} = \frac{3 - z}{2}$$

from AM-GM. Since z is the largest of the three numbers, it must at least 1 (otherwise the sum of the three would be less than 3). Using this in the above expression, $\sqrt{xy} \leq 1$, so that the maximum of xy is 1 as desired. This can be achieved when $x = y = z = 1$.

216. Rearranging the given expression we have

$$a + b \geq \sqrt{(a^2 + b^2)/2} + \sqrt{ab}.$$

Squaring both sides of this gives

$$a^2 + 2ab + b^2 \geq (a^2 + b^2)/2 + ab + 2\sqrt{ab(a^2 + b^2)/2},$$

which rearranges to $(a^2 + 2ab + b^2)/2 \geq \sqrt{4ab(a^2 + b^2)/2}$, or

$$\frac{(a + b)^2}{2} \geq \sqrt{2ab(a^2 + b^2)}.$$

Squaring out the left, we have

$$\frac{(a^2 + b^2) + (2ab)}{2} \geq \sqrt{(2ab)(a^2 + b^2)},$$

which is clearly true by AM-GM.

217. We see a product of n terms and an nth power. It looks like AM-GM. Rewrite the greater than side as

$$\left(\frac{(x + r_1) + (x + r_2) + \cdots + (x + r_n)}{n} \right)^n$$

Now, applying AM-GM to the terms $(x + r_1)$, $(x + r_2)$, ..., $(x + r_n)$, we have the desired result.

218. As written, the solution is very elusive. Let's try one of our little helping hints: take the reciprocal of each side, yielding (after rationalizing the denominator and remembering to reverse inequality sign) $\sqrt{n} + \sqrt{n-1} \geq 100$. Now the answer is much clearer. Since $\sqrt{2500} = 50$, for $n = 2500$ and all smaller n, we fail to satisfy the inequality but for $n = \mathbf{2501}$ the inequality is satisfied.

219. Seeing the absolute value signs, we consider the Triangle Inequality, or $|x + y| \leq |x| + |y|$. Note that since $|y| = |-y|$, we can write $|x| + |y| \geq |x - y|$ as well. In the problem, we have 10 terms of the form $|x - F_i|$. From the Triangle Inequality, we can write $|x - F_i| + |x - F_j| \geq |(x - F_i) - (x - F_j)| = |F_j - F_i|$. Note that we have gotten rid of the x. Continuing this, we can use the Triangle Inequality to combine all 10 terms:

$$f(x) = \sum_{i=1}^{10} |x - F_i| \geq |\pm (x - F_1) \pm (x - F_2) \pm \cdots \pm (x - F_{10})|,$$

where the $\pm$ signs show that we can use either plus or minus signs at each of these points and the inequality will still be valid. (This is a result of the fact that $|(x - F_i)| = |-(x - F_i)|$.) Since we want to find a constant such that $f(x) \geq c$, we must choose 5 of the $\pm$ signs to be negative and 5 to be positive to cancel out all of the x's. Since we can choose any five to be positive and still have a valid inequality, we must choose the five so that the resulting constant is as great as possible. (For example, if $z \geq 5$ and $z \geq 6$, the minimum value of z

is 6 and the inequality $z \geq 5$ is irrelevant.) Since our resulting sum is 5 positive Fibonacci numbers and 5 negatives, we choose the greatest 5 to be positive, so that

$$f(x) \geq (55 + 34 + 21 + 13 + 8) - (5 + 3 + 2 + 1 + 1) = \mathbf{119}.$$

Challenge: Can you find all x that make $f(x) = 119$?

220. Lemma: If $f(x)$ and $g(x)$ are such that $f(x) = a_n x^n + a_{n-1}x^{n-1} + \cdots + a_0$ and $g(x) = b_n x^n + b_{n-1}x^{n-1} + \cdots + b_0$ and $a_i \geq b_i$ for all i, then $f(x) \geq g(x)$ for all positive x. Proof: $f(x) - g(x) = (a_n - b_n)x^n + (a_{n-1} - b_{n-1})x^{n-1} + \cdots + (a_0 - b_0)$. Since $a_i \geq b_i$ for all i, $(a_i - b_i) \geq 0$, so the coefficients of $f(x) - g(x)$ are all positive. Thus, for all positive x, $f(x) - g(x) \geq 0$, and $f(x) \geq g(x)$.

Applying this lemma to the given problem, we see that if we can show that the coefficient of x^k on the left is greater than that of x^k on the right for all k, then we have proven the given inequality. On the left, the coefficient of x^k is the sum of the products of the roots taken $n - k$ at a time. (Recall the discussion of the relationship of the roots of a polynomial to its coefficients.) From the Binomial Theorem, the coefficient of x^k on the right hand side is $\binom{n}{k}(\sqrt[n]{r_1 r_2 \cdots r_n})^k$. Now, apply AM-GM to the terms in the sum which forms the coefficient of x^k on the left side. Since there are $\binom{n}{k}$ terms on the left, and each r_i appears in $\binom{n-1}{k-1}$ of the terms (since after choosing a specific r_i, we must choose $k - 1$ of the remaining $n - 1$ r_j's for the other $k - 1$ members of each term), we have

$$\frac{r_1 r_2 \cdots r_k + \cdots + r_{n-k+1}r_{n-k+2} \cdots r_n}{\binom{n}{k}} \geq \left((r_1 r_2 r_3 \cdots r_n)^{\binom{n-1}{k-1}} \right)^{1/\binom{n}{k}}$$

from the AM-GM Inequality. Multiplying this by $\binom{n}{k}$ on both sides and noting that $\binom{n-1}{k-1}/\binom{n}{k} = k/n$, we have

$$r_1 r_2 \cdots r_k + \cdots + r_{n-k+1}r_{n-k+2} \cdots r_n \geq \binom{n}{k}(r_1 r_2 r_3 \cdots r_n)^{k/n},$$

which is what we wanted to prove. Make sure you follow the algebra and the logic; it's a bit tricky. Make sure you also understand why the above expressions are the coefficients of the polynomials described in the original question.

221. Let the roots be r, s, and t. From the given form of the polynomial, we know $r + s + t = 12$ and $rst = 64$. Thus, the geometric mean of the three numbers equals the arithmetic mean. From the AM-GM Inequality (which we can use since these three numbers are positive), we know that if equality holds we must have $r = s = t$. Hence, the roots are all equal to 4. Finally, $a = rs + st + tr = \mathbf{48}$.

222. If we get rid of the radicals by squaring each side and then raising each side to the nth power, we have $n^n \leq (n!)^2$. We can write this out as

$$n \cdot n \cdot n \cdots n \cdot n \leq [1 \cdot 2 \cdots (n - 1) \cdot n][1 \cdot 2 \cdots (n - 1) \cdot n].$$

We can prove this if we can group the two bracketed products into n pairs so that one number in each pair comes from each set of brackets and each pair has a product greater than n. Make sure you see why this will complete the problem; there are n pairs on the right and n n's on the left. If each pair on the right has a product greater than or equal to n, then the right is greater than or equal to the left.

Now, how do we pair the terms? Since $1 \cdot 1$ is not greater than n, we don't want to pair k with k for each k. Let's try another way: pair 1 with n, 2 with $(n-1)$ and so on, so that we have

$$[(1)(n)][(2)(n-1)] \cdots [(n)(1)] = (n!)^2.$$

Now we must show that each of these products of the form $k(n-k+1)$ is greater than or equal to n. Since $k(n-k+1) = k(n-k) + k = (k-1)(n-k) + n$ and $(k-1)(n-k) \geq 0$ for all k from 1 to n, we have $k(n-k+1) \geq n$. Make sure you see this. Thus, $(n!)^2 \geq n^n$ and the problem is complete.

223. Seeing the product of sums, we think of Cauchy's Inequality, from which we have

$$(a+b+c+d)(h_a + h_b + h_c + h_d) \geq (\sqrt{ah_a} + \sqrt{bh_b} + \sqrt{ch_c} + \sqrt{dh_d})^2.$$

Since $V = ah_a/3$ (and similarly for the other faces), the right side above is $(\sqrt{3V} + \sqrt{3V} + \sqrt{3V} + \sqrt{3V})^2 = 48V$, completing the proof.

224. Expanding the left hand side yields

$$x^4 + y^4 + z^4 + 2x^2y^2 + 2y^2z^2 + 2z^2x^2 \leq n(x^4 + y^4 + z^4).$$

Since the x^2y^2 terms are on the less then side, we apply AM-GM using these as the geometric means, or $x^2y^2 = \sqrt{x^4y^4} = (x^4 + y^4)/2$. Hence,

$$2x^2y^2 + 2y^2z^2 + 2z^2x^2 \leq 2[(x^4 + y^4)/2] + 2[(y^4 + z^4)/2] + 2[(z^4 + x^4)/2],$$

and combining this with the above expression, we find

$$(x^2 + y^2 + z^2)^2 \leq 3(x^4 + y^4 + z^4),$$

so $n = \mathbf{3}$.

225. Let the distance travelled be z, the time of Car A be s, and that of Car B be t. Car B is easy; $ut/2 + vt/2 = z$, so $z/t = (u+v)/2$ and the average rate is the arithmetic mean of the two rates of the car. Let the time that Car A travels at rate u be r. Hence, $ur = v(s-r) = z/2$ and $ur + v(s-r) = z$. From the first equation, $r = vs/(u+v)$ and substituting this in the second gives $z/s = 2uv/(u+v)$. Perhaps you recognize this as the average rate of the car being the harmonic mean of the two rates it travels. We thus must show that

$$\frac{2uv}{u+v} \leq \frac{u+v}{2}.$$

Multiplying both sides by $2(u + v)$ and subtracting $4uv$, we have $(u - v)^2 \geq 0$, which is clearly true and we have solved the problem.

226. We wish to show that $ab > 4rR$. From the Triangle Inequality, we have $a + b > c$. (We think to use this because the problem involves a strict inequality). Since the problem also involves R and r, we use the law of sines and $[ABC] = rs$. The expression ab occurs in $[ABC] = (ab/2) \sin C$, so using this we have

$$ab = 2[ABC]/\sin C = 2rs/(c/2R) = 2rR(a + b + c)/c > 2rR(c + c)/c = 4rR,$$

as desired.

227. From Heron's formula we have $[ABC] = 15\sqrt{7}/4$. We can also write the area in terms of the sides and the given l, m, and n as $(al + bm + cn)/2 = 15\sqrt{7}/4$. Seeing this sum of products and the given sum of squares, we write out Cauchy's Inequality:

$$(a^2 + b^2 + c^2)(l^2 + m^2 + n^2) \geq (al + bm + cn)^2.$$

Using all of the given information on the sides, the area, and the sum $l^2 + m^2 + n^2$, we find that the left and the right sides of the above expression are equal. Thus, the equality condition for Cauchy's Inequality must hold, or $a/l = b/m = c/n$. Writing m and n in terms of l and using $l^2 + m^2 + n^2 = 225/44$, we find $l = \mathbf{30\sqrt{7}/77}$.

228. We are asked to show that for two positive numbers, $\text{RMS} - \text{AM} \geq \text{GM} - \text{HM}$. Adding AM to both sides and subtracting GM, after a bit of algebra on the less than side we have

$$\sqrt{\frac{a^2 + b^2}{2}} - \sqrt{ab} \geq \frac{(a - b)^2}{2(a + b)}.$$

Squaring both sides and simplifying the greater than side, we have

$$\frac{(a + b)^2}{2} - \sqrt{(2ab)(a^2 + b^2)} \geq \frac{(a - b)^4}{4(a + b)^2}.$$

Now we put the radical expression on the right and the other two on the left. On the left, we find a common denominator, multiply both sides by $2(a + b)^2$, and we find

$$\frac{2(a + b)^4 - (a - b)^4}{4(a + b)^2} \geq \sqrt{(2ab)(a^2 + b^2)} \quad \text{or}$$

$$\frac{2(a + b)^4 - (a - b)^4}{2} \geq \sqrt{(2ab)(a^2 + b^2)(4)(a + b)^4}.$$

The expression on the right is suggestive of AM-GM; we can get an AM on the left by factoring as the difference of squares:

$$\frac{(a + b)^4 + [(a + b)^4 - (a - b)^4]}{2} \geq \sqrt{(2ab)(a^2 + b^2)(4)(a + b)^4}, \quad \text{or}$$

$$\frac{(a + b)^4 + [4ab][2(a^2 + b^2)]}{2} \geq \sqrt{(2ab)(a^2 + b^2)(4)(a + b)^4},$$

where we note $(a+b)^4 - (a-b)^4 = [(a+b)^2 + (a-b)^2][(a+b)^2 - (a-b)^2]$. By AM-GM this final inequality is true, so since all steps are reversible, we have proven the inequality.

229. Seeing reciprocals, we try the AM-HM Inequality on a, b, and c, and we find

$$\frac{a+b+c}{3} \geq \frac{3}{\frac{1}{a} + \frac{1}{b} + \frac{1}{c}}.$$

Hence, $\frac{1}{a} + \frac{1}{b} + \frac{1}{c} \geq 3/2$. Now, seeing squares, we try RMS-AM, and we have

$$\sqrt{\frac{(a+1/b)^2 + (b+1/c)^2 + (c+1/a)^2}{3}} \geq \frac{a+1/b+b+1/c+c+1/a}{3} \geq 5/2.$$

Squaring and multiplying by 3 yields the desired inequality.

230. Let group i have p_i people. Hence, $p_1 + p_2 + \cdots + p_m = n$. Similarly, let s_k be the side length of the kth cake. Since no person has more than 25 cm^2 of cake, $s_k^2 \leq 25p_k$, or $s_k \leq 5\sqrt{p_k}$. The total amount of ribbon needed for the cakes is $R = 4s_1 + 4s_2 + \cdots + 4s_m$, which from above we know is less than or equal to $20\sqrt{p_1} + 20\sqrt{p_2} + \cdots + 20\sqrt{p_k}$. If we can now show that this second sum is less than or equal to $20\sqrt{mn}$, we will have

$$R \leq 20\sqrt{p_1} + 20\sqrt{p_2} + \cdots + 20\sqrt{p_k} \leq 20\sqrt{mn},$$

so $R \leq 20\sqrt{mn}$ as desired. Sums of products; looks like a job for Cauchy's Inequality, from which we have

$$[(\sqrt{p_1})^2 + (\sqrt{p_2})^2 + \cdots + (\sqrt{p_m})^2][1^2 + 1^2 + \cdots + 1^2] \geq (\sqrt{p_1} + \sqrt{p_2} + \cdots + \sqrt{p_m})^2$$
$$(p_1 + p_2 + \cdots + p_m)(m) \geq (\sqrt{p_1} + \sqrt{p_2} + \cdots + \sqrt{p_m})^2$$
$$nm \geq (\sqrt{p_1} + \sqrt{p_2} + \cdots + \sqrt{p_m})^2$$

Taking the square root of this and multiplying by 20 gives the desired inequality.

231. First, we write the area of a general triangle in two ways as follows:

$$[ABC] = rs = \sqrt{s(s-a)(s-b)(s-c)}.$$

From the AM-GM Inequality, $\sqrt[3]{(s-a)(s-b)(s-c)} \leq (s-a+s-b+s-c)/3 = s/3$. Hence,

$$rs = s\sqrt{\frac{(s-a)(s-b)(s-c)}{s}} = \sqrt{s}\left(\sqrt[3]{(s-a)(s-b)(s-c)}\right)^{3/2} \leq \sqrt{s}\sqrt{s^3/27},$$

and we have $r \leq s/3\sqrt{3}$ for any triangle. Applying this to each face of the tetrahedron, we find

$$r_A + r_B + r_C + r_D \leq \frac{\text{sum of semiperimeters}}{3\sqrt{3}}.$$

Since each side belongs to two triangles, the sum of the semiperimeters of the triangles is the sum of the sides of the tetrahedron, or 3. Thus, $r_A + r_B + r_C + r_D \le \sqrt{3}/3$ and equality holds when all sides are equal. We see this equality condition from the original AM-GM inequality, where $s - a = s - b = s - c$ implies the triangle is equilateral. Four equilateral faces means the tetrahedron is regular.

232. Let O be the circumcenter of $\triangle ABC$. Since $\angle AOB = 2\angle ACB$ and similarly for the other two angles of $\triangle ABC$, we can write

$$P = [BOC] + [AOC] + [AOB] = (r^2/2)(\sin 2A + \sin 2B + \sin 2C).$$

By equating angles inscribed in the same arc, we find that the interior angles of $A'B'C'$ are $(\angle A + \angle B)/2$, $(\angle B + \angle C)/2$, and $(\angle A + \angle C)/2$. Thus,

$$Q = (r^2/2)[\sin(A + B) + \sin(A + C) + \sin(B + C)].$$

Applying AM-GM to the sines and then using some of our trigometric goodies (watch the steps closely and make sure you understand the identity used in each one), we have

$$
\begin{aligned}
16Q^3 &= 16(r^6/8)[\sin(A + B) + \sin(B + C) + \sin(A + C)]^3 \\
&\ge 27r^6[2\sin(B + C)\sin(A + C)\sin(A + B)] \\
&= 27r^6[\cos(A - B) - \cos(A + B + 2C)]\sin(A + B) \\
&= 27r^6[\cos(A - B) + \cos C]\sin(A + B) \\
&= 27r^6[\cos(A - B)\sin(A + B) + \cos C\sin(A + B)] \\
&= (27/2)r^6[\sin 2A + \sin 2B + \sin(A + B + C) + \sin(A + B - C)] \\
&= (27/2)r^6(\sin 2A + \sin 2B + \sin 2C) \\
&= 27r^4(r^2/2)(\sin 2A + \sin 2B + \sin 2C) \\
&= 27r^4 P.
\end{aligned}
$$

Make sure you understand each of the steps! There are many subtle trigonometric identities, such as $\sin(A + B - C) = \sin(180° - 2C) = \sin 2C$, used here; make sure each is clear to you.

233. Let $S_k = x_1^k + x_2^k + \cdots + x_n^k$. From Cauchy's Inequality, we find

$$\left[\left(x_1^{(k+1)/2}\right)^2 + \left(x_2^{(k+1)/2}\right)^2 + \cdots + \left(x_n^{(k+1)/2}\right)^2\right]\left[\left(x_1^{(k-1)/2}\right)^2 + \left(x_2^{(k-1)/2}\right)^2 + \cdots + \left(x_n^{(k-1)/2}\right)^2\right]$$

$$\ge (x_1^k + x_2^k + \cdots + x_n^k)^2,$$

or $S_{k+1}S_{k-1} \ge S_k^2$. Starting from $k = 20$ and listing through $k = 92$, we have

$$S_{21}S_{19} \ge S_{20}^2$$

$$S_{22}S_{20} \geq S_{21}^2$$

$$\vdots$$

$$S_{93}S_{91} \geq S_{92}^2$$

Taking the product of all of these and cancelling out terms which appear on both sides, we have the desired $S_{19}S_{93} \geq S_{20}S_{92}$.

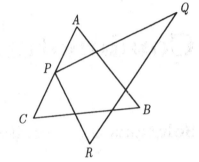

234. Labelling the sides and angles a, b, c, A, B, C as usual, we first can find $\angle RPQ = 90°$, $\angle PQR = \angle BCR = 30°$, and $\angle QRP = 60°$. The circumcenter of right triangle AMC is the midpoint of the hypotenuse, so $CP = b/2$. From the law of sines applied to $\triangle CRB$, we find $CR = a/\sqrt{3}$ (since $\angle BCR = \angle CBR = (180° - \angle CRB)/2 = (180° - \angle CMB)/2 = 30°$). Applying the law of cosines to $\triangle PCR$, we find

$$
\begin{aligned}
PR^2 &= PC^2 + CR^2 - 2(PC)(CR)\cos(C + 30°) \\
&= \frac{b^2}{4} + \frac{a^2}{3} - \frac{2ab}{2\sqrt{3}}(\cos C \cos 30° - \sin C \sin 30°)
\end{aligned}
$$

Now applying the law of cosines to $\triangle ABC$ to get $\cos C$ and noting that $2[ABC]/ab = \sin C$, we have (after a bit of algebra)

$$PR^2 = \frac{1}{4}\left(\frac{a^2}{3} + c^2 + \frac{4[ABC]}{\sqrt{3}}\right).$$

Since $PQ = (PR)\tan 60° = PR\sqrt{3}$ and $\triangle PQR$ is right, we have

$$[PQR] = \frac{(PQ)(PR)}{2} = \frac{PR^2\sqrt{3}}{2} = \frac{\sqrt{3}}{8}\left(\frac{a^2}{3} + c^2\right) + \frac{[ABC]}{2}.$$

Thus, $[PQR] - [ABC] = (\sqrt{3}/8)(a^2/3 + c^2) - [ABC]/2$. Applying AM-GM to $a^2/3$ and c^2, we find

$$[PQR] - [ABC] \geq \frac{\sqrt{3}}{8} \cdot 2\sqrt{\left(\frac{a^2}{3}\right)(c^2)} - \frac{[ABC]}{2}.$$

Simplifying, we have $[PQR] - [ABC] \geq ac/4 - [ABC]/2$. Since $[ABC] = (ac/2)\sin B$, we have $[PQR] - [ABC] \geq (ac/4)(1 - \sin B)$, so $[PQR] - [ABC] \geq 0$ (since $1 - \sin B \geq 0$), as desired.

Chapter 15

Combinatorics

Solutions to Exercises

15-1 Choosing k objects from a group of n without choosing some particular element A amounts to choosing the k objects from the $n-1$ non-A ones. Since this is choosing k objects from a group of $n-1$, it can be done in $\binom{n-1}{k}$ ways.

15-2 Let's try $n=9$, $k=4$ for a tough one. Evaluating, $\binom{9}{4} = 9\cdot 8\cdot 7\cdot 6/4\cdot 3\cdot 2\cdot 1 = 126$. Also, $\binom{8}{3} = 8\cdot 7\cdot 6/3\cdot 2\cdot 1 = 56$ and $\binom{8}{4} = 8\cdot 7\cdot 6\cdot 5/4\cdot 3\cdot 2\cdot 1 = 70$. Since $56+70 = 126$, the identity works in this case.

15-3 When $k=0$, we have $\binom{n}{0} = \binom{n-1}{0} + \binom{n-1}{-1}$. Since $\binom{n-1}{-1} = 0$, we have $1 = 1$, so Pascal's identity is still satisfied.

15-4 The counting argument is easy. To choose k things from a group of n is the same as to choose the $n-k$ elements you're *not* taking. The algebraic argument isn't much worse: we have $\binom{n}{k} = n!/k!(n-k)!$, while $\binom{n}{n-k} = n!/(n-k)!(n-(n-k))! = n!/(n-k)!k!$. The two are clearly the same.

15-5 For $n=8$ and $k=4$ we have

$$\binom{8}{4} + \binom{7}{3} + \binom{6}{2} + \binom{5}{1} + \binom{4}{0} = 70 + 35 + 15 + 5 + 1 = 126 = \binom{9}{4},$$

as desired. If $k = n-1$ the identity says that

$$\binom{n}{n-1} = \binom{n-1}{n-1} + \binom{n-2}{n-2} + \cdots + \binom{0}{0}.$$

This is obvious because the left hand side is n, while the right hand side is n 1's.

15-6 For $n = 8$ and $k = 4$ we have

$$\binom{3}{3} + \binom{4}{3} + \binom{5}{3} + \binom{6}{3} + \binom{7}{3} = 1 + 4 + 10 + 20 + 35 = 70 = \binom{8}{4},$$

as desired. If $k = 1$ we have

$$\binom{0}{0} + \binom{1}{0} + \cdots + \binom{n-1}{0} = \binom{n}{1},$$

which is obvious because the right hand side is n and the left is n 1's.

15-7 The first row is just 1; the second row is 1 1. We extend the table further not by evaluating $\binom{n}{k}$'s, but by simple addition:

```
                        1
                    1       1
                1       2       1
            1       3       3       1
        1       4       6       4       1
    1       5      10      10       5       1
  1     6      15      20      15       6       1
1     7      21      35      35      21       7       1
1   8     28      56      70      56      28       8       1
```

15-8 There are several equally good explanations. One is Pascal's identity, which forces $\binom{n}{k} = \binom{n}{n-k}$; clearly $\binom{n}{k}$ and $\binom{n}{n-k}$ are symmetrically placed entries in the triangle.

15-9 The sums are 1, 2, 4, and 8; clearly we have the powers of 2 here. This happens because of the identity $\binom{n}{0} + \binom{n}{1} + \cdots + \binom{n}{n} = 2^n$, since summing across a row of Pascal's triangle is just such a sum.

15-10 We do the induction on n. The base case of the induction is clear: certainly we can walk to $\binom{1}{1} = 1$ and $\binom{1}{0} = 1$ in 1 way each. For the inductive step, assume we can walk to $\binom{n-1}{k}$ in $\binom{n-1}{k}$ steps for any k. To get to $\binom{n}{j}$ for some j, we must pass through $\binom{n-1}{j-1}$ or $\binom{n-1}{j}$, because we only walk downward and to the left or right. Thus the number of ways we can walk to $\binom{n}{j}$ is the sum of the numbers of ways we can walk to $\binom{n-1}{j-1}$ and $\binom{n-1}{j}$. But these are $\binom{n-1}{j-1}$ and $\binom{n-1}{j}$ by the inductive assumption! Thus we can walk to $\binom{n}{j}$ in $\binom{n-1}{j} + \binom{n-1}{j-1} = \binom{n}{j}$ ways. (We used Pascal's identity in the last equation.)

15-11 This is virtually the same argument as in the text. Here we associate the o's with the possible last *left* branchings, and we are done by the same argument— since there must be one and only one last left branching and it must occur at one of the o's, the sum of the numbers of ways to get to the o's is equal to the number of ways to get to the •.

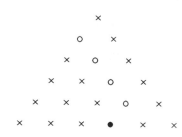

15-12 The fact that the sum of the bottoms of the combinations is always r suggests the use of a committee selection model. In fact, each term can be seen as the way to select an r-member committee, taking $r - k$ from a group of n candidates and k from a group of m candidates. Since we can take anywhere from 0 to r members from either group, this is just the number of ways to choose an r-member committee from a group of $n + m$ candidates, or $\binom{n+m}{r}$. We have hence proven that

$$\sum_{k=0}^{r} \binom{n}{r-k}\binom{m}{k} = \binom{n+m}{r},$$

as asked. (Try this with some small numbers, say $n = 4$, $m = 5$, and $r = 3$.)

Letting $m = n = r$, Vandermonde's identity is

$$\sum_{k=0}^{r} \binom{n}{n-k}\binom{n}{k} = \binom{2n}{n},$$

which by $\binom{n}{n-k} = \binom{n}{k}$ is

$$\sum_{k=0}^{r} \binom{n}{k}^2 = \binom{2n}{n}.$$

15-13 Since $(x + y)^2 = x^2 + 2xy + y^2$, $(x + y)^4 = (x^2 + 2xy + y^2)(x^2 + 2xy + y^2) = x^4 + 2x^3y + x^2y^2 + 2x^3y + 4x^2y^2 + 2xy^3 + x^2y^2 + 2xy^3 + y^4 = x^4 + 4x^3y + 6x^2y^2 + 4xy^3 + y^4$, which agrees with the Binomial Theorem, since $\binom{4}{0} = \binom{4}{4} = 1$, $\binom{4}{1} = \binom{4}{3} = 4$, and $\binom{4}{2} = 6$.

15-14 In $\sum$ form, the expansion is $\sum_{k=0}^{4} \binom{4}{k} x^k y^{4-k}$.

15-15 My logic is correct. The text gives the term as $\binom{4}{k} x^k y^{4-k}$, and I gave the term as $\binom{4}{4-k} x^k y^{4-k}$, but the two are the same since $\binom{4}{k} = \binom{4}{4-k}$.

15-16 For $n = 1$ we have $(x+y)^1 = \binom{1}{0}x + \binom{1}{1}y = x + y$, which is the correct expansion. For $n = 2$ we have $(x + y)^2 = \binom{2}{0}x^2 + \binom{2}{1}xy + \binom{2}{2}y^2 = x^2 + 2xy + y^2$, which is correct. For $n = 3$ we have $(x + y)^3 = \binom{3}{0}x^3 + \binom{3}{1}x^2y + \binom{3}{2}xy^2 + \binom{3}{3}y^3 = x^3 + 3x^2y + 3xy^2 + y^3$, which is—again!—correct.

15-17   We can use $\binom{n}{n-k} = \binom{n}{k}$ to write the earlier expansion as

$$(x+y)^n = \sum_{k=0}^{n} \binom{n}{k} x^{n-k} y^k.$$

This $\sum$ does not correspond exactly (but is still equivalent) to expanded version in the text, as a term-by-term expansion will show.

15-18   For the first one, we have

$$x^4 + \binom{4}{1} x^3 (2y) + \binom{4}{2} x^2 (2y)^2 + \binom{4}{3} x(2y)^3 + (2y)^4$$
$$= x^4 + 8x^3 y + 24x^2 y^2 + 32xy^3 + 16y^4.$$

For the second one, the term in question is $\binom{7}{4} x^4 2^3 = (35)(8)x^4 = 280x^4$, so the coefficient is **280**.

For the third one, the generic term will be $\binom{6}{k}(x^2)^k (1/x)^{6-k} = \binom{6}{k} x^{3k-6}$, so the x will vanish when $k = 2$. The coefficient will be $\binom{6}{2} = \mathbf{15}$.

To find the sum of the coefficients, we just let $a = b = 1$. (Do you see why?) Thus the sum of the coefficients in this case is $(1+1)^{10} = 2^{10} = \mathbf{1024}$.

15-19   Letting $x = 1$ and $y = -1$ in the Binomial Theorem yields

$$\binom{n}{0} - \binom{n}{1} + \binom{n}{2} - \binom{n}{3} + \cdots + (-1)^n \binom{n}{n} = 0,$$

which can be rearranged into

$$\binom{n}{0} + \binom{n}{2} + \binom{n}{4} + \cdots = \binom{n}{1} + \binom{n}{3} + \binom{n}{5} + \cdots$$

If n is odd, the identity becomes

$$\binom{n}{0} + \binom{n}{2} + \cdots + \binom{n}{n-1} = \binom{n}{1} + \binom{n}{3} + \cdots + \binom{n}{n}.$$

Applying $\binom{n}{k} = \binom{n}{n-k}$ to the left hand side makes it into the right hand side, so we're done right away.

15-20   Let $x = 2$ and $y = 1$ in the Binomial Theorem to get

$$(2+1)^n = \sum_{k=0}^{n} \binom{n}{k} 2^k 1^{n-k} = \sum_{k=0}^{n} \binom{n}{k} 2^k.$$

The last sum is the one we're trying to evaluate, so it equals $(2+1)^n = 3^n$.

15-21   The coefficient of $x^4yz^3w^2$ is the same as the number of ways in which the "word" $xxxxyzzzww$ can be arranged. This is $10!/4!1!3!2!$.

15-22   The coefficient of abc^2 is the same as the number of ways to rearrange $abcc$, which is $4!/1!1!2! = 4 \cdot 3 \cdot 2/2 = \mathbf{12}$.

15-23   Let the coefficients of the x, y, and z be j, k, and $n - j - k$ respectively. We want each of j and k to range from 0 to n, while still having $n - j - k$ be positive. Thus k can only range up to $n - j$, rather than all the way up to n. We thus write

$$\sum_{j=0}^{n}\sum_{k=0}^{n-j} \frac{n!}{j!\,k!\,(n-j-k)!} x^j y^k z^{n-j-k},$$

where we use the coefficient according to the exponents chosen. Can you see that every possible combination of exponents is attained by this sum?

Solutions to Problems

235. This is exactly the form of the identity

$$\sum_{k=1}^{n} k\binom{n}{k} = n2^{n-1},$$

which we proved in the text. Thus the sum is $\mathbf{100 \cdot 2^{99}}$.

236. We rewrite the given sum as $\sum_{k=0}^{n}\binom{n}{n-k}\binom{m}{k}$, then use, say, block walking. The sum describes all paths with $n - k$ steps left in the first n steps down, and k steps left in the next m steps down. Thus the sum describes all possible ways to take a total of n steps left in $n + m$ steps down, so it equals $\binom{n+m}{n}$.

237. Evaluate the inner sum first. We know that

$$\sum_{k=1}^{i}\binom{i}{k} = \binom{i}{1} + \binom{i}{2} + \cdots + \binom{i}{i} = 2^i - 1,$$

so that

$$\sum_{i=1}^{10}\sum_{k=1}^{i}\binom{i}{k} = \sum_{i=1}^{10}(2^i - 1) = (2 + 4 + 8 + \cdots + 2^{10}) - (1 + 1 + \cdots + 1) = 2046 - 10 = \mathbf{2036}.$$

238. According to the Binomial Theorem, the general term of the expansion looks like

$$\binom{16}{k}(xy)^k(-2y^{-3})^{16-k}.$$

Simplifying this, we get

$$\binom{16}{k}(-2)^{16-k}x^k y^{4k-48}.$$

We see that there is no power of y when $k = 12$; the coefficient is then $2^4\binom{16}{12} = 16\binom{16}{4}$.

239. This is really just sum manipulation. We write the given sum as $\displaystyle\sum_{k=0}^{n}\binom{k}{r} - \sum_{k=0}^{m-1}\binom{k}{r}$.

We proved in the text (using Pascal's identity over and over) that $\displaystyle\sum_{k=0}^{Q}\binom{k}{r} = \binom{Q+1}{r+1}$ for any Q; applying this to the two parts of the given sum yields $\binom{n+1}{r+1} - \binom{m}{r+1}$, as desired.

240. Let $n = 45$ (surprisingly, problems often look simpler with the numbers taken out), and write the given sum as $\displaystyle\sum_{k=0}^{n}(n-k-1)\binom{n}{k}$, which can be split into

$$\sum_{k=0}^{n}(n-k)\binom{n}{k} - \sum_{k=0}^{n}\binom{n}{k}.$$

The second sum is equal to 2^n. The first is, by the symmetry identity, the same as $\displaystyle\sum_{k=0}^{n}(n-k)\binom{n}{n-k}$; letting $j = n-k$, this becomes $\displaystyle\sum_{j=0}^{n}j\binom{n}{j}$, which we showed in the text is equal to $n2^{n-1}$. Thus the sum we want is $n2^{n-1} - 2^n = n2^{n-1} - 2\cdot 2^{n-1} = (n-2)2^{n-1}$. Substituting $n = 45$, our sum is $\mathbf{43 \cdot 2^{44}}$. (If you find all the $\sum$'s hard to follow, try writing the sums out. But if you do this, try to see how your manipulations correspond to manipulations of the $\sum$'s—in the long run you'll find $\sum$ to be a much more efficient notation.)

241. In this problem, we prove an identity from the text in a new way. Can you see which identity?

For the first part, once we include the first block in our group of n, we are left to pick $n-1$ other blocks. We have to pick these blocks from the remaining $n+k$. By elementary counting, we can pick $n-1$ blocks out of $n+k$ in $\binom{n+k}{n-1}$ ways.

The second part is similar. Once we pick the mth block, we need to pick $n-1$ more blocks. Since we can't choose any of the first m, we have $n+k+1-m$ blocks to choose from, so there are $\binom{n+k+1-m}{n-1}$ ways to make the choice.

For the third part, we use the first two parts. Consider the ways in which we can choose n blocks from a set of $n + k + 1$. In particular, break down the possible choices in terms of the position of the first block in the group. If the first block in our chosen group is block 1, part ii with $m = 1$ tells us that there are $\binom{n+k}{n-1}$ choices. If the first block is block 2, part ii with $m = 2$ tells us that there are $\binom{n+k-1}{n-1}$ choices. Continuing in this way, the total number of ways to choose a group of n from the total of $n + k + 1$ blocks is

$$\binom{n+k}{n-1} + \binom{n+k-1}{n-1} + \binom{n+k-2}{n-1} + \cdots + \binom{n-1}{n-1}.$$

But of course, we can also write the number of ways to pick n objects from the group of $n + k + 1$ as $\binom{n+k+1}{n}$. Thus we have proven that

$$\binom{n+k}{n-1} + \binom{n+k-1}{n-1} + \binom{n+k-2}{n-1} + \cdots + \binom{n-1}{n-1} = \binom{n+k+1}{n}.$$

Applying the identity $\binom{n}{k} = \binom{n}{n-k}$ to all the terms in this identity yields the desired identity; make sure you see how. [Note the method of proof: you can often easily prove combinatorial identities by *counting the same thing in two ways.*]

242. Each term is a coefficient times some numbers of a's, b's, c's, and d's. To find each coefficient we simply let $a = b = c = d = 1$. In doing so, our expansion reduces to the sum of coefficients, which is then $(1 + 1 + 1 + 1)^{10} = 4^{10}$.

243. This time let's expand the sums to see what's going on. The left hand side of the identity is

$$\binom{n}{1} + \binom{n+1}{2} + \binom{n+2}{3} + \cdots + \binom{n+m-1}{m},$$

which by a standard identity proved in the text is equal to

$$\binom{n+m}{m} - 1.$$

Similarly, the right hand side is

$$\binom{m}{1} + \binom{m+1}{2} + \binom{m+2}{3} + \cdots + \binom{m+n-1}{n} = \binom{m+n}{n} - 1.$$

But $\binom{n+m}{m}$ always equals $\binom{m+n}{n}$, so we're done!

244. The trick is to realize that $19^{92} = (20 - 1)^{92}$, which by the binomial theorem is

$$\binom{92}{92}20^{92} - \binom{92}{91}20^{91} + \cdots + \binom{92}{2}20^2 - \binom{92}{1}20 + \binom{92}{0}.$$

Finding the last three digits of this sum is equivalent to considering the sum (mod 1000). In (mod 1000), all but the last three terms vanish, since other terms contain 20 to some power 3 or higher, and are thus divisible by 1000. The third to last term is $\binom{92}{2}400 = 92 \cdot 91 \cdot 400/2 = 1674400$, which is congruent to 400 (mod 1000). The second to last term is $-\binom{92}{1}20 = 92 \cdot 20 = -1840$, which is congruent to -840. The last term is 1. The last three digits will thus be $400 - 840 + 1 = -439 \equiv 561$ (mod 100), and their sum will be **12**.

245. The given sum is equivalent to $\sum_{k=1}^{n}(-1)^{k+1}\binom{n}{k}$. (Write the sums out with $\cdots$ if you can't see why.) However, we proved in an exercise that $\sum_{k=0}^{n}(-1)^{k}\binom{n}{k} = 0$. We can get the given sum to look more like this by pulling out a minus sign, so the given sum is

$$-\sum_{k=1}^{n}(-1)^{k}\binom{n}{k} = -\left[\sum_{k=0}^{n}(-1)^{k}\binom{n}{k} - \binom{n}{0}\right] = -(-1) = 1,$$

as desired. (At the risk of being repetitive, we again urge you to write out the sums if this isn't 100% clear.)

246. We first evaluate the sum for n even. We then wish to evaluate

$$S = \binom{n}{1} + 3\binom{n}{3} + \cdots + (n-1)\binom{n}{n-1}$$

We can use the identity $\binom{n}{k} = \binom{n}{n-k}$ to write this as

$$S = (n-1)\binom{n}{1} + (n-3)\binom{n}{3} + \cdots + 1\binom{n}{1}.$$

We can then add the two representations of S to get

$$2S = n\left[\binom{n}{1} + \binom{n}{3} + \cdots + \binom{n}{n-1}\right].$$

In an exercise of the text, we showed that

$$\binom{n}{1} + \binom{n}{3} + \cdots + \binom{n}{n-1} = 2^{n-1},$$

so we have $2S = n2^{n-1}$, or $S = n2^{n-2}$. Note that since we have earlier shown also that

$$\binom{n}{1} + 2\binom{n}{2} + \cdots + n\binom{n}{n} = n2^{n-1},$$

$$\binom{n}{1} + 3\binom{n}{3} + 5\binom{n}{5} + \cdots + (n-1)\binom{n}{n-1} = n2^{n-2}$$ also proves that for even n,

$$2\binom{n}{2} + 4\binom{n}{4} + \cdots + n\binom{n}{n} = n2^{n-2}.$$

If n is odd, the sum is

$$S = \binom{n}{1} + 3\binom{n}{3} + \cdots + n\binom{n}{n}.$$

Do you see why this is different from the even case? Using $\binom{n}{k} = \binom{n}{n-k}$ straightaway accomplishes nothing. (Confirm this.) We pull out Pascal's identity instead, to write

$$S = \binom{n-1}{0} + \binom{n-1}{1} + 3\binom{n-1}{2} + 3\binom{n-1}{3} + \cdots + (n-1)\binom{n-1}{n-3} + (n-1)\binom{n-1}{n-2} + n\binom{n-1}{n-1}.$$

Since $n-1$ is even, we have already proven that

$$\binom{n-1}{1} + 3\binom{n-1}{3} + \cdots + (n-1)\binom{n-1}{n-2} = (n-1)2^{n-3}$$

and

$$2\binom{n-1}{2} + 4\binom{n-1}{4} + \cdots + (n-1)\binom{n-1}{n-1} = (n-1)2^{n-3}.$$

But S is the sum of these two sums and the leftover terms

$$\binom{n-1}{0} + \binom{n-1}{2} + \binom{n-1}{4} + \cdots + \binom{n-1}{n-1} = 2^{n-2}.$$

Hence for odd n, $S = (n-1)2^{n-3} + (n-1)2^{n-3} + 2^{n-2} = n2^{n-2}$, just as in the even case.

247. This one requires some serious cleverness, namely in writing the given sum as $\sum_{k=1}^{n} \binom{n}{n-k}\binom{n}{k-1}$. Once we do this, we can find the sum in many ways. One is committee selection. We have n cats and n dogs and we choose $n-k$ cats and $k-1$ dogs to get a term $\binom{n}{n-k}\binom{n}{k-1}$. Adding these up over all k, the sum is the total number of ways to select $n-1$ animals from the total of $2n$ (n cats plus n dogs). Thus the given sum is equal to $\binom{2n}{n-1}$.

248. The given quantity is

$$\frac{(2n+k)!(2n-k)!}{n!^2\,(n+k)!\,(n-k)!}.$$

We can write this expression as

$$\left(\frac{1}{n!^2}\right)\Big((2n+k)(2n+k-1)\cdots(n+k+1)\Big)\Big((2n-k)(2n-k-1)\cdots(n-k+1)\Big)$$

$$= \left(\frac{1}{n!^2}\right)\Big((2n+k)(2n-k)\Big)\Big((2n+k-1)(2n-k-1)\Big)\cdots\Big((n+k+1)(n-k+1)\Big).$$

Applying the AM-GM inequality to each term in parentheses, we find that each term is maximized for $k=0$. Thus the maximum value is $\left(\dfrac{2n}{n}\right)^2$.

249. This is perfectly suited for a committee selection-type model. Suppose we have n delegates at a conference. Each term $\binom{n}{k}\binom{n-k}{m-k}$ is the number of ways for Yalli to first choose k "best delegate" winners from the n total delegates, then choose $m - k$ "honorable mentions" from the $n - k$ non-best delegates. Observe that no matter what k is, Yalli always chooses m people for awards of some type. Thus the sum over k is the number of ways to have some number of best delegates and some number of honorable mentions, such that the total number of awards given is m.

Now we count them up another way. Let Yalli first choose the m people who will get *any award at all*, then choose some subset of those award winners to be best delegates. She can choose the m award winners from the n delegates in $\binom{n}{m}$ ways, then choose the subset of best delegates in 2^m ways (since each of the winners have 2 possible awards). Hence the given sum is equal to $2^m \binom{n}{m}$.

One note: our use of "best delegates" and "honorable mentions" is not entirely whimsical. It shows that a model close to your heart will often make things clearer.

250. To get rid of the distracting numbers, let's let $n = 22$, $m = 15$, and $r = 10$, so that our sum is

$$\sum_{k=0}^{r} \binom{n}{r-k}\binom{m}{k},$$

which by Vandermonde's identity (proven in an exercise) is $\binom{n+m}{r}$. Substituting numbers from the present problem, we can roll the sum up into $\binom{37}{10}$.

Chapter 16

Sequences and Series

Solutions to Exercises

16-1   The first is an arithmetic series with first term 2, last term $2n$, and n terms, so the sum is $\frac{n}{2}(2n+2) = \boldsymbol{n^2 + n}$. The second is an arithmetic series with first term 1, last term $2n-1$, and n terms, so the sum is $\frac{n}{2}[(2n-1)+1] = \boldsymbol{n^2}$.

16-2   We have

$$
\begin{aligned}
\sum_{i=1}^{n} i^3 &= 6\binom{i+1}{4} + 6\binom{i+1}{3} + \binom{i+1}{2} \\
&= 6\frac{(i+1)(i)(i-1)(i-2)}{24} + 6\frac{(i+1)(i)(i-1)}{6} + \frac{(i+1)(i)}{2} \\
&= \frac{(i+1)(i)[(i-1)(i-2)+4(i-1)+2]}{4} \\
&= \frac{(i+1)(i)(i^2+i)}{4} \\
&= \left(\frac{(i+1)(i)}{2}\right)^2,
\end{aligned}
$$

as desired. Note that this proves the unlikely-seeming result that

$$
1^3 + 2^3 + 3^3 \cdots + n^3 = (1+2+3+\cdots+n)^2.
$$

16-3   After 8 and 13 comes $8+13 = 21$, then $13+21 = 34$, then $21+34 = 55$, then 89, 144, 233, 377, 610, 987, ...

16-4   By the quadratic formula, the two roots of the equation are $\dfrac{1 \pm \sqrt{5}}{2}$. If we took the $-$ from the $\pm$, we would have $\dfrac{1 - \sqrt{5}}{2}$, which is negative and thus can't be the limiting ratio between two Fibonacci numbers. Thus we take the $+$ root.

16-5   For the first one, we just write

$$
\begin{aligned}
F_n &= F_{n-2} + F_{n-1} \\
&= F_{n-2} + F_{n-3} + F_{n-2} \\
&= F_{n-2} + F_{n-3} + F_{n-3} + F_{n-4} \\
&= F_{n-2} + F_{n-3} + F_{n-4} + F_{n-5} + F_{n-4} \\
&= \cdots \\
&= F_{n-2} + F_{n-3} + \cdots + F_1 + F_0 + F_1 \\
&= F_{n-2} + F_{n-3} + \cdots + F_1 + F_0 + 1.
\end{aligned}
$$

For the second, we proceed by induction. As the base case, for $n = 0$ we have $F_0^2 = 1 = F_0 F_1$. For the inductive step, assume it works for $n - 1$, so that $F_0^2 + F_1^2 + \cdots + F_{n-1}^2 = F_{n-1} F_n$. We then have $F_0^2 + F_1^2 + \cdots + F_n^2 = F_{n-1} F_n + F_n^2 = F_n(F_{n-1} + F_n) = F_n F_{n+1}$, so the identity holds for n.

The third is like the first: $F_{2n+1} = F_{2n} + F_{2n-1} = F_{2n} + F_{2n-2} + F_{2n-3} = F_{2n} + F_{2n-2} + F_{2n-4} + F_{2n-5} + \cdots = F_{2n} + F_{2n-2} + \cdots + F_2 + F_0$.

16-6   Probably the easiest way to see it is to consider very large n. Then one of the terms ar^{n-1} and bs^{n-1} will get very large compared to the other. The only way to compensate is to multiply both sides by 0.

16-7   This is simple enough. For r, we have

$$
r^2 - r - 1 = \frac{6 + 2\sqrt{5}}{4} - \frac{1 + \sqrt{5}}{2} - 1 = \frac{6 + 2\sqrt{5} - 2 - 2\sqrt{5} - 4}{4} = 0,
$$

as desired. The calculation for s is almost exactly the same.

16-8   For $n = 0$ the sum is $a + b = 2$. For $n = 1$ the sum is $ar + bs = r + s = 1$. For $n = 2$ the sum is $r^2 + s^2 = [(6 + 2\sqrt{5}) + (6 - 2\sqrt{5})]/4 = 12/4 = 3$, and for $n = 3$ the sum is $[(16 + 8\sqrt{5}) + (16 - 8\sqrt{5})]/8 = 4$. The first four terms of the sequence—2, 1, 3, 4—do indeed satisfy the Fibonacci relation.

16-9   Binet's formula gives

$$
F_0 = \frac{1}{\sqrt{5}} \left[\frac{1 + \sqrt{5}}{2} - \frac{1 - \sqrt{5}}{2} \right] = 1,
$$

$$F_1 = \frac{1}{\sqrt{5}}\left[\frac{6+2\sqrt{5}}{4} - \frac{6-2\sqrt{5}}{4}\right] = 1,$$

$$\text{and} \quad F_0 = \frac{1}{\sqrt{5}}\left[\frac{16+8\sqrt{5}}{8} - \frac{16-8\sqrt{5}}{8}\right] = 2,$$

as desired.

16-10 We write $G_n = ar^n + bs^n$, as we did for the Fibonacci sequence. In order that this sequence satisy the relation $G_{n+1} = G_n + 2G_{n-1}$, we must have $ar^{n+1} + bs^{n+1} = ar^n + bs^n + 2ar^{n-1} + 2bs^{n-1}$, which is rearranged into $ar^{n-1}(r^2 - r - 2) = -bs^{n-1}(s^2 - s - 2)$. Assuming $r \neq s$, this can only be satisfied if both r and s satisfy $x^2 - x - 2 = 0$, which by the quadratic formula has solutions $r = 2$ and $s = -1$. We then use $G_0 = 0$ and $G_1 = 1$ to write $a + b = 0$ and $ar + bs = 2a - b = 1$; solving the system gives $a = 1/3$ and $b = -1/3$. The solution is thus

$$G_n = \frac{1}{3}2^n - \frac{1}{3}(-1)^n.$$

16-11 The solution would be similar, except we would need to write X_n as the sum of *three* geometric series: $X_n = ar^n + bs^n + ct^n$. In order for X_n to satisfy the recursion relation, we would need r, s, and t to satisfy the cubic equation

$$x^3 - \alpha x^2 - \beta x - \gamma = 0.$$

If we could solve this equation to find r, s, and t, we would need three initial values, say A_0, A_1 and A_2, to find a, b, and c.

As the number of terms in the recursion grows, the degree of the polynomial which must be solved increases as well; even solving a cubic, to get the solution to a three-term recursion, is not easy.

16-12 A partial fraction decomposition on $\dfrac{n}{(n+1)(n+2)}$ reveals that it equals $\dfrac{2}{(n+2)} - \dfrac{1}{(n+1)}$, so

$$\begin{aligned}
\sum_{n=1}^{\infty} \frac{n}{(n+1)(n+2)} &= \sum_{n=1}^{\infty}\left(\frac{2}{(n+2)} - \frac{1}{(n+1)}\right) \\
&= \frac{2}{3} - \frac{1}{2} + \frac{2}{4} - \frac{1}{3} + \frac{2}{5} - \frac{1}{4} + \cdots \\
&= -\frac{1}{2} + \frac{1}{3} + \frac{1}{4} + \frac{1}{5} + \cdots
\end{aligned}$$

which **diverges** since the series $1 + \dfrac{1}{2} + \dfrac{1}{3} + \dfrac{1}{4} + \cdots$ diverges.

16-13   Having written our sum as the double sum given, we evaluate

$$\sum_{m=n}^{\infty} \frac{1}{3^m} = \frac{1/3^n}{1-(1/3)},$$

using the formula for the sum of an infinite geometric series. Putting this back in the other summation, our overall sum is

$$\frac{2}{3}\sum_{n=1}^{\infty} \frac{3}{2}\cdot\frac{1}{3^n} = \frac{2}{3}\cdot\frac{3}{2}\cdot\frac{1/3}{1-(1/3)} = \frac{1}{2}.$$

16-14

$\binom{-3}{4} = (-3)(-4)(-5)(-6)/(4)(3)(2)(1) = \mathbf{15};$

$\binom{-7/3}{3} = (-7/3)(-10/3)(-13/3)/(3)(2)(1) = \mathbf{-455/81}.$

16-15   We have $\binom{n}{k} = n(n-1)(n-2)\cdots(n-k+1)/k!$. If $k > n$, then $n-k+1 \le 0$, so 0 will appear somewhere in the product $n(n-1)(n-2)\cdots(n-k+1)$. Thus the product is 0, so $\binom{n}{k} = 0$ if $k > n$.

16-16 $\binom{-1}{n} = (-1)(-2)(-3)\cdots(-n)/(n)(n-1)\cdots(2)(1) = (-1)^n.$

16-17   We write

$$
\begin{aligned}
1/(2.12)^2 &= (2+.12)^{-2} = 2^{-2} + \binom{-2}{1}2^{-3}(.12) + \binom{-2}{2}2^{-4}(.12)^2 + \cdots \\
&= .25 + (-2)(.125)(.12) + (3)(.0625)(.12)^2 \cdots \\
&\approx .25 - .03 + .0027 = .2227.
\end{aligned}
$$

16-18   To first order, $1/101 = (100+1)^{-1} \approx (100-1)/100^2 = 99/10000 = .0099$. Using a calculator we get .009901—the first-order approximation is very good!

16-19   A second order approximation would take the first three terms into account, so would be

$$(A+\epsilon)^{-1} \approx A^{-1} - A^{-2}\epsilon + A^{-3}\epsilon^2 = \frac{A^2 - A\epsilon + \epsilon^2}{A^3}.$$

A "zeroth" order approximation would take only the first term; that is, $(A+\epsilon)^{-1} \approx 1/A$. Not too interesting, but a decent approximation if ϵ is small enough compared to A.

16-20   To first order,

$$\sqrt{A^2+\epsilon} = (A^2+\epsilon)^{1/2} \approx (A^2)^{1/2} + \binom{1/2}{1}(A^2)^{-1/2}\epsilon = A + \frac{\epsilon}{2A}.$$

To evaluate $\sqrt{17}$, we let $A = 4$ and $\epsilon = 1$ in the formula above to get $4 + 1/8 = \mathbf{4.125}$ as the approximation. Given that the actual value is $4.123\ldots$, this approximation isn't bad at all.

16-21 The reciprocals of the first sequence are $\frac{1}{2}$, 1, $\frac{3}{2}$, 2, ..., which is arithmetic. After getting a common denominator, the reciprocals of the second are $\frac{12}{3}$, $\frac{10}{3}$, $\frac{8}{3}$, $\frac{6}{3}$, which is again arithmetic. The reciprocals of the third are 2, 4, 8, 16, ..., which is not an arithmetic sequence. Thus the **first and second** are harmonic sequences.

Solutions to Problems

251. The sum of the first $3n$ positive integers is $(3n)(3n + 1)/2$; the sum of the first n is $(n)(n+1)/2$. We thus have $(3n)(3n + 1) = n(n + 1) + 300$, or $8n^2 + 2n - 300 = 0$. Dividing by the common factor of 2, we get $4n^2 + n - 150 = 0$, which factors as $(4n + 25)(n - 6) = 0$. Discarding the negative solution, we find $n = 6$. The sum of the first $4n$ positive integers is hence $(24)(25)/2 = \mathbf{300}$.

252. The reciprocals of the given sequence are $\frac{1}{6}$, $\frac{1}{3}$, $\frac{1}{2}$, ..., forming an arithmetic sequence with first term $\frac{1}{6}$ and common difference $\frac{1}{6}$. The eighth term in the arithmetic sequence is $\frac{1}{6} + 7(\frac{1}{6}) = \frac{8}{6} = \frac{4}{3}$; the eighth term in the harmonic sequence is the reciprocal of this, or $\mathbf{3/4}$.

253. Splitting it up, the sum becomes $\displaystyle\sum_{k=1}^{10} k^2 + \sum_{k=1}^{10} k + \sum_{k=1}^{10} 1 = \frac{(10)(11)(21)}{6} + \frac{(10)(11)}{2} + 10 = 385 + 55 + 10 = \mathbf{450}$.

254. This problem shows that products can telescope as well as sums. We have

$$\left(1 + \frac{1}{2}\right)\left(1 + \frac{1}{3}\right)\left(1 + \frac{1}{4}\right) \cdots \left(1 + \frac{1}{7}\right) = \left(\frac{3}{2}\right)\left(\frac{4}{3}\right)\left(\frac{5}{4}\right) \cdots \left(\frac{8}{7}\right).$$

In the right-hand expression, the numerator of each fraction is equal to the denominator of the next one; thus the two can cancel. We can cancel all the numerators except the last one and all the denominators except the first one, leaving $8/2 = \mathbf{4}$.

255. We write $a_2^2 - a_1 a_3 = 1$, so that $a_3 = (a_2^2 - 1)/a_1$. Furthermore, from $a_1^2 - a_0 a_2 = -1$, we get $a_2 = (a_1^2 + 1)/a_0 = 10$. Thus $a_3 = (100 - 1)/3 = \mathbf{33}$.

256. For any k, we can write

$$\frac{1}{k} + \frac{2}{k} + \cdots + \frac{k-1}{k} = \frac{1 + 2 + \cdots + (k-1)}{k} = \frac{k(k-1)/2}{k} = \frac{k-1}{2}. \qquad (*)$$

How does this apply? In our sum, we group the fractions like

$$\left(\frac{1}{2}\right) + \left(\frac{1}{3} + \frac{2}{3}\right) + \cdots + \left(\frac{1}{30} + \frac{2}{30} + \cdots + \frac{29}{30}\right),$$

and each quantity in parentheses is a sum of the type (∗). Thus the sum becomes

$$\frac{1}{2} + \frac{2}{2} + \frac{3}{2} + \cdots + \frac{29}{2} = \frac{1 + 2 + \cdots + 29}{2} = \frac{(29)(30)/2}{2} = \frac{435}{2}.$$

257. Each fraction is of the form $\dfrac{1}{n(n+2)}$, which can be written using partial fractions

as $\dfrac{1/2}{n} - \dfrac{1/2}{n+2}$. Thus the sum is

$$\frac{1}{2}\left(\frac{1}{2} - \frac{1}{4}\right) + \frac{1}{2}\left(\frac{1}{4} - \frac{1}{6}\right) + \frac{1}{2}\left(\frac{1}{6} - \frac{1}{8}\right) + \cdots + \frac{1}{2}\left(\frac{1}{18} - \frac{1}{20}\right) = \frac{1}{2}\left(\frac{1}{2} - \frac{1}{20}\right) = \frac{9}{40}.$$

258. Making the exponents all have base 2, we get

$$2^{1/3} 2^{2/9} 2^{3/27} 2^{4/81} \cdots = 2^{1/3 + 2/9 + \cdots}$$

Thus the problem comes down to evaluating the sum $S = (1/3) + (2/9) + (3/27) + \cdots$ To do this, we note that

$$S/3 = (1/9) + (2/27) + (3/81) + \cdots = S - [(1/3) + (1/9) + (1/27) + \cdots]$$

The infinite geometric series $(1/3) + (1/9) + (1/27) + \cdots$ is easily summed as $1/2$ (see Volume 1 if you don't know how to do this), so we have $S/3 = S - 1/2$, or $S = 3/4$. Hence the product we were asked to evaluate is $2^S = 2^{3/4} = \sqrt[4]{8}$.

259. We just evaluate the terms in succession: $a_3 = 2a_2 - 3a_3 = -8$, $a_4 = 2a_3 - 3a_2 = -13$, $a_5 = 2a_4 - 3a_3 = -2$.

260. Rationalizing the denominator of each term, we have

$$\frac{1}{\sqrt{2} + \sqrt{1}} + \frac{1}{\sqrt{3} + \sqrt{2}} + \frac{1}{\sqrt{4} + \sqrt{3}} + \cdots + \frac{1}{\sqrt{25} + \sqrt{24}}$$
$$= \frac{\sqrt{2} - \sqrt{1}}{1} + \frac{\sqrt{3} - \sqrt{2}}{1} + \frac{\sqrt{4} - \sqrt{3}}{1} + \cdots + \frac{\sqrt{25} - \sqrt{24}}{1},$$

which immediately telescopes into $\sqrt{25} - \sqrt{1} = 5 - 1 = 4$.

261. Since the Cesaro sum of $(a_1, a_2, \ldots, a_{99})$ is 1000, the sum $S_1 + S_2 + \cdots + S_{99}$ is $99(1000) = 99000$. Thus the Cesaro sum of $(1, a_1, a_2, \ldots, a_{99})$ is

$$\frac{1 + (1 + S_1) + (1 + S_2) + \cdots + (1 + S_{99})}{100} = \frac{100 + 99000}{100} = \mathbf{991}.$$

262. This is easily proven by induction. As the base cases, $v_1 = 2 = 2F_0$ and $v_2 = 4 = 2F_2$.

For the inductive step, assume that the relation $v_k = 2F_{2k-2}$ holds for all $k < n$. For n we use $F_n - F_{n-1} = F_{n-2}$ repeatedly to write

$$v_n = 3v_{n-1} - v_{n-2} = 3F_{2n-4} - F_{2n-6} = 2F_{2n-4} + F_{2n-5} = F_{2n-3} + F_{2n-4} = F_{2n-2},$$

as desired. Our induction is complete.

263. We are asked to evaluate

$$S = \frac{1}{2} + \frac{4}{4} + \frac{9}{8} + \frac{16}{16} + \frac{25}{32} + \cdots$$

We write

$$S/2 = \frac{1}{4} + \frac{4}{8} + \frac{9}{16} + \frac{16}{32} + \frac{25}{64} + \cdots,$$

and subtract this from S to find

$$S - S/2 = S/2 = \frac{1}{2} + \frac{3}{4} + \frac{5}{8} + \frac{7}{16} + \frac{9}{32} + \cdots$$

To sum this new series for $S/2$, we must play the game again, writing

$$S/4 = \frac{1}{4} + \frac{3}{8} + \frac{5}{16} + \frac{7}{32} + \frac{9}{64} + \cdots$$

and subtracting:

$$S/2 - S/4 = S/4 = \frac{1}{2} + \frac{2}{4} + \frac{2}{8} + \frac{2}{16} + \frac{2}{32} + \cdots$$

Since the sum of the geometric series $1/4 + 1/8 + 1/16 + \cdots$ is $1/2$, we have $S/4 = 1/2 + 2(1/2) = 3/2$, so $S = 4(3/2) = \mathbf{6}$.

264. A partial fraction decomposition changes our sum into $\displaystyle\sum_{n=3}^{\infty} \left(\frac{1}{4n-3} - \frac{1}{4n+1} \right)$, which telescopes straightforwardly:

$$\left(\frac{1}{9} - \frac{1}{13} \right) + \left(\frac{1}{13} - \frac{1}{17} \right) + \left(\frac{1}{17} - \frac{1}{21} \right) + \cdots = \frac{1}{9}.$$

265. We can expand the double sum as

$$\sum_{j=1}^{\infty}\sum_{k=1}^{\infty} \frac{1}{(j+k)^3} = \sum_{j=1}^{\infty} \left[\frac{1}{(j+1)^3} + \frac{1}{(j+2)^3} + \frac{1}{(j+3)^3} + \cdots \right]$$

$$= \left(\frac{1}{2^3} + \frac{1}{3^3} + \frac{1}{4^3} + \cdots \right) + \left(\frac{1}{3^3} + \frac{1}{4^3} + \frac{1}{5^3} + \cdots \right)$$

$$+ \left(\frac{1}{4^3} + \frac{1}{5^3} + \frac{1}{5^3} + \cdots \right) + \cdots$$

$$= \frac{1}{2^3} + \frac{2}{3^3} + \frac{3}{4^3} + \frac{4}{5^3} + \cdots$$

$$= \sum_{k=1}^{\infty} \frac{k-1}{k^3}$$

$$= \sum_{k=1}^{\infty} \left(\frac{1}{k^2} - \frac{1}{k^3} \right)$$

$$= \sum_{k=1}^{\infty} \frac{1}{k^2} - \sum_{k=1}^{\infty} \frac{1}{k^3}$$

$$= \boldsymbol{p - q}.$$

266. The product is $\left(\frac{2}{3}\right)\left(\frac{3}{4}\right)\left(\frac{4}{5}\right) \cdots \left(\frac{n-1}{n}\right)$, which telescopes into $\boldsymbol{2/n}$.

267. We have

$$1 + 2i + 3i^2 + \cdots + (n+1)i^n = [1 + 2i - 3 - 4i] + [5 + 6i - 7 - 8i] + \cdots + (n+1),$$

where there are $n/4$ of the expressions in brackets and an isolated $n + 1$. Each bracketed expression adds to $-2i - 2$, so the sum is $(n)(-2i - 2)/4 + (n+1) = \boldsymbol{(n + 2 - ni)/2}$.

268. Consider instead the sequence $g(n) = (-1)^n f(n)$. The first thing we note is that $g(n)$ satisfies the Fibonacci relation. Thus if we can find a and b such that $g(0) = aF_0 + bF_2$ and $g(1) = aF_1 + bF_3$, we will have $g(2) = g(1) + g(0) = a(F_0 + F_1) + b(F_2 + F_3) = aF_2 + bF_4$, $g(3) = g(2) + g(1) = a(F_1 + F_2) + b(F_3 + F_4) = aF_3 + bF_5$, and so on: thus, $g(n) = aF_n + bF_{n+2}$ for all n. Of course, this is dreaming until we can find such a and b. We need $g(0) = 3 = a + 2b$ and $g(1) = 1 = a + 3b$, so we immediately find $b = -2$ and $a = 7$; that is $g(n) = 7F_n - 2F_{n+2}$ for all n. For $n = 100$, we have $f(100) = g(100) = 7F_{100} - 2F_{102} = 5F_{100} - 2F_{101} = 3F_{100} - 2F_{99}$. This could also be written $F_{100} + 2F_{98}$, $F_{99} + 3F_{98}$, or in many other ways.

Do you see how this problem shows that any sequence A_n satisfying the Fibonacci relation can be written as $aF_{n+2} + bF_n$ for some integers a and b? An interesting result.

269. Use o to represent odd numbers and e for evens, and consider only the first four entries in each row. The first row is o, the second is ooo, the third is $oeoe$ (first four entries only), the fourth is $ooeo$. Each time we hit $ooeo$, the next row will be $oeee$ (figure out why). Each time we hit $oeee$, the next row is $oooe$; after $oooe$ comes $oeoe$. This is what we started with in the third row, so the rows will cycle through this pattern; $oeoe \rightarrow ooeo \rightarrow oeee \rightarrow oooe \rightarrow oeoe$. Thus every row after the third will have at least one even entry.

270. While you could certainly do this one algebraically, here's a nicer solution. Draw the grid

$$\begin{matrix} 1 \\ 1 & 2 \\ 1 & 2 & 3 \\ \vdots & \vdots & \vdots & \ddots \\ 1 & 2 & 3 & \cdots & n \end{matrix}$$

Now the sum across the kth row of the grid is $k(k+1)/2$, so the sum of all the numbers in the grid is

$$\frac{1(2)}{2} + \frac{2(3)}{2} + \cdots + \frac{n(n+1)}{2}. \tag{*}$$

On the other hand, the sum down the kth column of the grid is $(n-k+1)k$, so the sum of all the numbers in the grid is

$$1(n) + 2(n-1) + 3(n-2) + \cdots + n(1). \tag{**}$$

Comparing (*) and (**), we are immediately done.

271. Note that $a_n b_n = \frac{a_{n-1}^2}{b_{n-1}} \frac{b_{n-1}^2}{a_{n-1}} = a_{n-1} b_{n-1}$. This means that the product $a_n b_n$ is constant for all n, so is equal to the value at $n = 0$: $a_0 b_0 = 6$. Substituting $a_{n-1} = 6/b_{n-1}$ into the recursion for b_n, we have $b_n = b_{n-1}^3/6$. We thus have

$$b_8 = b_7^3/6 = (b_6^3/6)^3/6 = \cdots = \frac{b_0^{3^8}}{6^{3^7 + 3^6 + \cdots + 3^0}}.$$

Evaluating the power of 6 in the denominator as a geometric series, $3^7 + 3^6 + \cdots + 3^0 = (1 - 3^8)/(1 - 3) = 6560/2 = 3280$, this last fraction becomes $3^{6561}/6^{3280} = \mathbf{3^{3281}/2^{3280}}$.

272. The fourth term will have $k = 3$, so will be

$$\binom{1/3}{3} 1^{1/3 - 3} (-2x)^3 = \frac{\left(\frac{1}{3}\right)\left(-\frac{2}{3}\right)\left(-\frac{5}{3}\right)}{(3)(2)(1)}(-8x^3) = -\frac{40}{81}x^3.$$

The coefficient is **−40/81**.

273. We have $\Delta^1(u_n) = u_{n+1} - u_n = (n+1)^3 + (n+1) - n^3 - n = 3n^2 + 3n + 2$, $\Delta^2(u_n) = \Delta^1(\Delta^1(u_n)) = \Delta^1(3n^2 + 3n + 2) = 3(n+1)^2 + 3(n+1) + 2 - 3n^2 - 3n - 2 = 6n + 6$, $\Delta^3(u_n) = \Delta^1(6n + 6) = 6(n+1) + 6 - 6n - 6 = 6$, and $\Delta^4(u_n) = \Delta^1(6) = 6 - 6 = 0$. The answer is **4**.

274. We multiply the given equation by $(a + b)$ to get

$$(a + b)R_n = \frac{1}{2}(a^n + b^n)(a + b) = \frac{1}{2}(a^{n+1} + b^{n+1}) + \frac{1}{2}(ba^n + ab^n) = R_{n+1} + abR_{n-1}.$$

Since $a + b = 6$ and $ab = 1$, this becomes the recursion $6R_n = R_{n+1} + R_{n-1}$, or $R_{n+1} = 6R_n - R_{n-1}$. The initial conditions for the recursion are easily found: $R_0 = 1$ and $R_1 = (a+b)/2 = 3$.

Finding the units digit of a term is the same as finding the term (mod 10). Thus, let's calculate terms (mod 10): starting with R_0 and going up, we have 1, 3, $6(3) - 1 = 17 \equiv 7$, $6(7) - 3 = 39 \equiv 9$, $47 \equiv 7$, $33 \equiv 3$, 1, 3, 7, 9, 7, 3, 1, 3, 7, 9, and so on. The recursion repeats in groups of 6! Thus $R_{12345} \equiv R_{12345\,(\text{mod}\,6)} \equiv R_3 \equiv 9\,(\text{mod}\,10)$, so **9** is the units digit we seek.

275. We have

$$
\begin{aligned}
a_{100} &= a_{99} + 2(99) \\
&= a_{98} + 2(98) + 2(99) \\
&= \cdots \\
&= a_1 + 2(1 + 2 + 3 + \cdots + 99) \\
&= 2 + 2[(99)(100)/2] \\
&= \mathbf{9902}.
\end{aligned}
$$

276. This is actually a trick question: if the polynomial is equal to u_n for all n, then the sum of its coefficients can be found by substituting 1 for n in the polynomial. Hence the sum of the coefficients is equal to u_1, or **5**. We don't need the recursion information at all.

On the other hand, we can find the actual polynomial fairly easily. We write

$$
\begin{aligned}
u_n - u_{n-1} &= 3 + 4(n - 2) \\
u_{n-1} - u_{n-2} &= 3 + 4(n - 3) \\
u_{n-2} - u_{n-3} &= 3 + 4(n - 4) \\
&\vdots \\
u_2 - u_1 &= 3 + 4(0).
\end{aligned}
$$

Adding all these equations together, we get

$$u_n - u_1 = 3(n-1) + 4(1 + 2 + 3 + \cdots + (n-2)) = 3(n-1) + 2(n-2)(n-1) = 2n^2 - 3n + 1,$$

so that $u_n = 2n^2 - 3n + 1 + u_1 = 2n^2 - 3n + 6$.

277. We use a formula from complex numbers, writing

$$\sin x = \frac{e^{ix} - e^{-ix}}{2i}.$$

We then have

$$\sum_{n=0}^{\infty} \frac{\sin(nx)}{3^n} = \sum_{n=0}^{\infty} \frac{e^{nix} - e^{-nix}}{2i} \cdot \frac{1}{3^n}$$

$$= \frac{1}{2i} \sum_{n=0}^{\infty} \left(\frac{e^{ix}}{3} \right)^n - \frac{1}{2i} \sum_{n=0}^{\infty} \left(\frac{e^{-ix}}{3} \right)^n .$$

Since both sums are now infinite geometric series, this is just

$$\frac{1}{2i} \left[\left(\frac{1}{1 - (e^{ix}/3)} \right) - \left(\frac{1}{1 - (e^{-ix}/3)} \right) \right] .$$

Since $\sin x = 1/3$, $\cos x = 2\sqrt{2}/3$, so $e^{ix} = \cos x + i \sin x = (2\sqrt{2} + i)/3$ and $e^{-ix} = (2\sqrt{2} - i)/3$. Substituting in and rationalizing the denominators, we have

$$\frac{1}{2i} \left(\frac{9}{(9 - 2\sqrt{2}) - i} - \frac{9}{(9 - 2\sqrt{2}) + i} \right) = \frac{9}{2i} \left(\frac{[(9 - 2\sqrt{2}) + i] - [(9 - 2\sqrt{2}) - i]}{90 - 36\sqrt{2}} \right)$$

$$= \frac{1}{10 - 4\sqrt{2}}$$

$$= \frac{10 + 4\sqrt{2}}{68}$$

$$= \frac{5 + 2\sqrt{2}}{34}$$

Whew.

278. First of all we will prove by induction that $a_n = a_1 + n - 1$ for every $n \geq 1$. As the base cases, we have $a_2 = a_1 + 1$, $a_4 = a_2 + 1 = a_1 + 3$; since $a_1 + 1 = a_2 < a_3 < a_4 = a_1 + 3$ and all a_i are integers, $a_3 = a_1 + 2$. For the inductive step, suppose that $a_k = a_1 + (k - 1)$. Since $a_{2k} = a_k + k$, we have $a_{2k} = a_1 + (2k - 1)$. But $a_1 + (k - 1) = a_k < a_{k+1} < a_{k+2} < \cdots < a_{2k-1} < a_{2k} = a_1 + (2k - 1)$, so $a_{k+1} = a_k + 1 = a_1 + k$. This completes the induction, so $a_n = a_1 + (n - 1)$ for all $n \geq 1$.

Thus all we need is to find a_1. We will show that $a_1 = 1$ by contradiction. Assume that $a_1 > 1$. Then the numbers $(a_1 + 1)! + 2$, $(a_1 + 1)! + 3, \ldots$, $(a_1 + 1)! + a_1 + 1$ are composite. (Why?) Let p be the smallest prime number such that $p > (a_1 + 1)! + a_1 + 1$ and let $n = p - a_1 + 1$. Then $p = a_1 + n - 1 = a_n$, so that n is prime. On the other hand, $(a_1 + 1)! + 2 < p - a_1 + 1 < p - 1$, so that $p - a_1 + 1$ is composite, a contradiction. Since $a_1 > 1$ yields a contradiction, we must have $a_1 = 1$. Since $a_n = a_1 + n - 1$, we have $a_n = n$ for every n. In particular, $a_{1993} = \mathbf{1993}$.

279. Let such a number be $N = x_1 x_2 \cdots x_k$, where each digit x_i is an element of $\{1, 3, 4\}$ and $x_1 + x_2 + \cdots + x_k = n$. It is fairly clear that $a_n = a_{n-1} + a_{n-3} + a_{n-4}$. (Do you see why?) We thus have

$$a_{2n} = a_{2n-1} + a_{2n-3} + a_{2n-4} = a_{2n-2} + a_{2n-4} + (a_{2n-5} + a_{2n-3}) + a_{2n-4}$$

$$= a_{2n-2} + a_{2n-4} + (a_{2n-2} - a_{2n-6}) + a_{2n-4} = 2a_{2(n-1)} + 2a_{2(n-2)} - a_{2(n-3)}.$$

We define a new number $b_n = a_{2n}$. Then $b_n = 2b_{n-1} + 2b_{n-2} - b_{n-3}$. Clearly $b_1 = 1 = 1^2$, $b_2 = 4 = 2^2$, $b_3 = 9 = 3^2$, and so on. Now we must prove that the b_i are all squares.

Define a third sequence c_n by $c_1 = 1$, $c_2 = 2$, and $c_{n+2} = c_{n+1} + c_n$ for all n. We can show by induction that $b_n = c_n^2$ for all n. As base case, you can confirm for yourself that $b_1 = c_1^2$ and $b_2 = c_2^2$. For the inductive step, assume that $b_k = c_k^2$ holds for all $k < n$. Then

$$
\begin{aligned}
b_n &= 2b_{n-1} + 2b_{n-2} - b_{n-3} = 2c_{n-1}^2 + 2c_{n-2}^2 - c_{n-3}^2 \\
&= (c_{n-1} + c_{n-2})^2 + (c_{n-1} - c_{n-2})^2 - c_{n-3}^2 = c_n^2 + c_{n-3}^2 - c_{n-3}^2 = c_n^2.
\end{aligned}
$$

This completes the induction, so that $b_n = a_{2n} = c_n^2$ for every n.

280. To break down the number of pairings, consider $2(n+1)$ objects $a_1, a_1, a_2, a_2, \ldots,$ a_n, a_n, b, b. To each of the u_n pairings of $a_1, \ldots, a_n$ one can add (b, b). From each partition of the $a_1, \ldots, a_n$ one can form n new ones by replacing (a_i, a_j) with (a_j, b), (a_i, b). Among the $(n+1)u_n$ partitions thus obtained, some repetitions exist. If the original pairing contains two identical pairs (a_i, a_j), (a_i, a_j), $i \neq j$, then splitting each of them gives the same pairing of $a_1, a_1, a_2, \ldots, b$. There are $n(n-1)/2$ ways to select i and j, and for any such choice the remaining $2(n-2)$ objects can be paired in u_{n-2} ways. We must subtract this total number, $(n(n-1)/2)u_{n-2}$, of repetitions, leaving $u_{n+1} = (n+1)u_n - (n(n-1)/2)u_{n-2}$, as desired.

281. Letting $n = k$ and $n = k - 1$ for some $k \geq 2$ in the second given equation, we find

$$
\begin{aligned}
a_1 + \cdots + a_{k-1} &= (k-1)^2 a_{k-1} \\
a_1 + \cdots + a_k &= k^2 a_k.
\end{aligned}
$$

Subtracting the first from the second, we have, after a bit of algebra, $(k^2 - 1)a_k = (k-1)^2 a_{k-1}$. Since $k \geq 2$, we have

$$
a_k = \frac{k-1}{k+1} a_{k-1} = \frac{(k-1)(k-2)}{(k+1)(k)} a_{k-2} = \cdots = \frac{(k-1)!}{(k+1)\cdots 3} a_1 = \frac{1}{(k+1)k}.
$$

Hence we get $a_n = 1/n(n+1)$.

Chapter 17

Counting in the Twilight Zone

Solutions to Exercises

17-1   Are you convinced that our basic techniques will fail?

17-2   Let there be x setters, y spaniels, and z wolfhounds. The sequence representing this has x d's before the first __, y d's before the next __, and z d's after the last __. There is exactly one such sequence. Similarly, if we start from a sequence with x d's then a __, then y d's, then a __, then z d's, we can make exactly one choice for the breeder. If there are no setters, the sequence starts with a __; if no spaniels, the two __'s are adjacent; and if no wolfhounds, the sequence ends with a __. This is perfectly fine.

17-3   As before, we write a sequence with n d's and $r - 1$ __'s to represent each choice. (We use $r - 1$ __'s because we wish to partition the d's into r groups.) Again, counting the number of possible sequences is equivalent to counting the number of choices. Since we make our sequences by choosing $r - 1$ places to hold __'s out of $n + r - 1$ possible places in the sequence, our general formula is $\binom{n+r-1}{r-1}$.

17-4   If we let x_1 be the number of the first breed, x_2 be the number of the second breed, etc., the number of solutions to $x_1 + x_2 + \cdots + x_r = n$ is the number of ways we can choose n dogs from among r breeds. We've already solved this problem, so we know that the number of solutions to the given equation in nonnegative integers is $\binom{n+r-1}{r-1}$.

17-5   Suppose you're just in class A. Then you're only counted once in $+\#(A)$. If you're in A and B, you're added in both $+\#(A)$ and $+\#(B)$ and subtracted in $-\#(A \cap B)$. If you're in all three classes, you're included in everything, so you're added four times and subtracted three.

17-6   As an extesion of our three class discussion, you should find if we add a class D, the number of students is

$$\#(A) + \#(B) + \#(C) + \#(D)$$
$$-\#(A \cap B) - \#(A \cap C) - \#(A \cap D) - \#(B \cap C) - \#(B \cap D) - \#(C \cap D)$$
$$+\#(A \cap B \cap C) + \#(A \cap B \cap D) + \#(A \cap C \cap D) + \#(B \cap C \cap D)$$
$$-\#(A \cap B \cap C \cap D).$$

You should be able to construct the expression for adding class E now.

17-7   From the Principle of Inclusion-Exclusion, to find the total number of objects which are in at least one category (or $\#(A_1 \cup A_2 \cup A_3 \cup \cdots \cup A_n)$), we add the number of objects in each category, then subtract the number of objects which are in both A_i and A_j for all (i, j), and so on. Since $\#(A_i)$ is the same for all i, we need only determine it for one category then mulitply by the number of categories. Similarly, since $\#(A_i \cap A_j)$ is the same for all pairs of categories (i, j), we evaluate it for one pair of categories, then multiply by the total number of categories $\binom{n}{2}$. Continuing in this manner, we get the desired expression since there are $\binom{n}{3}$ groups of 3 categories, $\binom{n}{4}$ groups of 4 categories, and so on.

17-8   Don't go on unless you're sure that you understand this fact.

17-9   The generating for e_1 consists of only even powers; that of e_2 of only odd powers; and that of e_3 only prime powers. Thus our generating function is

$$(1 + x^2 + x^4 + x^6 + \cdots)(x + x^3 + x^5 + x^7 + \cdots)(x^2 + x^3 + x^5 + x^7 + \cdots).$$

17-10   The generating function for each die is $(x + x^2 + x^3 + x^4 + x^5 + x^6)$; thus, the generating function for rolling all the dice is $(x + x^2 + x^3 + x^4 + x^5 + x^6)^{10}$. We proceed as in the text to find the coefficient of x^{25}. We first factor out an x: $x^{10}(1 + x + x^2 + x^3 + x^4 + x^5)^{10}$. We thus want the coefficient of x^{15} in

$$(1 + x + x^2 + x^3 + x^4 + x^5)^{10} = \left(\frac{1 - x^6}{1 - x}\right)^{10} = (1 - x^6)^{10}(1 - x)^{-10}.$$

Since the exponents of x in $(1 - x^6)^{10}$ are multiples of 6, we have only three terms contributing to our total, namely $\left[\binom{10}{0}(x^6)^0\right]\left[-\binom{-10}{15}x^{15}\right]$, $\left[-\binom{10}{1}x^6\right]\left[-\binom{-10}{9}x^9\right]$, and $\left[\binom{10}{2}(x^6)^2\right]\left[-\binom{-10}{3}x^3\right]$. Hence, our desired number of rolls which produce 25 is

$$-\binom{10}{0}\binom{-10}{15} - \binom{10}{1}\binom{-10}{9} - \binom{10}{2}\binom{-10}{3}.$$

17-11   One 2 is 2, two 2's is 4, etc. Continuing in this way, we find our generating function for the number of 2's is $1 + x^2 + x^4 + x^6 + \cdots$.

17-12 For the x term, we only have one term: $x \cdot 1 \cdot 1 \cdot 1 = x$. For x^2, we have $x^2 \cdot 1 \cdot 1 \cdot 1 + 1 \cdot x^2 \cdot 1 \cdot 1 = 2x^2$; for x^3, we get $x^3 \cdot 1 \cdot 1 \cdot 1 + x \cdot x^2 \cdot 1 \cdot 1 + 1 \cdot 1 \cdot x^3 \cdot 1 = 3x^3$; and for x^4 we find

$$x^4 \cdot 1 \cdot 1 \cdot 1 + x^2 \cdot x^2 \cdot 1 \cdot 1 + 1 \cdot x^4 \cdot 1 \cdot 1 + x \cdot 1 \cdot x^3 \cdot 1 + 1 \cdot 1 \cdot 1 \cdot x^4 = 5x^4.$$

The only partition of 1 is 1; there are two partitions of 2 ($1 + 1$ and 2); there are 3 partitions of 3 ($1 + 1 + 1$, $1 + 2$, and 3); and there are 5 partitions of 4 ($1 + 1 + 1 + 1$, $1 + 1 + 2$, $2 + 2$, $1 + 3$, and 4). Notice how each expanded term of the generating function corresponds to one of the partitions. (For example, $x \cdot 1 \cdot x^3 \cdot 1$ corresponds to the $1 + 3$ partition of 4.)

17-13 Certainly we can. Our backwards counting approach is very flexible. Try inventing a simple three dimensional problem (like walking around on a cube).

17-14 Let Mike's initial vertex be 'home' and the other three 'away'. Let s_k be the number of ways he can get back to home after k moves starting from home and t_k be the number of ways to get home in k moves starting from an away vertex. Since from the home vertex, our next move takes us to any of 3 away vertices, we have $s_k = 3t_{k-1}$, or 3 times the number of ways he can get back home in $k - 1$ moves. From an away vertex, Mike can go straight home or to 2 other away vertices, so we find $t_k = s_{k-1} + 2t_{k-1}$. Clearly $s_1 = 0$ and $t_1 = 1$, so we can repeatedly use our recursions to solve the problem and find $s_6 = \mathbf{183}$.

17-15 For the odds we have the correspondence

1	2	3	4	5	6	7	8	9	10	11	...
1	3	5	7	9	11	13	15	17	19	21	...

and for the evens we have

1	2	3	4	5	6	7	8	9	10	11	...
2	4	6	8	10	12	14	16	18	20	22	...

These correspondences show that the set of positive even integers and that of positive odd integers are both the same size as the set of positive integers.

17-16 For the geometric proof, draw $\triangle ABC$ with $AC = b$ and $BC = a$. Let any line parallel to AB intersect AC at X and BC at Y. These parallel lines give us our correspondence between points on AC and BC. Analytically, take $0 < x < a$; we correspond this x to a number from 0 to b by bx/a.

Solutions to Problems

282. We started off with an easy one. We can split the five balls into three groups as in the problem in $\frac{1}{2}\binom{5}{2}\binom{3}{2}\binom{1}{1} = 15$ ways because we can pick 2 for the first group, two of the remaining 3 for the second group, and the last ball is for the last group. We then divide the product by 2 because the two groups of 2 are indistinguishable. Now we can put these three groups into numbered boxes in $3! = 6$ ways, for a total of $6(15) = \mathbf{90}$ ways to put the balls in the boxes.

283. There are $100/5 = 20$ multiples of 5 and $\lfloor 100/7 \rfloor = 14$ multiples of 7, for a total of 34; however, we have counted the multiples of 35 twice. Since we want to exclude these altogether, we subtract them twice for a total of $34 - 2 \cdot 2 = \mathbf{30}$.

284. After choosing the first square, we eliminate the other squares in that row and column. The remaining squares form a 4 by 4 grid. After choosing from among these squares, we have a 3 by 3 grid from which to choose the final square. Since we have $5^2 = 25$ ways to pick the first square, $4^2 = 16$ ways to pick the second, and $3^2 = 9$ ways to select the last, we have a total of $(25)(16)(9)/6 = \mathbf{600}$ ways to pick the squares, where we have divided by 6 because the 3 squares can be selected in $3! = 6$ orders.

285. We count the number of intersections by counting the maximum number of possible intersections of 100 lines, and then subtracting the number of intersections 'lost' to the parallel and concurrent lines. The maximum number of intersections occurs when each pair of line intersects at point through which no other lines pass. The number of such intersections is the number of ways to select the lines, or $\binom{100}{2} = 4950$. For the 25 parallel lines, there are 0 intersections where there could have been $\binom{25}{2} = 300$. For the concurrent lines, there is only one intersection where there could have been $\binom{25}{2} = 300$. Hence, we have 'lost' $600 - 1 = 599$ intersections and are left with a possible $4950 - 599 = \mathbf{4351}$.

286. We translate the given problem to one involving solutions in nonnegative integers by making the substitution $y_i = x_i - 1$. Since the x_i are positive integers, the y_i are nonnegative integers. Our given equation becomes

$$y_1 + y_2 + \cdots + y_8 = 11.$$

From the discussion in the chapter there are $\binom{18}{7} = \mathbf{31824}$ solutions to this equation in nonnegative integers.

287. We call the 'minimum element' of a set the element with the smallest subscript. First consider the case where a_1 is the minimum element. To form a desired set we can include any of the remaining elements. Since each element can either be in or out, there are $2^{11} = 2048$ such sets. If a_2 is the minimum element, only even-subscripted elements can be included. There are 5 of these, so there are $2^5 = 32$ desired sets with a_2 as the minimum element. Similarly, there are $2^3 = 8$ desired sets with a_3 as the minimum element, $2^2 = 4$ with a_4 as minimum element, $2^1 = 2$ with a_5, and $2^1 = 2$ with a_6. Each of the other 6 elements can form their own subset which satisfies the problem, so our total is

$$2048 + 32 + 8 + 4 + 2 + 2 + 6 = \mathbf{2102}.$$

288. The four countries can be ordered around the table in $(4 - 1)! = 6$ ways. The Americans and Russians can be ordered (in their little group) in $3! = 6$ ways. The Germans can be ordered in $4! = 24$ ways and the French in 2. The number of possible seating is thus $(6)(6)(6)(24)(2) = \mathbf{10368}$.

289. We solve this problem by counting the total number of possible seatings, then subtracting the ones in which Ginger sits next to Gilligan, his ape, or both. The number of possible seatings is simply 8!. To count the number of seatings in which Gilligan and Ginger are adjacent we consider the two as a unit, for a total of 7! seatings. Since Gilligan and Ginger can sit together in 2 orders, the total number of seatings in which they are adjacent is 2(7!). Similarly, Ginger can sit next to the ape in 2(7!) ways. Once again, we've overcounted by counting the cases of Ginger being between the two undesireables twice. Ginger can be seated between the two in the row in 2(6!) ways (consider the three as a unit and note that there are 2 ways to make the unit), so the number of admissible seatings is

$$8! - 2(7!) - 2(7!) + 2(6!) = 30(6!) = \mathbf{21600}.$$

290. The question is pretty tough as stands, so let's try to draw a one-to-one correspondence to a situation which is easily counted. Let x be a taken seat and o be an empty seat. Thus, $oxooxoooxooxoxooooo$ is a possible seating sequence. There aren't $\binom{20}{5}$ permissible sequences because there must be one o between each pair of x's. However, if we remove an o, or a seat, from between each pair of neighboring x's (forming $oxooxooxoxxooooo$ from the sequence above), we get a sequence with no restrictions. Similarly, we can go from a sequence of 11 o's and 5 x's with no restrictions to a sequence as in the problem by adding an o between each pair of neighboring x's. In this way we draw a one-to-one correspondence between the seating in the problem and the seating of 5 people in $20 - 4 = 16$ seats without restriction. (Make sure you see that this is a one-to-one correspondence; try to prove it.) Thus, there are $\binom{16}{5}$ ways to select the seats of the participants, and $5! = 120$ to put the people in the seats, for a total of $(120)(4368) = \mathbf{524160}$ seatings.

291. Guided by our counting on graphs discussion in the text, we work backwards. We can get to vertex 30 from 29 in only 1 way. Similarly, there's only one way to go from 25, 26, 27, or 28. From point 24 we can go to 25 or to 27. Each of these points have one path to 30, so there are 2 paths from 24. Similarly, if we start from 23, we have 2 paths via point 24 and 1 path via 28 (directly to 28). In this manner, we continue backwards finding the number of paths from each point on the grid. These numbers are shown on the grid beneath the numbered points. We see that the number of paths from point 1 is **671**.

1	2	3	4	5
671	616	511	365	190

10	9	8	7	6
55	105	146	175	190

11	12	13	14	15
55	50	41	29	15

20	19	18	17	16
5	9	12	14	15

21	22	23	24	25
5	4	3	2	1

30	29	28	27	26
1	1	1	1	1

292. We can just count these in the conventional casework way, but there is a significantly slicker way. Let A be the original set of points with integral components from 1 to 4, and B the set of points with integral components from 0 to 5. Clearly any line through four points of A also goes through two points of B. Now consider the points in B but not in A. Each of these points are on exactly one of the lines through four points in A. For example, the corners are on diagonals of the cube A, the points on the edges are on diagonals of square cross-sections, and the points on the interior of the faces are on the lines parallel to the coordinate axes through four points of A. Hence, we can draw a one-to-one correspondence between pairs of points in $B - A$ (meaning the points in B but not in A) and lines through four members of A. There are 6^3 points in B and 4^3 in A, so there are $(6^3 - 4^3)/2 = \mathbf{76}$ pairs of points in $B - A$. Extending this as suggested, we have $[(n+2)^3 - n^3]/2$ lines for $i, j, k \leq n$.

293. We can count the total number of ways to seat six people in a row by counting the number of ways none are seated properly, the number of ways one person is seated properly, two people are seated properly, etc. This leads us to the Principle of Inclusion-Exclusion. If we let $\#(A)$ be the number of ways the people can be seated with person A in the proper seat, the Principle of Inclusion-Exclusion becomes

$$6! = \binom{6}{1}\#(A) - \binom{6}{2}\#(A \cap B) + \binom{6}{3}\#(A \cap B \cap C) - \cdots - \binom{6}{6}\#(A \cap B \cap C \cap D \cap E \cap F) + X,$$

where the X is the number of seatings in which no one is in the proper seat. Here we note that $\#(A)$ is the same for each individual. Similarly, $\#(A \cap B)$ is the same for each pair. This accounts for $\binom{6}{2}\#(A \cap B)$ in the Principle of Inclusion-Exclusion since there are $\binom{6}{2}$ pairs. To evaluate $\#(A)$, we note that 1 person is fixed and the others can be seated in $5! = 120$ ways. Similarly $\#(A \cap B) = 4! = 24$ since the 4 non-fixed people can be seated in $4!$ ways. Hence, we have

$$X = 6! - \binom{6}{1}5! + \binom{6}{2}4! - \binom{6}{3}3! + \binom{6}{4}2! - \binom{6}{5}1! + \binom{6}{6},$$

so $X = \mathbf{265}$.

294.

    i. Here we are only interested in the number of 2's, 4's, 6's, etc., so our generating function is

$$(1 + x^2 + x^4 + \cdots)(1 + x^4 + x^8 + x^{12} + \cdots)(1 + x^6 + x^{12} + x^{18} + \cdots) \cdots.$$

    ii. We only want the odds, but only one of each; thus, each factor of the generating function terminates after two terms. Our generating function therefore is

$$(1 + x)(1 + x^3)(1 + x^5)(1 + x^7)(1 + x^9) \cdots.$$

    iii. The problem is essentially finding the partitions of a number containing only 1's, 5's, 10's, 20's, 50's, and 100's, so the generating function is

$$(1+x+x^2+\cdots)(1+x^5+x^{10}+\cdots)(1+x^{10}+x^{20}+\cdots)(1+x^{20}+x^{40}+\cdots)(1+x^{50}+\cdots)(1+x^{100}+\cdots).$$

iv. This one's a bit tricky. Whatever x, y, and z are, $2x$ is a multiple of 2, $3y$ is a multiple of 3, and $7z$ is a multiple of 7. Hence, each solution of $2x + 3y + 7z = n$ represents a partition of n with x 2's, y 3's, and z 7's. Since $z < 4$, the generating function factor for the 7's terminates after the fourth term. Thus, our full generating function is

$$(1 + x^2 + x^4 + x^6 + \cdots)(1 + x^3 + x^6 + x^9 + \cdots)(1 + x^7 + x^{14} + x^{21}).$$

295. Each term can be characterized by the number of a's, b's, c's, and d's it has. Let x_i be the number of i's the term has. Since each term is the product of 10 a's, b's, c's, and d's, we have $x_a + x_b + x_c + x_d = 10$. Each term in the expansion corresponds to a different solution (x_a, x_b, x_c, x_d). Hence, as discussed in the text, there are $\binom{13}{3}$ solutions to this equation and therefore **286** terms.

296. First note that if there are n elements in a set, then there are 2^n subsets of that set (since in forming a subset, we can either include or exclude each element). Hence, from $n(A) + n(B) + n(C) = n(A \cup B \cup C)$, we have $2^{|A|} + 2^{|B|} + 2^{|C|} = 2^{|A \cup B \cup C|}$, or $2^{101} + 2^{|C|} = 2^{|A \cup B \cup C|}$. Since $|C| > 0$, the only possible solution of this equation is $|C| = 101$ and $|A \cup B \cup C| = 102$. We can relate our determined expressions to the desired $|A \cap B \cap C|$ via the Principle of Inclusion-Exclusion:

$$|A \cup B \cup C| = |A| + |B| + |C| - |A \cap B| - |A \cap C| - |B \cap C| + |A \cap B \cap C|.$$

Solving for $|A \cap B \cap C|$, we find

$$|A \cap B \cap C| = -199 + |A \cap B| + |A \cap C| + |B \cap C|.$$

We now apply the Principle of Inclusion-Exclusion to the $|A \cap B|$ terms to get

$$\begin{aligned} |A \cap B \cap C| &= -199 + 2(|A| + |B| + |C|) - |A \cup B| - |A \cup C| - |B \cup C| \\ &= 403 - |A \cup B| - |A \cup C| - |B \cup C|. \end{aligned}$$

Each of the $|A \cup B|$ terms can be no larger than $|A \cup B \cup C| = 102$, so the smallest possible value of $|A \cap B \cap C|$ is $403 - 3(102) = $ **97**. Can you construct sets which satisfy this problem and our discovered minimum?

297. We'll derive the general result then apply it to the specific case in the problem. If we consider the boys indistinguishable and also the girls, our problem becomes finding the expected number of bg's or gb's in a sequence of m b's and n g's. Label the chairs from 1 to $m + n$. Consider the pair of chairs $(i, i+1)$. The probability that there is a boy and a girl in these chairs is the same as the expected number of boy-girl pairs in the two chairs (since there can be only boy-girl pair in the chairs at a time). To count the number of sequences with bg or gb in chairs $(i, i+1)$ we place the boy and girl in the chairs (2 ways, bg or gb) and then put the remaining $m - 1$ boys in the other $m + n - 2$ chairs in $\binom{m+n-2}{m-1}$ ways. Since there are $\binom{m+n}{m}$ ways to place the m b's in the $m+n$ places and $(m+n-1)$ adjacent pairs of chairs, our desired expected number is

$$\frac{(m+n-1)(2)\binom{m+n-2}{m-1}}{\binom{m+n}{m}} = \frac{2(m+n-1)(m+n-2)!m!n!}{(m+n)!(m-1)!(n-1)!} = \frac{2mn}{m+n}.$$

In the given case, we have $2(7)(13)/(7+13) = \mathbf{91/10}$.

298. First we count the number of sets of n u-cubes, no two of which are on the same level. Start from the top of the cube and work downward. There are n^2 choices from the top level. Eliminating all the cubes in the same level as the first chosen level, we are left with $(n-1)^2$ choices from the next level down. (Make sure you see this.) Continuing in this manner, we have $n^2(n-1)^2(n-2)^2\cdots 1^2 = (n!)^2$ sets of n u-cubes, no two of which are on the same level. Let A be the set of these sets.

Now we find the maximum number of these sets which have two or more u-cubes of the same color. If we can show that the number of such sets is less than the number of possible sets, we can conclude that there must be some sets with no two u-cubes of the same color. Suppose we pick two u-cubes of the same color. There are $n^3/4$ ways to pick the color and $\binom{4}{2} = 6$ ways to pick the pair of cubes from among the cubes of that color. To count the ways to pick the remaining cubes, we have, by the same argument as above, $[(n-2)!]^2$ ways to pick the remaining $n-2$ cubes to complete some member of the set A. Thus, our total number of members of A which have more than one u-cube of some color is no more than $6(n^3/4)[(n-2)!]^2$. (Make sure you see that this is the maximum possible number of such sets, not the exact number; we have overcounted because we have included several sets with at least two blocks of the same color much more than one time.) Hence, the maximum portion of the members of A which have more than one u-cube of the same color is

$$\frac{6(n^3/4)[(n-2)!]^2}{(n!)^2} = \frac{3n}{2(n-1)^2}.$$

For all $n \geq 4$, this fraction is less than 1. (Why?) Hence, there must be some portion of the members of A which have no two u-cubes of the same color.

299. To show that $2^n < f(n)$, we note that if we only take steps north and west, all of the paths thus formed are self-avoiding. Since at each juncture we have 2 choices (north or west), we have at least 2^n self-avoiding paths. If we count our paths by only excluding those in which we don't directly backtrack (i.e. go west then on the next step go east), we have 4 choices on the first step, then 3 on all subsequent steps, for a total of $4 \cdot 3^{n-1}$ paths. Unfortunately, this may not accurately count the self-avoiding paths because it is possible in this set-up to form loops rather than just backtracking to cross our on path. Hence, the number $4 \cdot 3^{n-1}$ is an upper bound and we have $2^n < f(n) \leq 4 \cdot 3^{n-1}$.

300. For $n = 1$, the sum is 2. Let $n \geq 2$. The first digit is 1, and there are $\binom{2n-1}{n-1} = \binom{2n-1}{n}$ ways to arrange the 1's among the remaining positions. Now consider any position except the first. If we put a 1 there, there are then $\binom{2n-2}{n-2} = \binom{2n-2}{n}$ numbers with a 1 in that position, so that when we add all the numbers there are $\binom{2n-1}{n}$ 2^{2n-1}'s and $\binom{2n-2}{n}$ of 2^k for the other k's. Our sum then is

$$\binom{2n-2}{n}(1 + 2 + 2^2 + \cdots + 2^{2n-2}) + \binom{2n-1}{n}2^{2n-1} =$$

$$\binom{2n-2}{n}(2^{2n-1} - 1) + \binom{2n-1}{n}2^{2n-1}.$$

Chapter 18

Again and Again

Solutions to Exercises

18-1   The continued power is

$$2^{2^{2^{2^2}}} = 2^{2^{2^4}} = 2^{2^{16}},$$

which is absolutely enormous. The continued fraction is

$$2 + \cfrac{1}{2 + \cfrac{1}{2 + \frac{2}{5}}} = 2 + \cfrac{1}{2 + \frac{5}{12}} = 2 + \frac{12}{29} = \frac{\mathbf{70}}{\mathbf{29}}.$$

The continued root can be evaluated only with a calculator, where it equals

$$\sqrt{2 + \sqrt{2 + \sqrt{2 + \sqrt{3.414}}}} \approx \sqrt{2 + \sqrt{2 + \sqrt{3.848}}} \approx \sqrt{2 + \sqrt{3.962}} \approx \sqrt{3.990} \approx \mathbf{1.998}.$$

(Can you guess where this continued root is heading?)

18-2   The first yields the equation

$$x = 2 + \frac{1}{x},$$

which gives the quadratic $x^2 - 2x - 1 = 0$. Solving for the positive root, we get $x = \mathbf{1 + \sqrt{2}}$.

The second yields the equation

$$x = 2 + \cfrac{1}{3 + \frac{1}{x}},$$

which simplifies (with some elbow grease) to the quadratic $3x^2 - 6x - 2 = 0$. Solving for the positive root, we get $x = 1 + \sqrt{15}/3$.

18-3 If it had been 2, the expression

$$\frac{1}{\text{something}}$$

would have had to be greater than 1, even though the "something" is greater than 1 (because it is a positive integer plus something else positive). It it had been 4, then 1/(something) would have had to be negative, an impossibility.

18-4 Removing the fractions one by one, the continued fraction does equal the proper fraction.

18-5 Since $29 \cdot 5 = 145 = 147 - 2$, we have

$$\frac{147}{29} = 5 + \frac{2}{29} = 5 + \frac{1}{29/2}.$$

Since $2 \cdot 14 = 28$, this yields

$$5 + \frac{1}{14 + \frac{1}{2}}$$

as the final continued fraction.

Since $7 \cdot 4 = 28 = 29 - 1$, the next fraction gives

$$\frac{29}{7} = 4 + \frac{1}{8}$$

immediately.

Since $12 \cdot 5 = 60 = 70 - 10$, the last one yields

$$\frac{70}{12} = 5 + \frac{10}{12} = 5 + \frac{5}{6} = 5 + \frac{1}{6/5} = 5 + \frac{1}{1 + \frac{1}{5}}.$$

18-6 We have $b_i = 1/(b_{i-1} - a_{i-1}) = 1/(b_{i-1} - \lfloor b_{i-1} \rfloor) = 1/\{b_{i-1}\}$.

18-7 We can take any continued fraction which terminates and roll up all the fractions until we get a single, rational, number. Thus this finite continued fraction cannot represent an irrational number.

18-8 We take π and subtract $a_1 = 3$. We take the reciprocal of what remains, to get 7.0625. We subtract $a_2 = 7$ and take the reciprocal of what remains to get 15.996595. We subtract $a_3 = 15$ and take the reciprocal of what remains to get 1.003417. We subtract $a_4 = 1$ and take the reciprocal of what remains to get 292.646, from which we take $a_5 = 292$.

We could go on, but eventually round-off errors would catch up with us, so we'll be satisfied with

$$\pi \approx 3 + \cfrac{1}{7 + \cfrac{1}{15 + \cfrac{1}{1 + \cfrac{1}{292 + \cdots}}}}$$

18-9   The method is the same as we used in the previous exercise. Enter the number you're finding the continued fraction for and subtract off its integer part, writing down the integer part as a_1. Take the reciprocal of what remains, and subtract off and write down the integer part a_2. Take the reciprocal of what remains and write down the integer part a_3. And so on. And so on. And... you get the picture.

18-10   The first few convergents are 3, $3 + \frac{1}{7} = \frac{22}{7}$, $3 + 1/(7 + 1/15) = 3 + \frac{15}{106} = \frac{333}{106}$. How good are these as approximations? This third one already yields 3.1415, an excellent approximation to π.

18-11   We prove it by induction. For the base case, we have $P_1 = a_1$, $Q_1 = 1$, $P_2 = a_1 a_2 + 1$, and $Q_2 = a_2$, so that

$$P_1 Q_2 - P_2 Q_1 = a_1 a_2 - (a_1 a_2 + 1)(1) = -1 = (-1)^1.$$

For the inductive step, we assume it holds for $k - 1$. For k we have

$$
\begin{aligned}
P_k Q_{k+1} - P_{k+1} Q_k &= P_k(a_{k+1} Q_k + Q_{k-1}) - (a_{k+1} P_k + P_{k-1}) Q_k \\
&= P_k Q_{k-1} - P_{k-1} Q_k = -(-1)^{k-1} = (-1)^k,
\end{aligned}
$$

and our induction is complete.

Solutions to Problems

301. Since

$$e^{x^{e^{x^{e^{x^{\cdot^{\cdot^{\cdot}}}}}}}} = 2,$$

we have

$$e^{x^2} = 2.$$

Taking natural logs of both sides, we have $x^2 = \ln 2$, or $x = \sqrt{\ln 2}$.

302. We have

$$c_n = n + \cfrac{1}{2n + \cfrac{1}{2n + \cdots}} = n + \cfrac{1}{n + n + \cfrac{1}{2n + \cdots}} = n + \cfrac{1}{n + c_n}.$$

Multiplying through by $n + c_n$, we have $c_n^2 + n c_n = n^2 + n c_n + 1$, or $c_n^2 = n^2 + 1$. Thus

$$\sum_{k=1}^{11} c_k^2 = \sum_{k=1}^{11} (n^2 + 1) = \sum_{k=1}^{11} n^2 + \sum_{k=1}^{11} 1 = \frac{11(12)(23)}{6} + 11 = \mathbf{517}.$$

303. Since $\lfloor\sqrt{k^2+1}\rfloor = k$, we have

$$\sqrt{k^2+1} = k + \frac{1}{A}$$

for some A. Solving for A, we have

$$A = \frac{1}{\sqrt{k^2+1}-k} = \frac{(\sqrt{k^2+1}+k)}{(\sqrt{k^2+1}-k)(\sqrt{k^2+1}+k)} = \sqrt{k^2+1}+k,$$

so that the continued fraction expansion is

$$\sqrt{k^2+1} = k + \frac{1}{A} = k + \cfrac{1}{k+\sqrt{k^2+1}} = k + \cfrac{1}{k+k+\frac{1}{k+\sqrt{k^2+1}}}$$

$$= k + \cfrac{1}{k+k+\frac{1}{k+k+\sqrt{k^2+1}}} = k + \cfrac{1}{2k+\cfrac{1}{2k+\frac{1}{2k+\cdots}}}$$

The period is **1**.

304. The golden ratio ϕ satisfies the quadratic equation

$$\phi^2 - \phi - 1,$$

so that $\phi = 1 + 1/\phi$, or

$$\phi = 1 + \frac{1}{\phi}$$

$$= 1 + \cfrac{1}{1+\frac{1}{\phi}}$$

$$= 1 + \cfrac{1}{1+\frac{1}{1+\frac{1}{1+\cdots}}}.$$

(You could also use the method of the text to find the continued fraction methodically.) The first five convergents are 1, $1 + 1/1 = 2$, $1 + 1/(1 + 1/1) = 1 + 1/2 = 3/2$, $1 + 1/(1 + 1/(1 + 1/1)) = 1 + 1/(3/2) = 1 + 2/3 = 5/3$, and $1 + 1/(1 + 1/(1 + 1/(1 + 1/1))) = 8/5$. (Do you see a pattern here? Can you prove that the nth convergent is F_n/F_{n-1}, where F_k is the kth Fibonacci number?)

305. We square the equation $A = \sqrt{6+2\sqrt{5}} - \sqrt{6-2\sqrt{5}}$, to get

$$A^2 = (\sqrt{6+2\sqrt{5}})^2 - 2\sqrt{6+2\sqrt{5}}\sqrt{6-2\sqrt{5}} + (\sqrt{6-2\sqrt{5}})^2 = 6+2\sqrt{5}-2\sqrt{16}+6-2\sqrt{5} = 4,$$

so that $A = 2$. We further have $B = A - \frac{1}{B}$, or $B^2 - AB + 1 = 0$, or $B = (A+\sqrt{A^2-4})/2 = 1$. Thus $A + B = \mathbf{3}$.

Chapter 19

Probability

Solutions to Exercises

19-1 If two events are mutually exclusive, they cannot both occur. Thus, $P(A \cap B) = 0$ and $P(A \cup B) = P(A) + P(B)$.

19-2 Applying the Principle of Inclusion-Exclusion, we must first add the probabilities of each of the events occurring, then subtract the probabilities of each pair of events occurring, and finally add the probabilities of all three events happening. Thus, we have

$$P(A \cup B \cup C) = P(A) + P(B) + P(C) - P(A \cap B) - P(A \cap C) - P(B \cap C) + P(A \cap B \cap C).$$

19-3 The square, or possible region, has area $4^2 = 16$. To satisfy the problem, the point must be outside the smaller square shown. (Make sure you see why.) The area of the desired region is then $16 - 2^2 = 12$. Hence the probability is $12/16 = \mathbf{3/4}$.

19-4 The segment CG represents those cases where the woman arrives at 12:00 and still meets her husband, since he arrives at 11:40 at the earliest for those points. Similarly, CH represents the cases where the man arrives at 11:50 and still is able to pick up his wife because she arrives between 11:40 and 12:00.

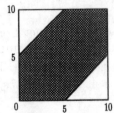

19-5 Graphing the two numbers against each other gives a 10 by 10 square of possible choices. We find the desired points as before. Let the vertical number be 0 and note that the horizontal can be between 0 and 5. Gradually increasing the vertical number yields the shaded region as the area of all points such that the positive difference between the horizontal and vertical numbers is less than $1/2$. The area of the possible region is 100 and that of the desired region is $100 - 25/2 - 25/2 = 75$; hence, our desired probability is $75/100 = \mathbf{3/4}$.

19-6   If we were only to consider integers, our problem would become a discrete one rather than continuous as we could count the individual cases of the choices of numbers. Our ratio of areas method would fail.

19-7   Convinced yet?

19-8   Still don't buy it?

19-9   Let event A be having the disease and event B be the test being positive. We are given

$$P(A) = 0.01, \quad P(B|A) = 0.9, \quad P(B|A') = 0.2,$$

where the last two are the probabilities of the test being positive given that I have the disease and that I don't, respectively. We are asked to find $P(A|B)$. Thus we must determine $P(A \cap B)$, the probability that I have the disease *and* the test is positive, and $P(B)$, the probability that the test is positive. We have $P(A \cap B) = P(A)P(B|A) = (0.01)(0.9) = 0.009$ (the probability I have the disease times the probability the test is positive when I am diseased). To find $P(B)$, we consider the two mutually exclusive cases of my being diseased and testing positive and my not being afflicted and testing positive: $P(B) = (0.01)(0.9) + (0.99)(0.2) = 0.207$. Hence, the probability that I am afflicted is $(0.009)/(0.207) = \mathbf{1/23}$. Kind of surprising, isn't it? We can improve the accuracy of testing by repeating the procedure on those individuals who test positive the first time.

Solutions to Problems

306. This is simply a counting problem. There are 52! ways to order the cards. To count the ways the two given cards can be adjacent, we consider the two cards as a unit, so we can order the 51 units (our 2 cards together plus the other 50 cards) in 51! ways. Since the two given cards can be ordered in two ways, our final probability is $[2(51!)]/52! = \mathbf{1/26}$.

307. Applying $P(A|B) = P(A \cap B)/P(B)$, we have

$$P = \frac{(1/2)(4/6)}{(1/2)(4/6) + (1/2)(3/8)} = \frac{\mathbf{16}}{\mathbf{25}}.$$

308. The winning team must win 3 of the first 5 games and then the last game (not 4 of the 6 games, since the winning team must win the last game). We can choose the winning team in 2 ways and the 3 games they win in $\binom{5}{3} = 10$ ways. The 6 games each have 2 possible outcomes, for a total of $2^6 = 64$ possible overall outcomes of the six games. Hence, our probability is $2(10)/64 = \mathbf{5/16}$.

309. Although this is a conditional probability problem, we can attack this best with our simple counting techniques. There are $3(3)(3) = 27$ ways to make three rolls over 3 and there are 3 ways (all 4's, all 5's, all 6's) to have a desired outcome, for a probability of $3/27 = \mathbf{1/9}$.

310. The only way we can have a desired outcome is if the center of the coin is directly in the center of one of the chessboard squares. Thus, the area of desired region is 0, since there is no two dimensional region of desireable points. Hence, our probability is **0**.

311. The described numbers can only be those with four 9's and a 7 and those with three 9's and two 8's. There are $\binom{5}{1} = 5$ of the former type and $\binom{5}{2} = 10$ of the latter. Of all of these, only 3 are divisible by 11. (Using the divisibility rule for 11 makes these easy to find.) Thus, our probability is $3/15 = \mathbf{1/5}$.

312. There are two distinct combinations which total six: 1-2-3 and 2-2-2. The latter can only occur in one way while the former can happen in 6 ways. (There are 6 ways to order the members of the set $\{1, 2, 3\}$.) Since all 7 of these cases are equally likely to occur, our probability is $\mathbf{1/7}$.

313. We can choose the 6 cards in $\binom{52}{6}$ ways. The two fives can be chosen in $\binom{4}{2}$ ways and the remaining 4 non-five cards in $\binom{48}{4}$ ways. Hence, our probability is

$$\frac{\binom{4}{2}\binom{48}{4}}{\binom{52}{6}}.$$

314. We find the probability that no two girls are adjacent and subtract from 1. There are 9! ways to seat the children in a circle. To count the number of ways to seat the children so that no two girls are adjacent, we consider one girl fixed and count the ways the rest of the students can be seated about her. Because no two girls can be next to each other, we know which 4 other seats contain girls and which boys. Thus, the number of ways we can seat the children in these is $(4!)(5!)$. (Once we fix the location of one girl, seating the others is like seating them in a row.) Hence, our probability is

$$1 - \frac{4!\,5!}{9!} = \frac{\mathbf{125}}{\mathbf{126}}.$$

315. Since all three people give the same answer, they are either all liars or all telling the truth. If they are all telling the truth, it is raining. Our desired probability then is the probability that all three are telling the truth divided by the probability that all three give the same answer, or

$$P = \frac{(4/5)^3}{(1/5)^3 + (4/5)^3} = \frac{\mathbf{64}}{\mathbf{65}}.$$

Compare this to our discussion of conditional probability with event B being all three people giving the same answer and event A being all three people being truth-tellers.

316. There are $\binom{54}{5}$ ways to select the cards. To find the number of ways to get 5 of a kind, we consider 2 cases: one joker plus 4 of a kind, and two jokers plus 3 of a kind. The former can occur in 13(2) ways, with 13 ways to choose the duplicated card and 2 ways to pick the joker. The latter can occur in 13(4) ways with 13 ways to pick the three of a kind and 4 ways to pick the three suits included among these. Hence,

$$P = \frac{13(2) + 13(4)}{54!/49!\,5!} = \frac{\mathbf{13(6!)(49!)}}{\mathbf{54!}}.$$

317. There are 500 possible choices. Since there are $\lfloor 500/7 \rfloor = 71$ multiples of 7, $\lfloor 500/11 \rfloor = 45$ multiples of 11, and $\lfloor 500/77 \rfloor = 6$ multiples of 77 less than 500, there are $71 + 45 - 6 = 110$ numbers between 0 and 500 which are multiples of 7 or 11 (by the Principle of Inclusion-Exclusion). The desired probability is then $110/500 = \mathbf{11/50}$.

318. Shown are five of the holes in the mesh; one hole plus the four surrounding it. Since the spark has a 1 mm radius, its center must be at least 1 mm from the wires which form the mesh. Thus, the center of the spark must be inside the shown shaded square which has side 3 mm (since the center must be at least 1 mm from each wire). Thus, the area of the desired region is 9 mm². The possible region is a bit tricky. We can't just consider the interior of the square mesh because that would exclude the possibility of the center of the spark actually hitting 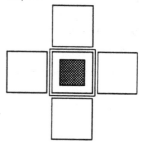 the wire mesh. Thus, we extend the possible region to the center of the wires which form the mesh as shown in the diagram. The possible region then is 0.5 mm further outside the hole in the mesh since the wires have diameter 1 mm. Hence, the probability is $9/36 = \mathbf{1/4}$. This approach is valid because we can cover the entire screen with these 36 mm² 'possible' regions, each containing 9 mm² 'desired' regions.

319. Without loss of generality, let $AB = 2$. Hence, $AM = 1$. Clearly either AP or PB is greater than or equal to AM. Let AP be this largest side. Thus, we require $PB + AM > AP$ in order for the three lengths to form a triangle. Letting $BP = x$, where $x \leq 1$ (since $BP \leq AP$), we have $x + 1 > 2 - x$, so $x > 1/2$ must be true for the three lengths to be the sides of a triangle. Our possible region has length 1 $(0 \leq x \leq 1)$ and our desired region has length 1/2 $(1/2 < x \leq 1)$ so our probability is $\mathbf{1/2}$.

320. We plot x and y on number lines, one ascending and one descending as shown. The bold portions of the lines show where the numbers will be rounded up. The described sum will only equal three when both x and y are rounded up. As the number lines make evident, both x and y are rounded up for a total length of 1 out of the possible 2.5 for a probability of $1/2.5 = \mathbf{2/5}$.

321. Since all lattice squares are identical, we look at one lattice square. In the diagram, circular arcs of length 1 have been drawn from each vertex; the points within each quarter-circle are within 1 unit of the vertex which is the center. The possible area is the area in the lattice square, or 1. The desired area is that area in the lattice square which is inside exactly two of the quarter-circles drawn. The Xed regions are regions inside either 4 (the center region) or 3 (the rest of the Xes) quarter-circles. The other regions are the ones we desire. Consider the region covered by the quarter-circles centered at A and B. The leftover region in the square but not in these quarter-circles is one of the four desired regions. We can find the area covered by the two quarter-circles by adding the area of the two and subtracting the area of their intersection. Doing this as discussed in Volume 1, we find the area contained in the quarter circles is $\pi/6 + \sqrt{3}/4$. Therefore, our desired area, and hence the probability (since the possible area is 1), is

$$4[1 - (\pi/6 + \sqrt{3}/4)] = 4 - \frac{2\pi}{3} - \sqrt{3}.$$

322. Let the three arcs $\overparen{AB}$, $\overparen{BC}$, and $\overparen{AC}$ have measures x, y, and z, where $x \geq y \geq z$. Since the three together form a circle, $x + y + z = 360°$. Since x is the largest arc, it must be at least 120°. The three points lie on a semicircle if this largest arc is greater than 180°. Since x is equally likely to be any value from 120° to 360° (we can see this by supposing we select the points by first choosing x, then y and then labelling the points), our possible range has length 240° and our desired region has length 180° (from 180° to 360°). Thus, our desired probability is **3/4**.

323. Since we have continuous variables, we turn to a graphical solution. Let the three numbers be (x, y, z), where $x, y \geq z$. First we find our possible range. Suppose $z = a$ for some a such that $0 < a < 1$. In the figure at right, the shaded region corresponds to all (x, y) such that both x and y are greater than or equal to z. We see that for any value of a we get a square for the desired area, where the square is the entire unit square when $z = 0$ and gets smaller as we increase z. Thus, we find that the possible region is a pyramid which has height 1 (z ranges from 0 to 1) and whose base is a square with side length 1 (corresponding to $z = 0$).

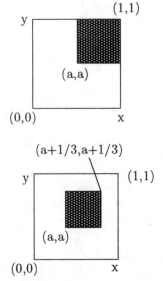

The desired range is a bit trickier. First, if $z > 2/3$, then we are in the desired region, since the largest number is at most 1, the difference between the largest and smallest cannot be larger than $1 - 2/3 = 1/3$. This corresponds to the entire possible region for $z > 2/3$ and is thus a pyramid with height 1/3 and square base with side length 1/3. For $z < 2/3$ consider the diagram, letting $z = a$. The shaded square shows all points for which neither x nor y is more than 1/3 greater than a. Any point outside this square has either x or y more than 1/3 greater than z. Thus, for all $z < 2/3$, the desired region is a square of area $(1/3)(1/3) = 1/9$. Since all these cross-sections have the same area, the volume of the solid formed by putting these together is $(1/9)(2/3) = 2/27$ since the solid has height 2/3. Our probability is a ratio of *volumes*. The volume of the possible region is $(1)(1^2)/3 = 1/3$ and that of the desired region is $2/27 + (1/3)(1/3)^2/3 = 7/81$, so our probability is $(7/81)/(1/3) = \mathbf{7/27}$.

Chapter 20

Find It and Make It

Solutions to Exercises

20-1 First let point C be a point such that its distances from lines l and m (CB and CA, respectively) are equal. Since CB and CA are distances to the respective lines, they are perpendicular to the lines. Since $AC = BC$, $\angle CBO = \angle CAO = 90°$, and $CO = CO$, we have $\triangle OCA \cong \triangle OCB$ by HL congruency. Hence, $\angle COB = \angle COA$, so any point in the locus is on one of the angle bisectors of the angle formed at O. Conversely, if C is on one of the angle bisectors at O, then from SA congruency applied to right triangles CBO and CAO, $CB = CA$, so C is on the locus. Hence, our locus is the angle bisectors.

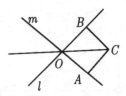

20-2 The locus is a pair of planes, one above and one below the given plane.

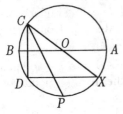

20-3 Continue CO to X. Since CX is a diameter, $\angle CDX = 90°$. Since DC is perpendicular to both AB and DX, we have $AB \parallel DX$. Since $\angle DCP = \angle PCX$, we have $\overset{\frown}{DP} = \overset{\frown}{PX}$ and point P is the midpoint of $\overset{\frown}{DX}$. Since $DX \parallel AB$, we have $\overset{\frown}{BD} = \overset{\frown}{AX}$ and point P is the midpoint of $\overset{\frown}{AB}$ as well. Hence, the locus is the endpoints of the diameter perpendicular to AB. (The other endpoint occurs when C is on the other side of AB.)

20-4 Did you really do the construction?

20-5 The incenter is the intersection of bisectors of the angles of the triangle. Thus, to get the incenter, we draw the angle bisectors of two of the angles and their intersection is the incenter. Similarly, we draw the perpendicular bisectors of two of the sides and find their intersection to get the circumcenter. To get the orthocenter, we draw the line from A perpendicular to BC and the line from B perpendicular to AC. Their intersection is the orthocenter. To get the median from A to BC, we locate the midpoint M of BC in the same way we find the perpendicular bisector. We then draw AM and similarly draw another median. Their intersection is the centroid. To draw the circumcircle, we draw a circle with center O (the circumcenter we found) and radius OA. The incircle is a bit tougher. We have the center, but the radius is the perpendicular distance from the incenter to the sides. Hence, we draw the perpendicular to a side and find where it meets the side (call this D). We then draw a circle with center I (the incenter) and radius ID.

20-6   First we make the square with side AB. We draw lines perpendicular to AB through A and B. We wish to find the point D on line l such that $AD = AB$. We do this by drawing an arc with center A and radius AB. The intersection of this with l is D. Drawing the line through D perpendicular to l, we find C as shown. Finding the square with diagonal AB is a bit less complicated. Since the diagonals of a square are perpendicular bisectors of each other, 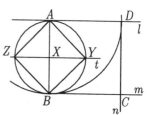 we draw t, the perpendicular bisector of AB. The vertices of a square are equidistant from the intersection of the diagonals, so we draw the circle with center X and radius XA. The intersections of this circle with line t give the other two vertices of the square.

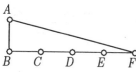

20-7   Since we can make a square, we can make a segment of length $\sqrt{2}$ by making a square with side length 1 and drawing the diagonal. This is a result of the Pythagorean Theorem. If we instead draw a rectangle with side lengths 1 and 2, the diagonal has length $\sqrt{5}$. We can continue in this way to note that the diagonal of a rectangle with side lengths 1 and 4 has length $\sqrt{17}$. Thus, we start with AB of length 1 and draw a line through B perpendicular to AB. We then draw a circle with center B and radius AB to get C on the perpendicular line so that $BC = AB = 1$. Drawing a circle with center C and radius AB locates D such that $BD = 2$. Similarly we can make E and F (or just a circle with center D and radius BD locates F). Connecting A to F gives us our desired segment since $AF = \sqrt{AB^2 + BF^2} = \sqrt{1 + 16} = \sqrt{17}$.

20-8   We use the construction in the previous example to divide AB into $p + q$ equal segments. We can then easily select the appropriate P from among the dividing points on AB. (Make sure you see how!)

20-9   Let the length of the desired segment be x. Hence we have $x = \sqrt{ab}$, or $(x)(x) = (a)(b)$, which reminds us of the Power of a Point Theorem. If we have two chords which intersect each other such that one is in pieces of lengths a and b and the other is in two equal pieces of length x, then $x^2 = ab$. The most common and useful instance of one chord bisecting another is when one chord is a diameter and the second chord is perpendicular to this diameter. Hence, we draw diameter AB by drawing

$AE = a$ then $EB = b$ on the same line. We find the midpoint M of this line and draw the circle with radius AM (and hence diameter AB). To get our second chord, we draw a line through E perpendicular to AB and let C and D be the points where the line meets the circle. Since AB is a diameter and $AB \perp CD$, we have $CE = DE$. From the Power of a Point Theorem, we have $CE = x^2 = (AE)(BE) = ab$; hence, CE is a segment with the desired length.

Solutions to Problems

324. Two triangles with the same base have the same area if their altitudes are the same. Hence, the locus is the set of points equidistant from the line containing the given base. The locus of points in a plane equidistant from a given line is a **pair of parallel lines**, or if the locus is in space, it is a **cylinder**.

325. We know that the center of a circle passing through three vertices of a triangle is the intersection of the perpendicular bisectors of the sides. Hence we just pick three points A, B, and C on the circle. The center then is the intersection of the perpendicular bisectors of AB and BC.

326. Start with segment BC. Since point A, the third vertex of the equilateral triangle, is the length BC away from C, it is on the circle with center C and radius BC. Similarly, A is on the circle with center B and radius BC. Hence we draw these two circles and the point A is the intersection of the two (either intersection will do).

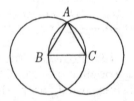

327. Call the point X. Any circle with radius a passing through X has a center which is a away from X; therefore, the locus of all possible points is the set of points a away from X, or the circle with center X and radius a.

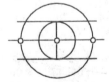

328. First we find the points equidistant from the two lines. Since the lines are parallel, the set of points equidistant from them is a third line, l, parallel to the first two and exactly between them. Let the radius of the circle be r. Thus, the third line from above is exactly r away from the other two. For a point then to be equidistant from the two lines and the circle, it must also be r away from the circle. The points which are r away from a circle with radius r are the center of the circle and the entire circle with radius $2r$ (make sure you see this). Line l passes through the center of the circle and also meets the circle with radius $2r$ in two points. Hence, there are **3** points in the plane which satisfy the problem.

329. We can make a 30° angle by bisecting a 60° angle. Since we can make an equilateral triangle, we can make a 60° angle. We then bisect one of the interior angles of the triangle to form a 30° angle.

330. We can fill half the tank exactly by tilting the tank as shown and filling it so that the water level connects the corners as shown in the first diagram. Make sure you see why the shaded triangle is half the area of the tank. Setting the tank level, we mark the height of half the tank with a line as shown in the second rectangle. We then tilt the tank again, filling until the water level connects the end of the chalk mark to the corner of the tank as shown in the

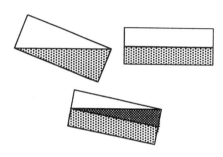

third diagram. The darker shaded area is clearly half the upper rectangle, or 25% of the whole tank. Hence, we have filled $50\% + 25\% = 75\%$ of the tank with water.

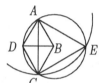

331. If we can find one side of the triangle, we can easily construct the rest of the triangle. If an equilateral triangle is inscribed in a circle, each side cuts off a 120° arc. We can find AC, one side of the triangle, by finding a 120° arc of the circle. We thus construct adjacent equilateral triangles BDC and ABD as shown. The resulting $\angle ABC$ has measure 120°. Hence, AC is one side of the triangle. The third vertex can be found in many ways; one way is to draw the circle with center A (or C) and radius AC (the third vertex is the intersection of this circle and circle B), another is to extend BD to meet the circle again. Make sure you see how both of these produces E, the third vertex of $\triangle ACE$.

332. Point G is the intersection of medians BE and CM of the original triangle. Choose any point X on the line l which C moves on and find Y, the centroid of $\triangle ABX$ as the intersection of medians AF and XM. Since $CM/GM = XM/YM = 3$, $\triangle CMX \sim \triangle GMY$ and thus $GY \parallel CX$. Hence, any centroid formed as in the problem is on the line through G parallel to line l and the desired locus is this line.

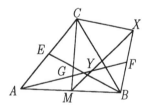

333. Draw a line through P to circle O at point Z. The midpoint of PZ is in the locus, so point Y is in the locus. We then connect Y to the midpoint of OP (point X in the diagram) because this forms similar triangles OZP and XYP (since $PX/PO = PY/PZ = 1/2$ and $\angle XPY = \angle OPZ$). Hence we have $XY/OZ = 1/2$ and $XY = r/2$. Similarly, we

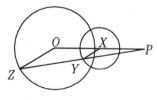

can show that any point in the locus is $r/2$ away from X. Thus, the locus is some portion of the circle with radius $r/2$ centered at X. (We might have guessed this by drawing several points on the locus.) We can show that every point on the circle is in the locus by drawing a line through P and an arbitrary point Y on the circle. Extending the line to Z, since $PX/PO = XY/OZ$ we have $\triangle OZP \sim \triangle XYP$ by SAS similarity. Hence, $PY/PZ = 1/2$ and Y is in the locus.

334. First note that $AA'B'A$ is a trapezoid and that OO' is perpendicular to AB. Since OO' is the median of $AA'B'A$, we have

$$OO' = (AA' + BB')/2 = (AG + GB)/2 = AB/2.$$

Hence, OO' has constant length and is always perpendicular to AB. Thus, there is only one point which can be O', regardless of the position of G. The locus is the point X on the circle on the same side of AB as A' such that $XO \perp AB$.

335. In order for a circle with center C to be tangent to two parallel lines, its center must be midway between the two lines. To find the lines through A and B which are parallel and have C midway between them, we note that the line through C parallel to our two lines must pass through the midpoint of AB. Hence, 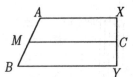 we construct the midpoint M of AB, then draw MC. The lines parallel to MC through A and B are the tangents. We construct the circle then by drawing the line through C perpendicular to the lines through A and B. Let X and Y be the intersections thus formed. Our circle is then the circle with center C and radius CX (since the radius is perpendicular to the tangent, CX is a radius of the desired circle).

336. In triangle ABC, $\angle ABC > \angle BAC$ if and only if $AC > BC$. Hence, the points B such that $BC < AC$ for a given AC compose the interior of the circle (except for the segment AC), and therefore the locus, centered at C with radius AC. (Make sure that you see that any point in the interior of the circle with center C and radius AC is closer to C than point A is.)

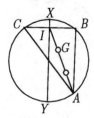

337. Given the centroid G and a vertex A, what else can we construct on the triangle? Let I be the midpoint of BC. Since $AG/GI = 2/1$, we can construct point I by finding the midpoint, M of AG, then drawing a circle with center G and radius GM. This intersects the ray from A through G at point I. Point I is then the midpoint of BC, but how do we find B and C? We know that the diameter through I is perpendicular to side BC since a diameter passing through the midpoint of a chord is perpendicular to the chord. Hence, we draw the diameter through I, then the line through I perpendicular to the diameter. The intersections of this line and the circle are points B and C.

338. We'll use analytic geometry to attack this problem. Without loss of generality, let the circles be

$$
\begin{aligned}
x^2 + y^2 &= r_1 \quad \text{and} \\
(x - a)^2 + y^2 &= r_2.
\end{aligned}
$$

Drawing a line through a point P and the center O of a circle of radius r, we find that the power of point P with respect to O is $(OP - r)(OP + r)$. Applying this to the point (x, y)

and the above circles, we have

$$\left(\sqrt{x^2+y^2}-r_1\right)\left(\sqrt{x^2+y^2}+r_1\right) = \left(\sqrt{(x-a)^2+y^2}-r_2\right)\left(\sqrt{(x-a)^2+y^2}+r_2\right)$$
$$x^2+y^2-r_1^2 = x^2-2ax+a^2+y^2-r_2^2.$$

Hence, all (x,y) which have the same power with respect to the two circles satisfy the equation $x=(r_1^2-r_2^2)/2a$. Thus, the locus is a line perpendicular to the line connecting the centers of the circles.

339. We can find three circles which pass through a single point by drawing the circles with centers A, B, and C which pass through the circumcenter P of $\triangle ABC$. Since $AP=BP=CP$, these circles all pass through P. We can then construct a triangle such that each of the drawn circles are tangent to two sides of the triangle by constructing the common tangents of the circles as shown. We draw these by constructing the perpendiculars to the sides of the triangle through the vertices (the six segments outside $\triangle ABC$). The intersections of these with the circles are the tangent points (such as M and N). Drawing the line through

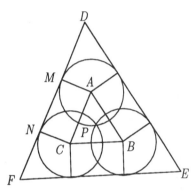

M and N we form the common tangent to circles A and C, because MN is perpendicular to AM and CN so MN is tangent to the circles. The intersections of these three tangents form $\triangle DEF$. The sides of $\triangle DEF$ are parallel to those of $\triangle ABC$. Since these triangles are similar and have the same orientation, corresponding lines in the triangles will be parallel. Hence, we locate X by drawing PE and PF. Since $XB \parallel PE$ and $XC \parallel PF$ (since corresponding lines are parallel), we draw lines through B and C parallel to EP and FP. The intersection of these lines is X. This is a tough construction; read through it a few times to make sure you understand it. Then get a compass and ruler and perform it.

340. Let points Y and Z be on segments AB and BC as shown. Since $\triangle ZYX \cong \triangle BAO$, we have

$$\angle YXZ + \angle YBZ = \angle BOC + \angle OBC + \angle OBA = 180°.$$

Thus, quadrilateral $BYXZ$ is cyclic. Since $\angle XYZ = \angle XBZ$, we find

$$\angle OBZ = \angle OBC = \angle XYZ = \angle XBZ.$$

From $\angle OBZ = \angle XBZ$, we deduce that O, B, and X are collinear. Thus we deduce the locus is a set of n line segments emanating from O equal in length and equally spaced about O. (Each line segment corresponds to a vertex of the polygon. For example, in the diagram point X is on the extension of BO past O.)

Chapter 21

Collinearity and Concurrency

Solutions to Exercises

21-1 Clearly $AB + BC = AC$ if B is on AC. If B is not on AC, then let X be the foot of the altitude from B to AC. By the Pythagorean Theorem,

$$AB + BC = \sqrt{AX^2 + XB^2} + \sqrt{XC^2 + BX^2} > AX + XC = AC.$$

Hence B is on AC if and only if $AB + BC = AC$.

21-2 Since AC is a straight line through B, $\angle DBC = 180° - \angle ABD$. Hence,

$$\angle EBD = \angle EBC + \angle CBD = 180° + (\angle EBC - \angle ABD).$$

Thus, $\angle EBD = 180°$ (and hence E, B, and D are concurrent) if and only if $\angle DBA = \angle EBC$.

21-3 In general, vectors $\vec{a}$ and $\vec{b}$ are in the same direction if one is a scalar times the other; that is if there exists some number n such that $\vec{a} = n\vec{b}$.

21-4 If we choose X to be the origin, then $\vec{x} = 0$, so that we need only prove that $\vec{y}$ and $\vec{z}$ are in the same direction. Yes, this usually simplifies our problem.

21-5 Each of the ratios, using the notion of directed segments, is negative for our initial diagram, so the product must be negative.

21-6 Create a number line through B and C such that $B = 0$ and $C = 1$. Let $X' = x$ be on segment BC. Hence, we have $BX'/CX' = (x - 0)/(1 - x) = c$. There is only one solution for x, $x = c/(c + 1)$. Hence, there's only one point X' on segment BC that satisfies $BX'/CX' = c$. If X' is on line BC but not on the segment, our ratio $BX'/CX' =$

$-(x-0)/(1-x) = c$, and we find $x = c/(c-1)$. (How is this related to directed segments?) Hence, there are two points on line BC which satisfy the problem, one on segment BC and one outside the endpoints B and C.

21-7 In the previous exercise you proved that there is one possible X' on segment BC and one other outside segment BC on line BC. For the former, BX'/CX' is negative and for the latter the ratio is positive. (Make sure you see this!) Now there is only one point which satisfies our restriction.

21-8 We can't apply the Angle Bisector Theorem as suggested because the heart of our problem is proving that AI is the bisector of $\angle CAZ$.

21-9 In saying that $\triangle AXC$ is right, we are assuming that point A is on HX (since HX is the perpendicular to BC through X). This is what we are trying to prove, so we can't assume it is true! Be very careful in using collinearity techniques on concurrency problems; it is very easy to make erroneous assumptions like this. Check your steps closely.

21-10 Let G be the intersection of medians AX and BY. We wish to show that the segment CZ, where Z is the midpoint of AB, passes through G. We'll do this by using our vector method of the previous section. From our discussion on vectors, we have

$$\vec{Z} = \frac{\vec{A} + \vec{B}}{2} \quad \text{and} \quad \vec{G} = \frac{\vec{A} + \vec{B} + \vec{C}}{3}.$$

Note that we can show that G has the above vector representation without assuming all three medians go through G; just two medians are enough to find the vector form of G. Hence,

$$\vec{Z} - \vec{C} = \frac{\vec{A} + \vec{B} - 2\vec{C}}{2} \quad \text{and} \quad \vec{G} - \vec{C} = \frac{\vec{A} + \vec{B} - 2\vec{C}}{3},$$

so that $\overrightarrow{CG} = (2/3)\overrightarrow{CZ}$. From this we conclude that C, G, and Z are collinear and AX, BY, and CZ are concurrent. Note that we can also conclude that the centroid divides each median in a $2 : 1$ ratio.

21-11 Suppose X, Y, and Z are on BC, AC, and AB such that

$$\frac{AY}{CY} \cdot \frac{CX}{BX} \cdot \frac{BZ}{AZ} = 1.$$

Let Z' be the point on AB such that AX, BY, and CZ' are concurrent. From Ceva's Theorem, we have

$$\frac{AY}{CY} \cdot \frac{CX}{BX} \cdot \frac{BZ'}{AZ'} = 1,$$

so that $BZ/AZ = BZ'/AZ'$, from which we deduce that Z and Z' are the same point using the notion of directed segments. This completes our proof of the converse of Ceva's Theorem.

21-12 Written in the alternative form, Menelaus's Theorem is easily distinguished from Ceva's Theorem.

21-13 Let X, Y, and Z be the points of interest (midpoints for medians and feet of angle bisectors for angle bisectors) of BC, AC, and AB, respectively. Medians are easy; $BX = CX$, $AY = CY$, and $AZ = BZ$ since the points are midpoints. The expression for Ceva's Theorem clearly completes this case. For angle bisectors, we look for a way to evaluate the ratios. The Angle Bisector Theorem gives us our answer: $BX/CX = BA/CA$, $AY/CY = AB/CB$, and $BZ/AZ = BC/AC$. Multiplying these gives us the desired result.

Solutions to Problems

341. The sum of all of our Greek angles is $180°$ since together they form a triangle. Using the given equalities, we have $2(\alpha + \beta + \delta) = 180°$, so $\alpha + \beta + \gamma = 90°$. Hence, from $\triangle ADB$, $\angle ADB = 180° - (\alpha + \beta + \delta) = 90°$. In the same manner, we can show that BE and CF are also altitudes. Finally, from these angle equalities, we can use the sine form of Ceva's Theorem to prove the altitudes are concurrent. Yet another method to prove the concurrency of altitudes...

342. Applying Menelaus's Theorem to $\triangle ECB$, since A, P, and D are collinear and are on sides EB, EC, and BC, respectively, of the triangle, we have

$$\frac{PE}{CP} \cdot \frac{CD}{DB} \cdot \frac{AB}{AE} = 1.$$

The first ratio is $1/r$, the second is $3/1$, and the last is $(AE + EB)/AE = 1 + 2/3 = 5/3$. Hence, we find $r = \mathbf{5}$.

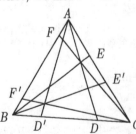

343. What a messy diagram... and we didn't even include the angle bisectors! Since we are dealing primarily with angles, we'll use the sine form of Ceva's Theorem which we proved in the chapter. Since AD, BE, and CF are concurrent, we have

$$\frac{\sin \angle DAC}{\sin \angle DAB} \cdot \frac{\sin \angle BCF}{\sin \angle ACF} \cdot \frac{\sin \angle ABE}{\sin \angle EBC} = 1.$$

Suppose X on BC is the foot of the angle bisector from A. Since AD' is the reflection of AD in AX, $\angle D'AX = \angle DAX$. Hence

$$\angle D'AB = \angle XAB - \angle XAD' = \angle XAC - \angle XAD = \angle DAC.$$

Similarly, we can show five other angle congruencies like this one. Using these, we have

$$\frac{\sin \angle D'AB}{\sin \angle D'AC} \cdot \frac{\sin \angle ACF'}{\sin \angle BCF'} \cdot \frac{\sin \angle CBE'}{\sin \angle E'BA} = \frac{\sin \angle DAC}{\sin \angle DAB} \cdot \frac{\sin \angle BCF}{\sin \angle ACF} \cdot \frac{\sin \angle ABE}{\sin \angle EBC} = 1.$$

Hence, if AD, BE, and CF are concurrent, then so are AD', BE', and CF'.

344. Since $HC = HZ$ and $CZ \perp AB$, AB is the perpendicular bisector of CZ. Hence, $AZ = AC = AX$ and $BZ = BC = BY$. Thus, AZ and BZ are medians of triangles CZX and CZY, respectively, which are half the sides to which they are drawn. Hence, triangles CZX and CZY are right, so that $\angle XZY = \angle CZX + \angle CZY = 90° + 90° = 180°$ and X, Z, and Y are collinear.

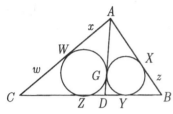

345. For the first part, we determine BD in terms of the sides of the triangle. Labelling AW, CW, and BX as shown and letting $DG = y$, we have, since tangents from a point to a circle are equal, $AW = AG = AX = x$, $CW = CZ = w$, $DG = DZ = DY = y$, and $BY = BX = z$. Hence, $BD = z + y$, $BC = a = w + 2y + z$, $AC = b = x + w$, and $AB = c = x + z$. From these and a little algebra, we find $AB + BC - AC = 2z + 2y = 2BD$. Hence, $BD = (a + c - b)/2$, so that D must be the point where the incircle of $\triangle ABC$ is tangent to BC. Thus, the perpendicular to BC through D passes through the center of the incircle, as do the angle bisectors l and m. Hence, the three lines in question are concurrent at the incenter of $\triangle ABC$. The second part of the problem follows easily from observations made above. The other points defined like D are the other two points where the incircle is tangent to $\triangle ABC$. Hence, $BD = BI = s - b$, $CD = CH = s - c$, and $AH = AI = s - a$, and Ceva's Theorem completes the problem.

346. Seeing cosines involved, we think to try the sine form of Ceva's Theorem. Thus, we need to find all our Greek angles in the diagram in terms of the angles of the triangle. Since the line through A is an angle bisector, $\alpha = \phi = A/2$. The line through C is just an altitude, so $\theta = 90° - B$ and $\epsilon = 90° - A$. Finally, the line through B is a bit tougher. Let O be the circumcenter and draw the circumcircle. We find $\angle AOB = 2\angle C$. Since $\triangle AOB$ is isosceles, $\beta = \angle OBA = (180° - 2\angle C)/2 = 90° - C$. Similarly, $\delta = 90° - A$. Now we apply the sine form of Ceva, finding that these lines are concurrent if and only if

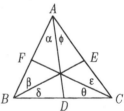

$$\frac{\sin \alpha}{\sin \phi} \cdot \frac{\sin \epsilon}{\sin \theta} \cdot \frac{\sin \delta}{\sin \beta} = \frac{\sin A/2}{\sin A/2} \cdot \frac{\sin(90° - A)}{\sin(90° - B)} \cdot \frac{\sin(90° - A)}{\sin(90° - C)} = 1.$$

Applying the identity $\sin(90° - x) = \cos x$ attains the desired result.

347. As we saw in an earlier chapter, the orthocenter and the centroid have fairly simple vector representations upon taking the circumcenter as the origin. This highly suggests that vectors may be the best way to go for this problem. Using our vectors, we have

$$\overrightarrow{OG} = \frac{\vec{A} + \vec{B} + \vec{C}}{3} \quad \text{and} \quad \overrightarrow{OH} = \vec{A} + \vec{B} + \vec{C}.$$

Clearly, $\overrightarrow{OH} = 3\overrightarrow{OG}$, so O, G, and H are collinear since $\overrightarrow{OH}$ and $\overrightarrow{OG}$ are in the same direction. Since $\overrightarrow{OH}$ has three times the length of $\overrightarrow{OG}$, we conclude $2(OG) = GH$, completing the second part of the problem.

348. As we showed in a previous problem in the chapter on locus and construction, the locus of all points with equal powers with respect to two circles is a straight line. If the two circles intersect, then this line must contain the common chord of the circles, since the endpoints of the chord have power 0 with respect to each circle. Let the circles in the diagram in the problem be C_1, C_2, and C_3, labelled clockwise from the upper left. Let I be the intersection of AD and BE. Since I is on AD, it has the same power with respect to C_1 and C_2. Since it is on BE, it has the same power with respect to C_2 and C_3. Thus, I has the same power with respect to both C_1 and C_3 and hence is on CF, so the three segments are collinear at I.

349. Triangles, lines, and concurrency—looks like a job for Ceva! Let X', Y', and Z' be the points where AX, BY, and CZ intersect the sides of the triangles as shown. Seeing angles, we think of the angle form of Ceva's Theorem. From the law sines applied to $\triangle ABX$ and $\triangle ACX$, we find

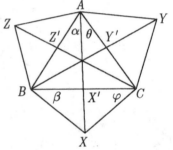

$$\frac{\sin\alpha}{BX} = \frac{\sin(B+\beta)}{AX} \quad \text{and} \quad \frac{\sin\theta}{CX} = \frac{\sin(C+\varphi)}{AX}.$$

Applying the law of sines to $\triangle BCX$ gives $(\sin\beta)/CX = (\sin\varphi)/BX$ and combining this and the two above equalities yields

$$\frac{\sin\alpha}{\sin\theta} = \frac{BX\sin(B+\beta)}{CX\sin(C+\varphi)} = \frac{\sin\varphi\sin(B+\beta)}{\sin\beta\sin(C+\varphi)}.$$

We find similar expressions for the ratios of sines at the other vertices and find that the product of the three yields 1, so by the converse of the sine form of Ceva's Theorem, AX, BY, and CZ are concurrent. If you aren't comfortable with the sine form of Ceva and would rather use lengths, note that $BX'/X'C = (c\sin\alpha)/(b\sin\theta)$ (from the law of sines applied to $\triangle ABX$ and $\triangle AXC$ and $\sin\angle AXB = \sin\angle AXC$) and proceed as above to find the three ratios appearing in Ceva's Theorem. Once again, their product is 1 and the lines are concurrent.

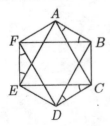

350. From the given equal angles, $ABCD$, $ABEF$, and $CDEF$ are all cyclic quadrilaterals. Let the three circumcircles be C_1, C_2, and C_3. If any two of these are the same circle, then all three must be the same circle. Make sure you see this; suppose C_1 and C_2 are the same. If so, then $CDEF$ is also inscribed in this circle since its vertices are also vertices of at least one of the other 2 quadrilaterals. Hence, either these three circles are distinct, or they are all the same. From a previous problem, if the three circles are different, then the common chords AB, CD, and EF must be concurrent. Clearly this is impossible for a convex hexagon, so the circles must all be the same. Finally, BC, DE, and AF are chords subtending arcs of equal measure (since $\angle CAB = \angle ECD = \angle FEA$) and thus must have equal length.

Chapter 22

Geometry Tidbits

Solutions to Exercises

22-1 Draw planes X and Y such that they are perpendicular. In plane X draw segments AB and CD such that AB is perpendicular to Y and CD is parallel to Y. Thus, when we project plane X into plane Y, the image of AB is point and that of CD is still a segment. Since the ratio of images $A'B'/C'D'$ is 0 and the ratio of the original segments is nonzero, we have our desired example.

22-2 No. Again let the planes be X and Y. If the planes are parallel, a projection from X to Y leaves the figure unchanged (make sure you see this). Otherwise they intersect in some line, call it l. Now break up the original region into rectangles, no matter how small, with one pair of sides parallel to l and the other pair perpendicular to l. Upon projection from plane X to plane Y, the sides parallel to l remain unchanged (again, make sure you see why), while those perpendicular (and hence the area) are all scaled by the same factor. Hence, no matter how figures are oriented, upon a projection all of them are scaled by the same factor.

22-3 No. The image of a line segment under an orthogonal projection cannot be longer than the original segment. This is a simple consequence of the Pythagorean Theorem: suppose $A'B'C'$ is the image of ABC. If we move plane $A'B'C'$ (straight up or straight down) so that A coincides with A', right triangle ABB' has hypotenuse AB and legs BB' and AB' (or $A'B'$). Hence, $A'B' \leq AB$.

22-4 Let line l be in the plane projected by a central projection into another plane such that m is the image of l. Clearly E, the intersection of the lines, is its own image. Let $\angle OED = 90°$, $\angle AEC = 60°$, $\angle OBA = 45°$, and $\angle OAE = 90°$. Letting

$OE = 12$, we find $AE = 6\sqrt{3}$, $OA = AB = 6$, so $BE = 6\sqrt{3} - 6$. We also find $CE = 12\sqrt{3}$ and $DE = 12(2 - \sqrt{3})$, so $DC = 24\sqrt{3} - 24$. Hence, $AB/BE \ne CD/DE$.

22-5 You should find that OA' gets larger and larger as OA gets smaller and smaller and that OA' shrinks as OA grows.

22-6 We seek the point X on OP such that $(OX)(OP) = r^2$, 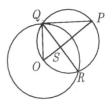 where r is the radius of the circle. Writing this as $OX/r = r/OP$, we think to hunt for similar triangles. By constructing the circle with diameter OP we locate points Q and R, the intersections of this circle with circle O. Since OP is a diameter, $\triangle OQP$ is right. Drawing QR which intersects OP at S, we have $QS \perp OP$ (why?), so $\triangle OQP \sim \triangle OSQ$. Hence we have $OQ/OS = OP/OQ$, or $(OS)(OP) = r^2$ as desired. Thus, point S is the inversion of P with respect to O. What if P is inside circle O?

22-7 Any two circles are similar and have the same orientation, so any pair of circles are homothetic to each other. We can find the center by drawing lines through corresponding parts and finding where they intersect. We can easily prove that two such lines go through Q, the point of tangency by noting that the common tangent and the lines through the centers of the circles both go through the point of tangency.

22-8 By SAS similarity we find $\triangle AEF \sim \triangle ACB$. Hence, 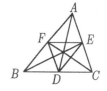 $FE \parallel BC$ and similarly we find that the sides of $\triangle ABC$ are parallel to those of $\triangle DEF$. Hence, the triangles ABC and DEF are both similar and homothetic. To find the center of homothecy, consider the midpoint M of FE. By SAS similarity ($AF/AB = FM/BD$ and $\angle AFM = \angle ABD$) we have $\triangle AFM \sim \triangle ABD$ so that point M is on AD. Similarly we can show that the medians of $\triangle DEF$ are on the same lines as the medians of $\triangle ABC$. The center of homothecy is the intersection of these lines, the centroid of the triangles.

22-9 Draw one ray from P, r_1, pointing directly 'up' and let the area of the region be K. We wish to create another ray, r_2, from P such that the area of Γ between r_1 and r_2 is $K/12$. We do so by letting r_2 be initially coincident with r_1, in which case the area between the two is 0. Rotate r_2 clockwise and let x be the area inside Γ between r_1 and r_2 (measuring clockwise from r_1). As r_2 rotates from r_1 all the way around the circle back to r_1, x varies continuously from 0 to K. Hence, for some r_2 we must have $x = K/12$. We fix r_2 at this position and hunt for r_3 by rotating clockwise from r_2 and so on.

22-10 Are you convinced that the theorem isn't very easily proven?

22-11 We can't use this approach on an infinite number of points because we have chosen the three points with the minimum α. If we have an infinite number of points, there is not necessarily a minimum value of α! A simple counterexample is the set of lattice points on a Cartesian plane (i.e. the points (i, j) where i and j are integers.)

Solutions to Problems

351. Let G be the centroid of ABC. Let $AD = 3x$. Then, $GD = x$, $AG = 2x$, $AD' = 3x$, and $GD' = 5x$. Hence, D', E' and F' are dilations of D, E, and F with ratio -5, meaning that $GD' = 5(GD)$ and D' is on the other side of G from D. Thus, $D'E'F'$ is homothetic to ABC (since $\triangle D'E'F' \sim \triangle DEF \sim \triangle ABC$ and lines through corresponding parts are concurrent) with center G and ratio $D'G/AG = 5/2$. Thus, $[D'E'F']/[ABC] = (5/2)^2$ and $[D'E'F'] = \mathbf{75}$.

352. Two parallel lines never intersect; rather, they only meet at the 'point at infinity.' Since their images are circles through the center which do not intersect anywhere but the center (because the lines only intersect at the point at infinity, whose image is the center of inversion), the images are circles through the center of inversion which are tangent at the center. This provides a way of proving that lines are parallel (or that circles are tangent).

353. A circle with radius one has circumference 2π. Consider the four arcs in which the vertices of the quadrilateral divides the circle. Since their sum is 2π, at least one has length less than or equal to $\pi/2$. The central angle of this arc is then less than or equal to $\pi/2$ and hence the chord is less than or equal to $\sqrt{1+1} = \sqrt{2}$.

354. Assume that F is two-dimensional. If its image upon projection onto α is a straight line, F must be perpendicular to α. Similarly F must be perpendicular to β. Hence, α must be parallel to β, a contradiction. We conclude that F cannot be two-dimensional.

355. Let the right angle be at A. From SAS similarity, $\triangle AEF \sim \triangle ABC$. Since $AB = AE$, $\triangle AEF \cong \triangle ABC$. Let the altitude from A to EF be AX and to BC be AY. Since $AY = DY$ by reflection and $AX = AY$ from the congruent triangles, we have $XD = 3(AY)$. Hence, triangles DEF and ABC have congruent bases (EF and BC) and altitudes DX and AY such that $DX/AY = 3$. Finally, $[DEF] = 3[ABC] = \mathbf{3}$.

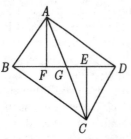

356. It is very important to note that proving that the area of an orthodiagonal quadrilateral is half the product of its diagonals does *not* solve this problem. We are asked to prove the converse of this fact. We do this by drawing the altitudes from A and C to diagonal BD and showing that their feet coincide, so the line from C perpendicular to BD passes through A and the diagonals are perpendicular. Let E and F be the aforementioned altitude feet as shown. We are given $[ABCD] = (AC)(BD)/2$. From the diagram, $[ABCD] = [(AF)(BD) + (EC)(BD)]/2$. Setting the two expressions for $[ABCD]$ equal to each other, we conclude that $AF + EC = AC$. Thus,

$$AC = AG + CG = \sqrt{AF^2 + FG^2} + \sqrt{EC^2 + EG^2}.$$

Since $AC = \sqrt{AF^2} + \sqrt{CE^2}$, we deduce that $FG = EG = 0$, so F, G, and E are the same point and the quadrilateral $ABCD$ is indeed orthodiagonal. Make sure you understand the general method we employed here in showing that points E and F are the same.

357. First we show that a line tangent to a circle at the center of inversion is parallel to the image, line l, of the circle. Let the tangent be line m. Consider the images of l and m. The image of l is the original circle and the image of m is m itself. Since the images of l and m intersect only at the center of inversion, l and m only intersect at the point at infinity. Hence, lines l and m are parallel. Since the tangents of the two circles in the original problem are perpendicular, the images of the circles are lines parallel to these two and are thus perpendicular as well.

358. Let the points where the circles intersect be A, B, C, D, E, and F, connected as shown in the diagram. Since the measure of an arc is twice an inscribed angle, we can write

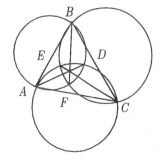

$$\angle ACB = \angle ECB + \angle ECA = (\overarc{EB} + \overarc{AE})/2$$

$$\angle ABC = \angle ABF + \angle FBC = (\overarc{AF} + \overarc{FC})/2$$

$$\angle BAC = \angle BAD + \angle CAD = (\overarc{BD} + \overarc{CD})/2.$$

Summing these, we find that the sum of the desired arcs is $2(\angle ACB + \angle ABC + \angle BAC) = 2(180°) = 360°$, so the boundary's measure is invariant.

359. Let H be the midpoint of altitudes AD and BE. Thus, $ABDE$ is a parallelogram, so $AE \parallel BD$, which is a contradiction to ABC being a triangle. Hence, the orthocenter cannot be the midpoint of two altitudes. Remember that if any two lines bisect each other, they are the diagonals of a parallelogram; it will come in handy!

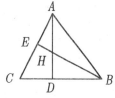

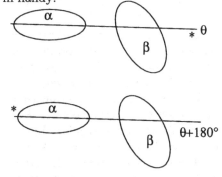

360. As we showed in the chapter, given any orientation, there exists a line that bisects the area of a given region. Let the regions be α and β. It is not hard to see from the proof in the book that the line of a given orientation that bisects the area of α is unique. As we slide a line up from below α to above α, the area below it increases continuously from 0 to $[\alpha]$ and thus at only one point can it bisect the area of $[\alpha]$. Start with an orientation, say θ, and the line with orientation θ that bisects the area of α. Choose θ such that the line passes through β. (We can do this by choosing a point in β and finding the line through this point which bisects the area of α.) Let x be the area of β to the right of the line bisecting the area of α, where we initially arbitrarily choose which side is right. In the diagram, where the top is our initial orientation θ, the right side is indicated by a star. As we rotate from θ to $\theta + 180°$ (finding the line which bisects the area of α for each orientation) we come to the second diagram, where our bisecting line is the same as the first, but the star, which rotates along with the line, is on the other side. Now the area of β to the right of the bisecting line is $[\beta] - x$. Hence, as we continuously change orientation from θ to $\theta + 180°$, the area in β to the right of the line goes continuously from x to $[\beta] - x$. At some point in between, this area must be $[\beta]/2$. This line is the desired line which bisects both figures.

361. Since AC is common to both triangles, it is tangent to both incircles. Let these points of tangency be E and F, where AE is tangent to $\triangle ABC$. We will show that these two points are the same, so the two circles are tangent. As discussed in Volume 1,

$$AE = (AB + AC - BC)/2 \text{ and}$$
$$AF = (AC + AD - CD)/2.$$

Subtracting these gives $AE - AF = [(AB + CD) - (BC + DA)]/2$. This last quantity is 0 because $ABCD$ is circumscribed about a circle. Hence $AE = AF$ and E and F are the same point since both are on segment AC.

362. Draw a line through 2 of the points A and B. Let x be the number of the $2n - 2$ points (the original $2n$ minus the two on the line) on the right side of the line (where we choose the right side arbitrarily). As many times before, we spin the line 180° (so that the line always goes through A) and the result is $2n - 2 - x$ of the points on the right side. Since in spinning we go from x to $2n - 2 - x$ by 1's, we must hit $n - 1$ somewhere. If we do this for all $2n$ points, we get at least n different lines (2 points are 'used' for each line).

363. Extend side AD of a triangle which fits the description of the problem to point B on the larger circle. Since $\triangle ABC$ and $\triangle ADC$ share an altitude, $[ADC]/[ABC] = AD/AB$. Since the two circles are homothetic with center A, $AD/AB = 1/3$. Finally, we see that by maximizing $[ABC]$, we maximize $[ADC]$. The maximum area of a circle inscribed in a circle of radius 3 is equilateral and has side length $3\sqrt{3}$, so its area is $27\sqrt{3}/4$. Hence, the maximum value of $[ADC]$ is $\mathbf{9\sqrt{3}/4}$.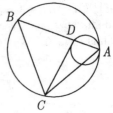

364. The argument here is the same as for the Pancake Theorem. Choose a line with orientation α which bisects the area of S. Let x be the length of the boundary to the left of the line, rotate the orientation from α to $\alpha + 180°$ (finding the area bisecting line for each orientation). The length of the boundary to the left of the line must at some point be half the length of the boundary of S and we have found our desired line.

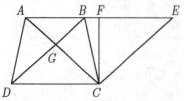

365. Draw CE parallel to BD. Since $ABCD$ is an isosceles trapezoid and $BECD$ is a parallelogram, $AC = BD = EC$, so altitude CF is a median since $\triangle ACE$ is isosceles. Since $CF = (AB + CD)/2 = (AB + BE)/2 = AE/2$, $\triangle ACE$ is a right triangle (the median from C is half the opposite side). Since $AC \perp CE$, $AC \perp BD$ and $ABCD$ is orthodiagonal.

366. Let the smooth convex figure be S. Given any orientation θ, there are two tangents to S with that orientation, one on either side of S. Draw these two tangents. Draw also the two tangents with orientation $\theta + 90°$. The intersection of these lines with the first two lines forms a rectangle. Designate the sides of the rectangle with orientation θ as the length and the other side as the width. Let x be the ratio of the length to the width. As we rotate the initial orientation from θ to $\theta + 90°$, this ratio will go from x to $1/x$. (Why?) At some point the ratio must be 1 and the rectangle is a square.

367. Instead of projecting a single plane as we have done several times, in this problem we project three planes (three sides of the drilled cube) onto one plane. Hold the cube so that you are looking directly through the hole. What you are looking at is what results when you project the cube down upon a plane perpendicular to the axis of the drill. The figure is a portion of this projection. The circle centered at A (which is the image of vertex A') is the hole formed by the drill and thus has radius 1.

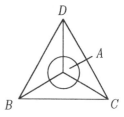

Points B, C, and D are the images of the cube vertices connected to vertex A' by edges of the cube.

Let the original cube vertices be B', C', and D'. The orientation of segment $B'D'$ is perpendicular to the orientation of the drill and hence is parallel to the image plane. Any segment which is orthogonally projected onto a parallel plane has an image of equal length. Thus, $BD = B'D' = 3\sqrt{2}$. Hence, BCD is equilateral and $[BCD] = 9\sqrt{3}/2$. Now the ratio of $[BCD]$ to the area of the shown circle is equal to the ratio of $[B'C'A'] + [B'D'A'] + [D'C'A']$ to the area of the portion of the faces on these three faces which are zapped by the drill. Thus,

$$\frac{\text{area lost to drill}}{[B'C'A] + [B'D'A] + [D'C'A]} = \frac{\pi}{9\sqrt{3}/2}.$$

From this we find that the area lost on these three faces is $\pi\sqrt{3}$ (since $B'C'A$ and the other two are isosceles right triangles with side length 3). Hence, on each face, $\pi\sqrt{3}/3$ is lost to the drill, leaving $\mathbf{9 - \pi\sqrt{3}/3}$.

368. The original diagram is on the left. Seeing lots of circles with special intersections, we try an inversion with respect to the third circle. The image of the other two circles are lines since the circles pass through the center of inversion. These lines are perpendicular since the circles are orthogonal (proven in an earlier prob-

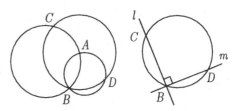

lem) and they meet on the circle of inversion (at B, which is its own image) because the original circles intersect at B. Points C and D are their own images. Since $\angle CBD$ is right and inscribed, it is inscribed in a semicircle. Hence, CD is a diameter of the image circle. Since C, D, and the circle of inversion are their own images, CD is the diameter of the original circle as desired.

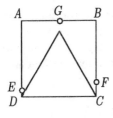

369. First we show that it is impossible to cover the square with three triangles. Since there are four vertices of the square, two of them must be covered with one triangle. This can only be done when a side of the triangle is a side of the square as shown. Consider points E, F, and G on the sides of the square such that $AG = 0.5$, $ED = 0.01$ and $FC = 0.02$. A simple application of the Pythagorean Theorem reveals that no two of these three points are within 1 unit of each other and hence we need three different triangles to cover all three. Our minimum number is **4** then, and the second diagram shows that this is indeed possible.

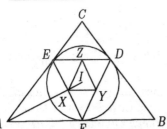

370. First note that if circle α is obtained by inverting circle β with respect to circle γ, then the centers of α, β, and γ are collinear. (Why?) We can show that the circumcircle of $\triangle ABC$ is the image of the circumcircle of $\triangle XYZ$ upon inversion with respect to incircle I by showing that points A, B, C are the inverses of X, Y, Z. (Remember, we only need three points to determine a circle; this is why we need only show that three points on one circle are the images of three points on the other!) Let segment AI intersect EF at M. Hence, $\angle EAM = \angle FAM$ (AI is an angle bisector), $AM = AM$, and $EA = FA$ (equal tangents), so $\triangle EAM \cong \triangle FAM$. From this, $EM = FM$ and M is the same point as X. Since $\angle AFI = \angle FXI = 90°$, we have $\triangle AFI \sim \triangle FXI$ so that $(IX)(IA) = (IF)^2$. Since IF is the radius of inversion and I the center, this proves that A is the image of X. Similarly, we show that B and C are the images of Y and Z and our proof is complete.

371. To construct the first outer medial triangle of $\triangle ABC$, we construct the line through A parallel to BC, the line through B parallel to AC, and the line through C parallel to AB. The intersections of these lines form our triangle. For the second part, since we want to contain all the points inside the first outer medial triangle, we look for a triangle with some maximal quantity, such as maximum area or maximum perimeter. Since we are dealing with the region inside the triangle, we'll try area. Because there are

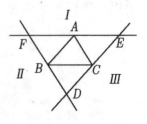

a finite number of points, there is some group of three points among the n such that these three form the triangle of largest area possible among all those formed by connecting 3 of the n points. Let this triangle be ABC and its first outer medial triangle be DEF. Let the region on the opposite side of line EF from BC be region I, and let regions II and III be defined similarly as shown. Clearly all points outside DEF lie in at least one of these regions. Consider point P in region I. The distance from P to BC (the distance from a point to a line is the length of the altitude from the point to the line) is greater than that from A to BC, so $[PBC] > [ABC]$. Since $[ABC]$ is the triangle of maximal area among those formed by the original n points, P cannot be among those points. Similarly, none of the remaining $n - 3$ points can be outside DEF and we have found our desired triangle.

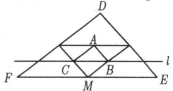

For the third part, we want no points inside so we minimize the area. Let $\triangle ABC$ be the triangle of minimum area among those with all vertices among the n points and let $\triangle DEF$ be its second outer medial triangle. Let point P be one of the other n points. First, it cannot be inside $\triangle ABC$, or it would be closer to BC than point A; hence, we would have $[PBC] < [ABC]$, a contradiction. Next, it cannot be between line l and segment EF. By SSS congruency we have $\triangle ABC \cong \triangle MCB$, so that EF is the same distance from BC as point A is. Thus, any point between l and EF is closer to BC than point A. For a point P in this region we would then have $[PBC] < [ABC]$, a contradiction as before. Similarly we can eliminate the other regions of $\triangle DEF$ and $\triangle ABC$ is proven to be our desired triangle.

372. Consider any point P inside $\triangle ABC$. Draw two lines through P parallel to the directions of the sides of the rectangle and let the four points of intersection of these lines with the sides of the triangle be D, E, F, and G. By the Pigeonhole Principle (which creeps into a great many problems), at least two of these points must be in the same rectangle (of the three that cover the sides). Let the points be D and E and the rectangle which contains them both be R_i. If these are on the same line through P, then R_i also contains P because every point on DE will also be in R_i. If D and E are on perpendicular lines through P, the rectangle formed with opposite vertices at D and E and sides parallel to the sides of R_i is contained entirely within R_i. Since P is also a vertex of this rectangle with vertices at D and E, P is in R_i as well. Since point P is arbitrarily chosen within $\triangle ABC$, all points in $\triangle ABC$ are contained in at least one of the rectangles.

Chapter 23

Number Theory

Solutions to Exercises

23-1 The quotient $(b/a_1)/(b/(a,b)) = (a,b)/a_1$. Hence, if $a_1|(a,b)$, this quotient is an integer, so $b/(a,b)|b/a_1$.

23-2 Since $(2,6) = 2$, we have to divide the modulus, 6, by 2 when we divide everything else by 2. This jives with the previous example, where we had to divide 6 by 2 to get $10 \equiv 1 \,(\text{mod} \, 3)$.

23-3 In the first one, the modulus is 20 and we are dividing by 6. Since $(20,6) = 2$, we have to divide the modulus by 2. We are thus left with $a \equiv b \,(\text{mod} \, 10)$.

In the second one, we can divide out 23. Since $(23,5) = 1$, the modulus remains the same and we have $1 \equiv 6 \,(\text{mod} \, 5)$.

In the third one, we are dividing by 6 and the modulus is 9. Since $(6,9) = 3$, we divide the modulus by 3 to get $2 \equiv 5 \,(\text{mod} \, 3)$.

23-4

i. First we subtract 45 from both sides to get $1235x \equiv 9045 \,(\text{mod} \, 24)$. We then mod both sides out by 24 (divide by 24 and keep the remainder) to get some smaller, manageable numbers: $11x \equiv 21 \,(\text{mod} \, 24)$. All we need to do is divide both sides by 11. However, 11 doesn't divide 21, so we add 24 to the right side until it is divisible by 11: $21 \equiv 45 \equiv 69 \equiv 93 \equiv 117 \equiv 141 \equiv 165 = 11 \cdot 15$. We thus have $11x \equiv 11 \cdot 15 \,(\text{mod} \, 24)$, so that $x \equiv 15 \,(\text{mod} \, 24)$ is a general solution.

ii. As above, we subtract 45 from both sides to get $1235x \equiv 9045 \,(\text{mod} \, 11)$. We then mod both sides by 11 to get $3x \equiv 3 \,(\text{mod} \, 11)$. Dividing both sides by 3, we have $x \equiv 1 \,(\text{mod} \, 11)$. as the general solution.

iii. We subtract 45 from both sides to get $1235x \equiv 9042 \,(\mathrm{mod}\,11)$. We mod both sides out by 11 to get $3x \equiv 11 \,(\mathrm{mod}\,11)$. This becomes $3x \equiv 0 \,(\mathrm{mod}\,11)$, so that $x \equiv 0 \,(\mathrm{mod}\,11)$ is the general solution.

iv. We have $1232x \equiv 9045 \,(\mathrm{mod}\,24)$, or $8x \equiv 21 \,(\mathrm{mod}\,24)$. To divide a 2 from both sides, we try adding 24 to the left: $21 \equiv 45 \equiv 69 \equiv \cdots$. But the right side will never be divisible by 2 when we add 24's to it, since 24 is divisible by 2. Thus the equation has no solutions.

23-5   We solve the first congruence: $3x \equiv 4 \equiv 11 \equiv 18 \,(\mathrm{mod}\,7)$, or $x \equiv 6 \,(\mathrm{mod}\,7)$. This has the general solution $x = 6 + 7j$. Unfortunately, the second congruence has no solution, since adding any number congruent to 5 is of the form $8k + 5$, and thus cannot be divisible by 4, as $4x$ is. Thus the system has **no solutions**. Just for fun, let's solve the first and third congruences alone. For the third, we have $5x \equiv 6 \equiv 15 \,(\mathrm{mod}\,9)$, so that $x \equiv 3 \,(\mathrm{mod}\,9)$. This has the general solution $x = 3 + 9k$; combining this with the solution of the first congruence, we have $3 + 9k = 6 + 7j$. This leads us to the additional linear congruence $3 = 6 + 7j \,(\mathrm{mod}\,9)$, or $7j \equiv -3 \equiv 6 \equiv 15 \equiv 24 \equiv 33 \equiv 42 \,(\mathrm{mod}\,9)$, or $j \equiv 6 \,(\mathrm{mod}\,9)$. Thus $j = 6 + 9l$ for any l; substituting this into $x = 6 + 7j$, we have $x = 6 + 7(6 + 9l) = 48 + 63l$ for any l.

23-6   In mod 7, the squares are 0, 1, 4, $9 \equiv 2 \,(\mathrm{mod}\,7)$, $16 \equiv 2$, $25 \equiv 4$, and $36 \equiv 1$: the quadratic residues are **0, 1, 4, and 2**. In mod 8, the squares are 0, 1, 4, $9 \equiv 1$, $16 \equiv 0$, $25 \equiv 1$, $36 \equiv 4$, $49 \equiv 1$: the quadratics residues are **0, 1, 4**. In mod 9, they are 0, 1, 4, $9 \equiv 0$, $16 \equiv 7$, $25 \equiv 7$, $36 \equiv 0$, $49 \equiv 4$, and $64 \equiv 1$: the squares are **0, 1, 4, 7**.

23-7   The second m positive integers will have the same squares (mod $2m + 1$) as the first m: the square of $2m + 1 - k$ is $(2m + 1)^2 - 2(2m + 1) + k^2 \equiv k^2 \,(\mathrm{mod}\,2m + 1)$. Thus if the numbers 1 through m all have different squares, we have $m + 1 = (n + 1)/2$ quadratic residues: these m plus 0.

23-8   The first 16 squares are 1, 4, 9, 16, 25, 36, 49, 64, 81, 100, 121, 144, 169, 196, 225, 256. In mod 11, the first 10 are 1, 4, 9, 5, 3, 3, 5, 9, 4, 1. Adding in 0, we have $6 = (11 + 1)/2$ quadratic residues—the maximum. In mod 17, the squares are 1, 4, 9, 16, 8, 2, 15, 13, 13, 15, 2, 8, 16, 9, 4, 1, so we have $9 = (17 + 1)/2$ quadratic residues including 0. Again the maximum.

23-9   In mod 3, the residues are 0, 1, and $2^2 \equiv 1$. Thus **0 and 1** are the residues. (The important lesson here is that no square is ever congruent to 2 (mod 3).) We found in an earlier example that the quadratic residues (mod 8) are 0, 1, and 4—these are the only possible squares (mod 8). This is another exceedingly useful tool: to prove some expression cannot be a square, just prove it is congruent to, say, 3 (mod 8).

23-10   For $n = 16 = 2^4$ the product is $(1 + 2 + 4 + 8 + 16) = $ **31**. For $n = 20 = 2^2 \cdot 5$ it is $(1 + 2 + 4)(1 + 5) = 7 \cdot 6 = $ **42**. For $n = 28 = 2^2 \cdot 7$ it is $(1 + 2 + 4)(1 + 7) = 7 \cdot 8 = $ **56**.

23-11   The key is the distributive law. For example, consider the above product for $s(28)$. We have $(1 + 2 + 4)(1 + 7)$, Which on expansion by the distributive law is $(1)(1) + (1)(7) + (2)(1) + (2)(7) + (4)(1) + 4(7)$. We get all possible combinations of prime powers, which is to say all possible divisors!

23-12   Since $1 + x + x^2 + \cdots + x^n = (x^{n+1} - 1)/(x - 1)$, the product becomes

$$s(n) = \left(\frac{p_1^{e_1+1} - 1}{p_1 - 1} \right) \left(\frac{p_2^{e_2+1} - 1}{p_2 - 1} \right) \cdots \left(\frac{p_k^{e_k+1} - 1}{p_k - 1} \right).$$

23-13   The "$d|n$" underneath the Σ means that the sum is taken over all d which divide n. If we add up 1 for all such d, we get the number of d which divide n, which is the number of divisors. If we add up d for all such d, we get the sum of the d which divide n, which is the sum of the divisors.

23-14 $s(24) = s(2^3 \cdot 3) = (1 + 2 + 4 + 8)(1 + 3) = 15 \cdot 4 = 60 > 2 \cdot 24$; 24 is abundant. $s(26) = s(2 \cdot 13) = (1 + 2)(1 + 13) = 3 \cdot 14 = 42 < 2 \cdot 26$; 26 is deficient. $s(28) = s(2^2 \cdot 7) = (1 + 2 + 4)(1 + 7) = 7 \cdot 8 = 56 = 2 \cdot 28$; 28 is perfect.

23-15   Since $2^{k+1} - 1$ is assumed to be prime, $2^k(2^{k+1} - 1)$ is a complete factorization. Thus the sum of the divisors is

$$(1 + 2 + 4 + \cdots + 2^k)\left(1 + (2^{k+1} - 1)\right) = (2^{k+1} - 1)(2^{k+1}),$$

which is twice our original number. Thus any number of this form is perfect.

23-16   For $k = 1$ we have $2^1(2^2 - 1) = 2 \cdot 3 = 6$. For $k = 2$ we get $2^2(2^3 - 1) = 2 \cdot 7 = 28$. To find the next perfect number, we need to find k such that $2^{k+1} - 1$ is prime. $2^4 - 1 = 15$ is not prime, but $2^5 - 1 = 31$ is. Thus the next perfect number is $2^4(2^5 - 1) = 16 \cdot 31 = \mathbf{496}$.

23-17   We take powers: $1^1 = 1$, so 1 has period **1**; $2^2 = 4$, $2^3 = 8 \equiv 1$, so 2 has period **3**; $3 \to 9 \equiv 2 \to 6 \equiv -1 \to -3 \to -9 \equiv -2 \to -6 \equiv 1$ (where $\to$ represents going from one power to the next), so 3 has period **6**; $4 \to 16 \equiv 2 \to 8 \equiv 1$, so 4 has period **3**. Similarly 5 has period **6**, and 6 has period **2**.

23-18   We must show that $a^6 \equiv 1 \,(\mathrm{mod}\,7)$ for $a = 1, 2, \ldots, 7$. The sixth powers are 1, $64 \equiv 1$, $3^6 = (3^3)^2 \equiv (-1)^2 \equiv 1$, $4^6 \equiv (-3)^6 \equiv 3^6 \equiv 1$, $5^6 \equiv (-2)^6 \equiv 1$, and $6^6 \equiv (-1)^6 \equiv 1$.

23-19   Fermat's Theorem is the key to this universal type of problem. We know that $6^{22} \equiv 1 \,(\mathrm{mod}\,23)$, so that

$$6^{1000} \equiv 6^{1000 \,(\mathrm{mod}\,22)} \equiv 6^{10} \equiv (6^5)^2 \equiv 7776^2 \equiv 2^2 \equiv 4 \,(\mathrm{mod}\,23).$$

23-20   The period of a number (mod 23) must divide $23 - 1 = 22$, so must be **1, 2, 11, or 22**. The period of a number (mod 17) must divide 16, so must be **1, 2, 4, 8, or 16**. The period of a number (mod 7) must divide 6, so must be **1, 2, 3, or 6**.

23-21   Since g has period $p - 1$, the numbers $g^{(p-1)/d_1}$, $g^{(p-1)/d_2}, \ldots$ have periods d_1, $d_2, \ldots$ respectively. Why? Clearly these numbers taken to the respective powers all yield $g^{p-1} \equiv 1$. Can these numbers be taken to smaller powers yield 1? Suppose $(g^{(p-1)/d_k})^c \equiv 1 \,(\mathrm{mod}\,p)$ for $c < d_k$. Then $g^{c(p-1)/d_k} \equiv 1$ for $c(p - 1)/d_k < p - 1$, violating the assertion that g has period $p - 1$. Thus the given numbers have the desired periods.

23-22 20 has the prime factors 2 and 5, so the numbers relatively prime to it are those divisible by neither 2 nor 5, namely 1, 3, 7, 9, 11, 13, 17, 19. The numbers relatively prime to 15 are divisible by neither 3 nor 5, so are 1, 2, 4, 7, 8, 11, 13, 14. The numbers relatively prime to 12 are divisible by niether 2 nor 3, so are 1, 5, 7, and 11 only.

23-23 As we found in the previous exercise, there are 4 numbers less than 12 and relatively prime to 12, so that $\phi(12) = \mathbf{4}$. Since 11 is prime, every number less than it is relatively prime to it. There are 10 positive numbers less than 11, so $\phi(11) = \mathbf{10}$.

23-24 For p prime, every number less than p is relatively prime to it. There are $p - 1$ positive numbers less than p, so $\phi(p) = \boldsymbol{p - 1}$. For p prime, Euler's generalization yields $a^{\phi(p)} \equiv 1 \,(\mathrm{mod}\, p)$, or $a^{p-1} \equiv 1 \,(\mathrm{mod}\, p)$. This is exactly Fermat's Theorem.

23-25 Every number less than p^k is relatively prime to p^k, except the multiples of p. Between 1 and p there are $p - 1$ numbers not divisible by p; between $p + 1$ and $2p$ there are $p - 1$, and so on. There are p^{k-1} such sets of p integers, each containing $p - 1$ integers relatively prime to p, for a total of $p^{k-1}(p - 1)$ numbers less than p^k and relatively prime to it. Hence $\phi(p^k) = p^{k-1}(p - 1)$. (Try this for $p = 3$ and $k = 2$.)

23-26 We factor $6876 = 2^2 \cdot 1719 = 2^2 \cdot 3^2 \cdot 191$. Thus

$$\phi(6876) = 6876 \left(1 - \frac{1}{2}\right)\left(1 - \frac{1}{3}\right)\left(1 - \frac{1}{191}\right) = 6876 \cdot \frac{1}{2} \cdot \frac{2}{3} \cdot \frac{190}{191} = \mathbf{2280}.$$

23-27 With $a = b = 2$, we have $3! = 6 \equiv 2 \,(\mathrm{mod}\, 4)$. But for any higher $a = b$, the factorial $(a^2 - 1)!$ contains a at least twice, so the factorial is congruent to 0. (Try it for $a = 3$ or $a = 4$.)

Solutions to Problems

373. 24 divides a number if 8 and 3 divide it. We can factor $p^2 - 1$ into $(p - 1)(p + 1)$. Since p is a prime greater than 3, p is odd. Thus either $p \equiv 1 \,(\mathrm{mod}\, 4)$ or $p \equiv 3 \,(\mathrm{mod}\, 4)$. In each case one of $p + 1$ and $p - 1$ is congruent to 0 (mod 4) and one is congruent to 2. The one which is congruent to 0 is divisible by 4, and the other is even; thus 8 divides $p^2 - 1$. To show 3 divides $p^2 - 1$ we use a similar argument. Since p is a prime greater than 3, p is not divisible by 3, so either $p \equiv 1 \,(\mathrm{mod}\, 3)$ or $p \equiv 2 \,(\mathrm{mod}\, 3)$. In either case one of $p - 1$ and $p + 1$ is congruent to 0 (mod 3), and is thus divisible by 3. Thus the product $(p - 1)(p + 1)$ is divisible by 3.

374. Since $n - 4$ is divisible by 5, $n \equiv 4 \,(\mathrm{mod}\, 5)$. Thus $n^2 \equiv 16 \equiv 1 \,(\mathrm{mod}\, 5)$ and $n^4 \equiv 1 \,(\mathrm{mod}\, 5)$. Hence $n^2 - 1 \equiv 0$, $n^2 - 4 \equiv -3 \equiv 2$, $n^2 - 16 \equiv -15 \equiv 0$, $n + 4 \equiv 8 \equiv 3$, and $n^4 - 1 \equiv 0$. All those congruent to 0 are divisible by 5, so the **first, third, and fifth** are divisible.

375. For some integers q, we can write $1059 = q_1 d + r$, $1417 = q_2 d + r$, and $2312 = q_3 d + r$. We thus have $1417 - 1059 = 358 = (q_2 - q_1)d$ and $2312 - 1417 = 895 = (q_3 - q_2)d$. This means that d divides both 358 and 895. Factored, $358 = 2 \cdot 179$ and $895 = 5 \cdot 179$. Since d divides both, it must equal 179. Dividing 179 into 1059, we find $r = 164$ as the remainder. Thus $d - r = 179 - 164 = \mathbf{15}$.

376. If 7 divides $x^2 + 15x + 1$, we have $x^2 + 15x + 1 \equiv 0 \,(\mathrm{mod}\,7)$, or $x^2 + x + 1 \equiv 0 \,(\mathrm{mod}\,7)$. Substituting in 0, 1, 2, ..., 6 for x to find solutions, we discover that $x \equiv 2$ and $x \equiv 4$ are the solutions. The solutions less than or equal to 100 are thus

$$2, \ 4, \ 9, \ 11, \ 16, \ 18, \ \ldots, \ 93, \ 95, \ 100,$$

the sum of which can be divided into the two arithmetic series $2 + 9 + 16 + \cdots + 100 = \frac{15}{2}(102) = (15)(51) = 765$ and $4 + 11 + 18 + \cdots + 95 = \frac{14}{2}(99) = (7)(99) = 693$. The answer is the sum of these two, or **1458**.

377. Since $n = 2$ gives $32 - 2 = 30$, this is the largest number which must divide $n^5 - n$ for any n. To see that 30 does divide $n^5 - n$ for all n, we realize that $30 = 2 \cdot 3 \cdot 5$, so we have only to show that 2, 3, and 5 divide.

So consider the equation successively in mods 2, 3, and 5. In mod 2, $n \equiv 0$ or 1, so $n^5 - n \equiv 0^5 - 0 \equiv 0$ or $1^5 - 1 \equiv 0$. Since $n^5 - n \equiv 0 \,(\mathrm{mod}\,2)$ no matter what n is, 2 always divides. For $n = 3$, n is congruent to either 0, 1, or 2; testing each of these gives the same result, so 3 always divides. For 5, Fermat's Theorem guarantees that $n^5 \equiv n \,(\mathrm{mod}\,5)$ for any n; do you see why? Alternatively, we can test 0, 1, 2, 3, and 4 (or, easier, $-2, -1, 0,$ 1, and 2) to see that each yields a result congruent to 0 $(\mathrm{mod}\,5)$. Since 2, 3, and 5 divide $n^5 - n$ for all n, 30 does as well. Since this is also the largest possible candidate, **30** is the answer.

378. The units digits of powers of 7 go 7, 9, 3, 1, 7, 9, 3, 1, ..., repeating in sets of 4. Thus the units digits of $7^{(7^7)}$ is equal to the units digit of $7^{[(7^7 (\mathrm{mod}\,4)]}$. To evaluate $7^7 \,(\mathrm{mod}\,4)$, we write $7^7 \equiv 3^7 \equiv (-1)^7 \equiv -1 \equiv 3 \,(\mathrm{mod}\,4)$. Hence the units digit of $7^{(7^7)}$ is equal to the units digit of 7^3, or **3**.

379. Consider the elements of S $(\mathrm{mod}\,7)$; then our criterion is that S can't contain any two elements whose sum is congruent to 0 $(\mathrm{mod}\,7)$. We cannot take both an element congruent to 1 and an element congruent to 6; we must choose one or the other. The same holds true for the pairs $(2, 5)$ and $(3, 4)$. Since there are 8 elements congruent to 1 (1, 8, 15, ..., 50) and only 7 for the others, we take all the elements congruent to 1, 2, and 3, for 22 elements. What about elements congruent to 0? We can take one, but taking two would yield a sum congruent to 0. Thus to the other 22 we can add one element congruent to 0, for **23** total elements.

380. $f(x)$ is congruent to 0 when divided by 6 if $x^2 + 3x + 2 \equiv 0 \,(\mathrm{mod}\,6)$. Testing 0, 1, ..., 5, we get the remainders 2, 0, 0, 2, 0, 0. We thus have four solutions between 0 and 5, four between 6 and 11, four between 12 and 17, four between 18 and 23, then one more, at 25. The total is **17** elements.

381. There aren't any. Since all the numbers 2, 3, ..., n divide $n!$, we can see that 2 divides $n! + 2$, 3 divides $n! + 3$ and so on. Each number greater than $n! + 1$ and less than

$n! + n$ has a divisor other than 1 or itself, so there are **0** prime numbers in this range.

382. Finding the last three digits of 9^{105} is equivalent to evaluating $9^{105} \pmod{1000}$. By the Binomial Theorem, we have

$$9^{105} = (10-1)^{105} = \binom{105}{105}10^{105} - \binom{105}{104}10^{104} + \cdots - \binom{105}{2}10^2 + \binom{105}{1}10^1 - \binom{105}{0}.$$

Since $10^k \equiv 0 \pmod{1000}$ for $k \geq 3$, only the last three terms of the expansion matter (mod 1000). These last three terms are $-\binom{105}{2}100 = -(105)(104)(100)/2$, which is divisible by 1000 and thus congruent to 0, $\binom{105}{1}10 = 1050 \equiv 50$, and $-\binom{105}{0} \equiv -1$. Thus the last two digits are found by looking at $50 - 1 \equiv 49$, so are **049**.

383. The product telescopes: the 3 in $\frac{3}{1}$ cancels with the 3 in $\frac{5}{3}$, the 4 in $\frac{4}{2}$ cancels with the 4 in $\frac{6}{4}$, and so on. What's left is $\sqrt{(n+1)(n+2)/2}$. Since $n+1$ and $n+2$ are consecutive integers, they are relatively prime, so the only way $(n+1)(n+2)/2$ can be a perfect square is if either $(n+1)/2$ and $n+2$ are perfect squares or $n+1$ and $(n+2)/2$ are perfect squares. In either case we seek two perfect squares x and y such that $2x$ and y are consecutive integers. Writing down the first few squares, 1, 4, 9, we see that 4 and 9 are just such squares. We thus let $(n+1)/2 = 4$ and $n+2 = 9$, so $n = 7$. (Another pair of squares, 25 and 49, yields $n = 48$ as the next largest solution. The equation $x^2 = 2y^2 \pm 1$ is the Pell equation, so we could find infinitely many solutions n.)

384. Since Adam's schedule repeats every 4 days and Ben's every 10, the overall schedule repeats every 20 days. In this 20-day period, Ben rests on days 8, 9, 10, 18, 19, and 20, while Adam rests on days 4, 8, 12, 16, 20. In each 20-day period they share 2 rest days. In the first 1000 days, or 50 even 20-day periods, they thus share **100** rest days.

385. Looking at the powers of 7 (mod 100) to get the last two digits, we have $7^1 \equiv 07$, $7^2 \equiv 49$, $7^3 \equiv 343 \equiv 43$, and $7^4 \equiv (43)(7) \equiv 307 \equiv 07$. Thus the last two digits repeat in cycles of 3, so $7^{9999} \equiv 7^{9999 \pmod 3} \equiv 7^3 \equiv \mathbf{43} \pmod{100}$.

386. Two consecutive integers n and $n+1$ have sum $2n+1$; setting this equal to 1000, we get $n = 999/2$, which is not an integer. Three consecutive integers n, $n+1$, and $n+2$ have sum $3n+3$; $3n+3 = 1000$ yields $n = 997/3$, which is again not an integer. For $n = 4$ we have $4n+6 = 1000$, or $n = 994/4 = 497/2$. For $n = 5$ we get $5n+10 = 1000$, or $n = 990/5 = 198$—at last an integral solution. Hence $n = \mathbf{5}$ is the smallest solution.

387. We can see that 17 divides $9x+5y$ by noting that $9x+5y = 17x+17y-4(2x+3y)$. Each term on the right is divisible by 17, so $9x+5y$ is.

388. The squares (mod 10) can easily be verified to be 0, 1, 4, 5, 6, 9, and 0, so that d must be one of these digits. Moreover, in (mod 4) any number is congruent to its last two digits, or $10+d$. But a square must be congruent to 0 or 1 (mod 4), so that $10+d$ must be 12, 13, 16, or 17. Since d cannot be 2, 3, or 7, d must be 6. Thus our proposed square ends with the digits 19916. Since any number is congruent to its last four digits (mod 16), our number is congruent to $9916 \equiv 12 \pmod{16}$. But all even squares are congruent to 0 or

4 (mod 16), so this cannot be a square. [We came across using (mod 16) only after finding that (mod 8) didn't give any new information; always feel free to play around. To see that all even squares are congruent to 0 or 4 (mod 16), note that all even numbers are of either the form $4k$ or the form $4k + 2$. The square in the first case is $16k^2 \equiv 0 \,(\text{mod}\,16)$, while the square in the second case is $16k^2 + 16k + 4 \equiv 4 \,(\text{mod}\,16)$. All in all, a pretty slick solution.]

389. The simplest way to do it is to look at the fifth power of each digit (mod 10). We have $0^5 \equiv 0$, $1^5 \equiv 1$, $2^5 = 32 \equiv 2$, $3^5 = 243 \equiv 3$, $4^5 = 1024 \equiv 4$, $5^5 \equiv 5$, $6^5 \equiv (-4)^5 \equiv -4 \equiv 6$, $7^5 \equiv (-3)^5 \equiv -3 \equiv 7$, $8^5 \equiv (-2)^5 \equiv -2 \equiv 8$, and $9^5 \equiv (-1)^5 \equiv -1 \equiv 9$. No matter what a number q is, it will be congruent to one of these digits (mod 10), so $q^5 \equiv q \,(\text{mod}\,10)$, and 10 divides $q^5 - q$.

390. We use the result of the previous problem—that $q^5 \equiv q \,(\text{mod}\,10)$ for all q. As long as q is not divisible by 5, we can divide a q from both sides of this to get $q^4 \equiv 1 \,(\text{mod}\,5)$. (Note that we have to divide the modulus by 2, since q might be even.) Thus, if neither x nor y is divisible by 5, we have $x^4 \equiv 1 \,(\text{mod}\,5)$ and $4y^4 \equiv 4(1) \equiv 4 \,(\text{mod}\,5)$ and $x^4 + 4y^4 \equiv 1 + 4 \equiv 5 \equiv 0 \,(\text{mod}\,5)$.

391. If x is the multiple of 5, then $x^4 + 4y^4 \equiv 0 + 4 \equiv 4 \,(\text{mod}\,5)$, so it is not divisible by 5. If y is the multiple of 5, then $x^4 + 4y^4 \equiv 1 + 0 \equiv 1$, so it is not divisible by 5.

392. Every odd prime can be written as either $6n + 1$ or $6n + 5$ (not $6n + 3$ because it's divisible by 3). For the former, $6n + 1 + 2 = 3(2n + 1)$, so $p + 2$ is not composite in this case. Hence, $p = 6n + 5$ and $p + 1 = 6n + 6$ is divisible by 6 as desired.

393. Let $n = 10x + y$ where x and y are integers and $0 \leq y \leq 9$. Hence, $n^2 = 100x^2 + 20xy + y^2$, so the tens digit of n^2 is odd if and only if the tens digit of y^2 is. This only occurs if $y = 4$ or $y = 6$. In both cases, the units digit of n^2 is **6**.

394. Since $a_1 = 1$ is not prime, $a_2 = 1001$ is not prime, and a_n is clearly divisible by 3 if n is, so we need only consider $n > 3$ such that n is not divisible by 3.

We have $a_n = 1 + 10^3 + 10^6 + \cdots + 10^{3(n-1)} = \frac{10^{3n}-1}{10^3-1} = \frac{(10^n-1)(10^{2n}+10^n+1)}{999}$. Since $10^n - 1$ is divisible by 9, we need only show that $10^{2n} + 10^n + 1$ is divisible by 111 to prove our assertion. We first note that $10^3 = 1000 \equiv 1 \,(\text{mod}\,111)$, so $10^{3m} \equiv 1 \,(\text{mod}\,111)$, $10^{3m+1} = 10^{3m} \cdot 10 \equiv 10 \,(\text{mod}\,111)$, and $10^{3m+2} \equiv 100 \,(\text{mod}\,111)$ for any positive integer m.

Since n is not divisible by 3, we consider the two cases $n = 3k + 1$ and $n = 3k + 2$. In the first cast we have $10^n \equiv 10^{3k+1} \equiv 10 \,(\text{mod}\,111)$ and $10^{2n} \equiv 10^{3(2k)+2} \equiv 100 \,(\text{mod}\,111)$. Thus in this case $10^{2n} + 10^n + 1 \equiv 100 + 10 + 1 \equiv 0 \,(\text{mod}\,111)$. In the second case we similarly get $10^n \equiv 100$ and $10^{2n} \equiv 10 \,(\text{mod}\,111)$, so $10^{2n} + 10^n + 1 \equiv 0 \,(\text{mod}\,111)$ in this case as well. Since 9 always divides $10^n - 1$ and 111 always divides $10^{2n} + 10^n + 1$, the fraction $a_n = (10^n - 1)(10^{2n} + 10^n + 1)/999$ is an integer for $n > 1$. Furthermore, since $10^{2n} + 10^n + 1 > 10^n - 1 > 999$ for $n > 3$, the above factoriation shows that all a_n with $n > 3$ can be expressed as the product of two integers larger than 1; hence, a_n is not prime.

395. We need to prove both the "if" and the "only if" parts. For the "only if," we start with $p | (a^2 - a - 3)$. Let $b = 3a - 1$; then $b^2 - b + 25 \equiv (3a - 1)^2 - (3a - 1) + 25 \equiv$

$9a^2 - 9a + 27 \equiv 9(a^2 - a + 3) \equiv 0 \,(\mathrm{mod}\, p)$, where the last equivalence follows from the assumption that $a^2 - a + 3 \equiv 0 \,(\mathrm{mod}\, p)$.

To prove the "if," we start with $p|(b^2 - b + 25)$. We need two cases. If $p \neq 3$, then there exists some r such that $3r \equiv 1 \,(\mathrm{mod}\, p)$. We let $a = r(b + 1)$; then $a^2 - a + 3 \equiv r^2(b+1)^2 - r(b+1) + 3 \equiv r^2(b+1)^2 - (3r)r(b+1) + 3(3r)^2 \equiv r^2[(b+1)^2 - 3(b+1) + 27] \equiv r^2(b^2 - b + 25) \equiv 0 \,(\mathrm{mod}\, p)$.

If $p = 3$, we just let $b = 2$ and $a = 1$; then $a^2 - a + 3 = 3$, which 3 divides, and $b^2 - b + 25 = 27$, which 3 divides.

We have thus proven that if $p|(a^2 - a + 3)$ for some a, then $p|(b^2 - b + 25)$ for some b.

396. We set $y_k = x_k x_{k+1} x_{k+2} x_{k+3}$, with the modification that the k can wrap around as in $y_{j-1} = x_{j-1} x_j x_1 x_2$. Each y_i is equal to either 1 or -1 and $y_1 + y_2 + \cdots + y_n = 0$. Hence n is even: $n = 2m$. Also, $y_1 y_2 \cdots y_n = (-1)^m$; but each x_j appears four times in this product, so the product is $+1$. Thus m is also even: $m = 2p$, so $n = 4p$ is divisible by 4.

397. First $d(n)$. Let $m = p_1^{e_1} \cdots p_k^{e_k}$ and $n = q_1^{f_1} \cdots q_l^{f_l}$ be the factorizations of the relatively prime integers m and n. Since m and n are relatively prime, all the q's are different from all the p's, so the factorization of the product mn is $p_1^{e_1} \cdots p_k^{e_k} q_1^{f_1} \cdots q_l^{f_l}$. We thus have

$$
\begin{aligned}
d(m) &= (e_1 + 1)(e_2 + 1) \cdots (e_k + 1) \\
d(n) &= (f_1 + 1)(f_2 + 1) \cdots (f_k + 1) \\
d(mn) &= (e_1 + 1)(e_2 + 1) \cdots (e_k + 1)(f_1 + 1)(f_2 + 1) \cdots (f_k + 1),
\end{aligned}
$$

so clearly $d(mn) = d(m)d(n)$ for relatively prime m and n.

For $s(n)$ we do nearly the same thing. With m, n, and mn as above, we have

$$
\begin{aligned}
s(m) &= (1 + p_1 + p_1^2 + \cdots + p_1^{e_1}) \cdots (1 + p_k + p_k^2 + \cdots + p_k^{e_k}) \\
s(n) &= (1 + q_1 + q_1^2 + \cdots + q_1^{f_1}) \cdots (1 + q_k + q_k^2 + \cdots + q_k^{f_k}) \\
s(mn) &= (1 + p_1 + p_1^2 + \cdots + p_1^{e_1}) \cdots (1 + p_k + p_k^2 + \cdots + p_k^{e_k}) \\
&\quad \times (1 + q_1 + q_1^2 + \cdots + q_1^{f_1}) \cdots (1 + q_k + q_k^2 + \cdots + q_k^{f_k})
\end{aligned}
$$

so $s(mn) = s(m)s(n)$ for relatively prime m and n.

398. Rather than use long division on the polynomials, we note that if the polynomial $f(x)$ divides $g(x)$, then the integer $f(p)$ divides $g(p)$ for any fixed p. Thus, substituting $p = 0$ tells us that $m|30$; substituting $p = 1$ yields $(m + 3)|66$. Just these first two yield, upon testing divisors of 30, either $m = 3$ or $m = 30$. $p = -1$ gives $(m - 3)|0$, which yields no information, but $p = 2$ gives $(p + 12)|5280$, which fails for $p = 30$. Thus **3** is the only remaining candidate.

399. If $a < b$ and $b > 2$, $2^b - 1$ is greater than $2^a + 1$, so cannot divide it. If $a = b$, $2^b - 1$ clearly cannot divide $2^a + 1$ because their difference is only 2. For the case where $a > b$, we write $a = bq + r$ for integers $q \geq 1$ and $0 \leq r < b$. We then write

$$\frac{2^a + 1}{2^b - 1} = \frac{2^{bq+r} + 1}{2^b - 1} = 2^r \frac{2^{qb} - 1}{2^b - 1} + \frac{2^r + 1}{2^b - 1}.$$

Now $(2^b - 1) | (2^{qb} - 1)$ for any q and b (do you see why?), so the first term is an integer. The second term, on the other hand, is never an integer, because $2^r + 1 < 2^b - 1$. Thus the sum is not an integer, so $2^b - 1$ cannot divide $2^a + 1$.

400. It suffices to show that at least one of $2d - 1$, $5d - 1$, and $13d - 1$ is not a square. Assume for the sake of contradiction that all three are squares; then we have $2d = x^2 + 1$, $5d = y^2 + 1$, and $13d = z^2 + 1$ for some x, y, and z. Clearly x is odd; then $x^2 \equiv 1 \pmod 8$ and $2d \equiv x^2 + 1 \equiv 2 \pmod 8$. Thus d is odd. This forces y and z to be even: $y = 2u$, $z = 2v$. Since $z^2 - y^2 = 8d$, we have $(v - u)(v + u) = 2d$. But $v - u$ and $v + u$ have the same parity, so they must both be even for their product to be even. Since both are even, their product is moreover divisible by 4. But that product is also equal to $2d$, for d an odd integer. Thus the product cannot be divisible by 4, so we have a contradiction.

401. Let p be any prime; we show that p divides the numerator at least as much as it divides the denominator. The largest α for which p^α divides the denominator, $n!$, is $\lfloor n/p \rfloor + \lfloor n/p^2 \rfloor + \cdots$. (This is fairly clear based on our discussion of factorials in Volume 1; read back over that if you need to.) If p divides b, then p can be cancelled from the quotient. If p does not divide b, then it must divide one of the factors $a, a+b, \ldots, a+(p-1)b$. (Why?) Altogether there are at least $\lfloor n/p \rfloor$ factors in the numerator divisible by p (one for each block of p consecutive factors); similarly there are at least $\lfloor n/p^2 \rfloor$ factors divisible by p^2, and so on for higher powers of p. Altogether the product $a(a + b)(a + 2b) \cdots (a + (n - 1)b)$ has p as a factor at least α times. Since any prime divides the numerator at least as many times at it divides the denominator, the fraction is an integer.

402. We write n as the sum of consecutive integers as

$$n = k + (k + 1) + \cdots + (k + l) = \frac{(2k + l)(l + 1)}{2}.$$

If l is odd, $2k + l$ is odd. If l is even, $l + 1$ is odd. Hence, any number which is the sum of consecutive integers has an odd factor and thus cannot be a power of 2. If n is not a power of 2 we can write n as $2^x(2y + 1)$. If $y < 2^x$, then we can write n as

$$n = (2^x - y) + (2^x - y + 1) + \cdots + (2^x + y - 1) + (2^x + y).$$

If $y \geq 2^x$, we can write

$$n = (y - 2^x + 1) + (y - 2^x + 2) + \cdots + (2^x + y).$$

Chapter 24

Diophantine Equations

Solutions to Exercises

24-1 The solutions are given by $(x, y) = (4k, 3k)$ for any k.

24-2 The graph is shown at right, with the solutions highlighted in black. The solutions are obtained by starting at $(0,0)$ and moving right 3, down 2, left 3, up 2, and so on.

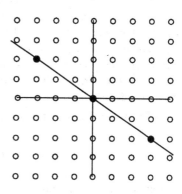

24-3 Starting with $(0,0)$, we have $(3,2)$, $(6,4)$, $(9,6),\ldots$. With $b = 6$, $a = 4$, the greatest common divisor is $g = 2$, yielding the solutions $(3k, 2k) = (-3, -2)$, $(0,0)$, $(3,2),\ldots$.

24-4 Dividing out a common factor of 2, the given equation becomes $2x = -3y$. Thus the graph is the same as the graph we drew above. Rather than getting the solutions by moving right 6 and down 4, we get them by going right 3 and down 2 as before. Thus the common factor of 2 does not change the solutions; we just divide it out before we start.

24-5 We have $5(2) + 3(-1) = 7$, so $(2, -1)$ is a solution.

24-6 Substituting in, we have $a(r) + b((c - ar)/b) = ar + c - ar = c$, so $(r, (c - ar)/b)$ is a solution. (You might wonder why we need to specify that r is a solution of $ar \equiv c \pmod{b}$. This is necessary to make $(c - ar)/b$ an integer. Do you see how?)

24-7

    i. Dividing out the common factor of 2, the equation becomes $3x + 2y = 2$. To find a specific solution, we solve $3x \equiv 2 \equiv 0 \pmod{2}$. One solution is $x = 0$, yielding $(x, y) = (0, 1)$

as a solution of the equation. To get more solutions, we add a multiple $-2k$ to x and a multiple $3k$ to y. This yields $(-2k, 3k+1)$ as the general solution of the equation. Putting in various k, we can get some solutions if we have a mind to: $(-4, 7)$, $(-2, 4)$, $(2, -2)$.

ii. In this case, the left side is always divisible by 2 but the right side never is. Thus the equation has no solutions.

24-8 No. The only positive y which doesn't make $3x + 7y$ greater than 12 is $y = 1$, but substituting $y = 1$ yields $3x = 5$. There is no x which satisfies this equation.

24-9 We fill in the same grid as in the text, with x along the top and y down the side:

	0	1	2	3
0	0	m	$2m$	$3m$
1	n	$n + m$	$n + 2m$	$n + 3m$
2	$2n$	$2n + m$	$2n + 2m$	$2n + 3m$
3	$3n$	$3n + m$	$3n + 2m$	$3n + 3m$

All $c \equiv 0 \pmod{m}$ with $c \geq 0$ can be obtained from the first row; $c \equiv n \pmod{m}$ with $c \geq n$ can be obtained from the second row; and so on until all $c \equiv (m-1)n \pmod{m}$ with $c \geq (m-1)n$ can be obtained from the last row.

We can thus get all $c \geq n(m-1)$; the largest c we can't get is the largest $c \equiv n(m-1)$ which is still less than $n(m-1)$. (Compare to the argument in the text if following all these letters bogs you down.) The largest c congruent to $n(m-1) \pmod{m}$ which is less than $n(m-1)$ is $n(m-1) - m = mn - m - n$, as desired.

Since this argument is quite abstract, we strongly recommend that you go through it for, say, $3x + 7y = c$. What is the largest c we can't get? Get a feel for why we can't get this c, and why this is the largest such c.

24-10 We have $x = \sqrt{z^2 - y^2} = \sqrt{(r^2 + s^2)^2 - (r^2 - s^2)^2} = \sqrt{(2r^2)(2s^2)} = 2rs$.

24-11 If r and s have a common factor d, then d divides $2rs$, $r^2 - s^2$, and $r^2 + s^2$. But it was specified that the triangle was primitive, meaning that x, y, and z can have no common divisors, so d cannot exist. Thus r and s must be relatively prime.

24-12 For $(3, 4, 5)$, we have $2rs = 4$, so that $rs = 2$, implying that $r = 2$ and $s = 1$.

For $(6, 8, 10)$, we similarly have $rs = 6/2 = 3$ or $8/2 = 4$. Since $r \neq s$, the possibilities are $r = 4$, $s = 1$ and $r = 3$, $s = 1$. The second pair produces the correct triangle.

For $(5, 12, 13)$, we have $rs = 12/2 = 6$, so that either $r = 6$, $s = 1$ or $r = 3$, $s = 2$. The latter gives the correct triangle.

24-13 Clearly $r < 10$, since otherwise $z = r^2 + s^2 = 100 + s^2$ is greater than 100. Moreover, one of r and s must be even, or else all three sides of the triangle will be even. We further need r and s to be relatively prime, and $r > s$. We find the pairs $(2, 1)$, $(4, 1)$, $(6, 1)$, $(8, 1)$, $(3, 2)$, $(5, 2)$, $(7, 2)$, $(9, 2)$, $(4, 3)$, $(8, 3)$, $(5, 4)$, $(7, 4)$, $(9, 4)$, $(6, 5)$, $(8, 5)$, $(7, 6)$, $(8, 7)$, and $(9, 8)$. Not all these are OK, though, since some of them make $z > 100$. In particular, $(8,7)$ and $(9,8)$ make $r^2 + s^2 > 100$. We are left with 16 pairs (r,s), and thus **16** primitve Pythagorean triples.

24-14 Not both r and s can be odd, since otherwise $2rs$, $r^2 - s^2$, and $r^2 + s^2$ are all even, whereas we know that the three are relatively prime. Both r and s cannot be even for the same reason. Moreover, we cannot have r even and s odd, since then we have $y_0^2 \equiv r^2 - s^2 \equiv -1 \equiv 3 \,(\mathrm{mod}\,4)$, which is not possible. The only remaining possibility is that s is even and r odd.

24-15 Since r and s are relatively prime and $t = s/2$, r and t must clearly be relatively prime.

24-16 We already established that r and t are relatively prime, so their square roots, r_1 and t_1, must certainly be relatively prime as well. Moreover, we know that r is odd, so that its square root r_1 is odd. (Of course this exercise is simple, but it makes sure that you follow what's going on.)

24-17 We know that $y_0^2 = r^2 - s^2$; substituting in several definitions, we get $y_0^2 = (r_1^2)^2 - (2t)^2 = (r_1^2)^2 - (2t_1^2)^2$. This can be rearranged to get the desired equation.

24-18 If some common factor divided both $2t_1^2$ and y_0^2, then it would also divide r_1 and t, and hence r and s. But r and s are relatively prime, so such a common factor cannot exist. Thus $2t_1^2$ and y_0^2 are relatively prime.

24-19 Because $z_0 = r^2 + s^2 = r_1^4 + s^2 > r_1^4 > r_1$.

24-20 You might have found the solutions $(x,y) = (1,1)$, $(3,2)$, $(7,5)$, for example. (Make sure you see why these are solutions.)

24-21 In this case we can factor $x^2 - E^2 y^2 = 1$ as $(x - Ey)(x + Ey) = 1$. Since $x - Ey$ and $x + Ey$ are integers, the only way this can be is if $x - Ey = x + Ey = \pm 1$. Thus $y = 0$, $x = \pm 1$ are the only two solutions, both of which can be considered trivial.

24-22 Using the continued fraction

$$\sqrt{2} = 1 + \cfrac{1}{2 + \cfrac{1}{2 + \cfrac{1}{2 + \cdots}}}$$

with period 1, we find the convergents $\frac{1}{1}$, $\frac{3}{2}$, $\frac{7}{5}$, $\frac{17}{12}$ and the corresponding Pell solutions $(1,1)$, $(3,2)$, $(7,5)$, and $(17,12)$. The first corresponds to the $-$ sign, the second to $+$, the third to $-$, and the fourth to $+$.

We can do the others similarly; the only tough part is finding the continued fraction expansion. Using the usual method for continued fractions, we find

$$\sqrt{3} = 1 + \cfrac{1}{1 + \cfrac{1}{2 + \cfrac{1}{1 + \cfrac{1}{2 + \cdots}}}} \qquad (\text{period } 2),$$

$$\sqrt{5} = 2 + \cfrac{1}{4 + \cfrac{1}{4 + \cfrac{1}{4 + \cdots}}} \qquad (\text{period } 1),$$

and

$$\sqrt{6} = 2 + \cfrac{1}{2 + \cfrac{1}{4 + \cfrac{1}{2 + \frac{1}{4 + \cdots}}}} \qquad \text{(period 2).}$$

Since $\sqrt{5}$'s continued fraction has period 1, every convergent will be a solution. We find $(2,1)$, corresponding to $-$, $(9,4)$, corresponding to $+$, and $(38,17)$, corresponding to $-$.

For $\sqrt{3}$ and $\sqrt{6}$, we want every *second* convergent, because the continued fractions are period 2. (What do we get for the other convergents?) For $\sqrt{3}$ we get the solutions $(2,1)$, corresponding to $+$, and $(7,4)$, corresponding to $+$. For $\sqrt{6}$ we get $(5,2)$, corresponding to $+$, and $(49,20)$, corresponding to $+$.

24-23 We proceed by induction. For $n = 1$, we get $a = x_0$, $b = y_0$, which is a solution by assumption. For any solution (m,n), multiplying $(m + \sqrt{D}\,n)$ by $(x_0 + \sqrt{D}\,y_0)$ yields

$$(mx_0 + Dny_0) + (nx_0 + my_0)\sqrt{D},$$

for the pair $(mx_0 + Dny_0, nx_0 + my_0)$. Testing this pair as a solution, we have

$$(mx_0 + Dny_0)^2 - D(nx_0 + my_0)^2 = m^2(x_0^2 - Dy_0) - Dn^2(x_0^2 - Dy_0^2) = (\pm 1)(m^2 - Dn^2) = \pm 1,$$

as desired.

This allows us to make the inductive step. Assume that $(x_0 + \sqrt{D}\,y_0)^k$ yields a solution; we have shown that multiplying this by $x_0 + \sqrt{D}\,y_0$ will yield another solution. Thus if $(x_0 + \sqrt{D}\,y_0)^k$ yields a solution, $(x_0 + \sqrt{D}\,y_0)^{k+1}$ also yields a solution. By induction $(x_0 + \sqrt{D}\,y_0)^n$ yields a solution for any n.

24-24 The squares x^2 and y^2 are both congruent to 0 or 1 (mod 4), so their sum is congruent to 0, 1, or 2. Since 100000003 is congruent to 3 (mod 4), it cannot be the sum of the two squares.

Solutions to Problems

403. To solve this Pell equation, we need the continued fraction expansion of $\sqrt{8}$. We can get this without computation by recalling that

$$\sqrt{2} = 1 + \cfrac{1}{2 + \cfrac{1}{2 + \cdots}},$$

so that

$$\sqrt{8} = 2\sqrt{2} = 2 + \cfrac{2}{2 + \cfrac{1}{2 + \frac{1}{2 + \cdots}}} = 2 + \cfrac{1}{1 + \cfrac{1}{4 + \cfrac{2}{2 + \frac{1}{2 + \cdots}}}} = 2 + \cfrac{1}{1 + \cfrac{1}{4 + \cfrac{1}{1 + \frac{1}{4 + \cdots}}}}$$

(Of course, we could find this continued fraction in the usual way, but this method is a little easier.) Since the period of the continued fraction is 2, we get the first solution to our equation from the second convergent: $2 + \frac{1}{1} = \frac{3}{1}$. Testing $(x, y) = (\mathbf{3}, \mathbf{1})$, we find that it is indeed a solution.

We can find more solutions without the continued fraction by taking powers of $3 + \sqrt{8}$. The square is $17 + 6\sqrt{8}$, yielding $(x, y) = (\mathbf{17}, \mathbf{6})$ as the next solution. (Test it; does it work?)

404. We seek the number of solutions to $4x + 3y = 1776$ such that x and y are nonnegative integers. Letting $y = 0$, we find the solution $(444, 0)$; succeeding solutions can be found by decreasing x by 3 and increasing y by 4. The next few solutions are thus $(441, 4)$, $(438, 8)$, and so on. This process continues until we reach $(0, 592)$. How many solutions does this entail? The arithmetic sequence $444, 441, \ldots, 0$ has $444/3 + 1 = \mathbf{149}$ terms.

405. We can rearrange the given equation into $n = m(n - 1)$, or $m = n/(n - 1)$. For m to be an integer, we must have $n = 0$ or $n = 2$ (do you see why?). Thus we have the **2** solutions $(m, n) = (2, 2)$ and $(0, 0)$.

406. Clearly the right side of the equation is congruent to 1 (mod 3). The left side factors into $m(m + 5)(m + 1)$. One of m, $m + 1$, and $m + 5$ must be divisible by 3 (why?), so the left side of the equation is always congruent to 0 (mod 3). Hence the equation has **no solutions**.

407. We factor 1984 as $2^6 \cdot 31$ to see that $\sqrt{1984} = 8\sqrt{31}$. Since x and y are integers and $\sqrt{x} + \sqrt{y} = 8\sqrt{31}$, we must have $\sqrt{x} = a\sqrt{31}$ and $\sqrt{y} = b\sqrt{31}$. Furthermore, we must have $a + b = 8$ and $b > a$ (since the problem stipulates that $y > x$). The only pairs (a, b) are $(1, 7)$, $(2, 6)$, and $(3, 5)$, so there are **3** solutions.

408. Assume for the sake of contradiction that $3q$ can be expressed as a sum of squares, and let $q = a_0^2 + b_0^2$ and $3q = c_0^2 + d_0^2$. Further suppose that q is the smallest positive integer with the desired property. All squares are congruent to either 0 or 1 (mod 3), so $c_0^2 + d_0^2 = 3q \equiv 0 \pmod{3}$ implies that $c_0^2 \equiv d_0^2 \equiv 0$, which in turn implies that c_0 and d_0 are divisible by 3. We thus write $c_0 = 3c_1$ and $d_0 = 3d_1$. Then $3q = 9(c_1^2 + d_1^2)$, so $q = 3(c_1^2 + d_1^2)$ is divisible by 3. Writing $q = 3q_1$, we have $q_1 = c_1^2 + d_1^2$ and $3q_1 = q = a_0^2 + b_0^2$. In q_1 we have thus constructed a smaller positive integer with the desired property, which is a contradiction to our assumption that q is the smallest. Hence there is no such q.

409. First of all, we use the fact that a square is always congruent to 0 or 1 (mod 4). In order, the given pairs are congruent to 3, 1, 1, 3, and 1, so 07 and 63 are immediately out. Furthermore, any square which ends in 5 must end in 25: if the nonsquared number was congruent to $10x + 5 \pmod{100}$, then the square is congruent to $100x^2 + 100x + 25 \equiv 25 \pmod{100}$. Thus 85 is out. The remaining two, 29 and 41, can be the last two digits of a square: $27^2 = 729$ and $21^2 = 441$. Thus **29 and 41** are answers.

410. Any Pythagorean triangle is a multiple of a primitive triangle, with sides $2rs$, $r^2 - s^2$, and $r^2 + s^2$. If the sides of our triangle are $2Crs$, $C(r^2 - s^2)$, and $C(r^2 + s^2)$, then the area is $C^2rs(r^2 - s^2) = C^2rs(r + s)(r - s)$ and the perimeter is $2Crs + 2Cr^2 = 2Cr(r + s)$. Setting the area equal to the perimeter, we have $C^2rs(r + s)(r - s) = 2Cr(r + s)$, or, cancelling

$Cr(r+s)$ from both sides, $Cs(r-s) = 2$. The possibilities are $C = 2$, $s = 1$, $r - s = 1$; $C = 1$, $s = 2$, $r - s = 1$; and $C = 1$, $s = 1$, $r - s = 2$. The first case gives $(C, r, s) = (2, 2, 1)$, so that the triangle we obtain has sides $2(2)(2)(1) = 8$, $2(2^2 - 1^2) = 6$, and $2(2^2 + 1^2) = 10$. The second case gives $(C, r, s) = (1, 2, 3)$, yielding the sides $2(2)(3) = 12$, $3^2 - 2^2 = 5$, and $3^2 + 2^2 = 13$. The third case gives $(C, r, s) = (1, 1, 3)$, yielding the sides $2(1)(3) = 6$, $3^2 - 1^2 = 8$, and $3^2 + 1^2 = 10$—this is the same triangle as we got in the first case. Thus there are only **2** solutions: $(5, 12, 13)$ and $(6, 8, 10)$.

411. Since 3^m, 3^n, and 1 are all odd, their sum, $3^m + 3^n + 1$, is odd as well. Thus we write $3^m + 3^n + 1 = k^2$, for k some odd integer. This yields $3^m + 3^n = (k^2 - 1) = (k - 1)(k + 1)$. The right hand side of this equation is always divisible by 8 (since k is odd, it is between a multiple of 4 and a multiple of 2). However, powers of 3 are always congruent to either 1 or 3 (mod 8), so the left side of the equation is congruent to $1 + 1 \equiv 2$, $1 + 3 \equiv 4$, or $3 + 3 \equiv 6 \pmod{8}$. Hence the left side of the equation can never be divisible by 8, while the right hand side always is, so $3^m + 3^n + 1$ can never be a perfect square.

412. We could square the numbers, add them, and take the square root, but that wouldn't be much fun. Instead we divide out the common factors until the legs are relatively prime. Dividing out 2, the legs are 204 and 10403, and these are relatively prime. We thus set $2rs = 204$, so that $rs = 102 = 2 \cdot 3 \cdot 17$. The only way to get $r^2 - s^2$ large enough is to take $r = 102$, $s = 1$, whence $r^2 - s^2 = 10404 - 1 = 10403$. The hypotenuse of the primitive triangle is $r^2 + s^2 = 10405$, and the hypotenuse of the original triangle is twice this, or **20810**.

413. For $x > 5$, $x!$ has units digit 0. Since $1! = 1$, $2! = 2$, $3! = 6$, and $4! = 24$, $1! + 2! + 3! + \cdots + x!$ thus has units digit $1 + 2 + 6 + 24 + 0 + 0 + \cdots = 33 \to 3$ for $x \geq 4$. We wish for this to equal a perfect square; but a perfect square cannot have units digit 3. Thus the only possible solutions are for $x \leq 3$. In fact, we find the only two solutions, $(\mathbf{1}, \mathbf{1})$ and $(\mathbf{3}, \mathbf{3})$, by testing these values of x.

414. Only one of the two legs of a primitive Pythagorean triangle is even, the one of the form $2rs$. Not both of r and s can be odd, because $r^2 - s^2$ would also be even if r and s were both odd. Since one of r or s is even, $2rs$ is divisible by 4, so cannot equal 90. Thus no primitive Pythagorean triangle can exist with one leg 90. (Can you find a non-primitive Pythagorean triangle with one leg 90?)

415. If the sides are $2rs$, $r^2 - s^2$, and $r^2 + s^2$, then the area is $rs(r^2 - s^2) = rs(r+s)(r-s)$ and the perimeter is $2rs + 2r^2 = 2r(r + s)$. Setting the area equal to twice the perimeter, we have $rs(r + s)(r - s) = 4r(r + s)$, or, cancelling $r(r + s)$ from both sides, $s(r - s) = 4$. Since s and $r - s$ are integers, the only possibilities are $s = 1$, $r - s = 4$; $s = 2$, $r - s = 2$; and $s = 4$, $r - s = 1$. The first case is not primitive, since both r and s are odd then. In the second case, we have $s = 2$, $r = 4$, so again the triangle is not primitive. In the third case, $s = 4$ and $r = 5$, so the sides of the triangle are $2(4)(5) = 40$, $5^2 - 4^2 = 9$, and $5^2 + 4^2 = 41$. The only triangle with the desired property is $(\mathbf{9}, \mathbf{40}, \mathbf{41})$.

416. Every Pythagorean triangle is some multiple of a primitive triangle, so we only need to prove it for primitive triangles. We consider r and s (mod 5). If either is congruent to 0, then we are done because $2rs$ is congruent to 0. If the two are congruent to one another, then we are done because $r^2 - s^2$ is congruent to 0. If $r \equiv -s \pmod 5$, then we are done because $r^2 - s^2$ is congruent to 0. What's left? Only the pairs $(r, s) \equiv (1, 2)$, $(3, 4)$, $(1, 3)$, and $(2, 4)$. Testing these shows that $r^2 + s^2$ is congruent to 0 (mod 5) for each.

417. In (mod 5), the possible fourth powers are $0^4 \equiv 0$, $1^4 \equiv 1$, $2^4 \equiv 16 \equiv 1$, $3^4 \equiv (-2)^4 \equiv 1$, and $4^4 \equiv (-1)^4 \equiv 1$—that is, only 0 and 1. So consider the five numbers a through e. If e^4 is congruent to 0 (mod 5), then a^4 through d^4 must all be congruent to 0 (mod 5). If e^4 is congruent to 1, then one of a^4 through d^4 must be congruent to 1 and the other three to 0. In either case, at least three of the numbers are divisible by 5.

418. Since $n^a + n^b = n^c$, a and b must be less than c. We thus divide through by a to get $1 + n^{b-a} = n^{c-a}$. Looking at this equation (mod n), we must have $b - a = 0$, since otherwise n^{b-a} and n^{c-a} would both be divisible by n and we would have $0 \equiv 1 \pmod n$. With $b - a = 0$, we get $2 = n^{c-a}$, which forces $n = 2$, $c = a + 1$. The expression $a^n + b^n - c^n$ becomes $a^2 + a^2 - (a+1)^2$, or $a^2 - 2a - 1$. The largest this can be with $a < 11$ is for $a = 10$, which yields $100 - 20 - 1 = \mathbf{79}$.

419. Since $14x^2$ and 7^{1990} are divisible by 7, $15y^2$ must be also. Hence we let $y = 7y_1$ and we have $14x^2 + 15 \cdot 49y_1^2 = 7^{1990}$. Dividing by 7 gives us $2x^2 + 105y_1^2 = 7^{1989}$, so x is divisible by 7 as well. We let $x = 7x_1$ and we find, after dividing by 7, that $14x_1^2 + 15y_1^2 = 7^{1988}$. We can continue like this over and over until we finally come to $14x_i^2 + 15y_i^2 = 7^0 = 1$. This equation clearly has no integer solutions, so the original equation has no integer solutions.

420. Multiplying the equation by 5 and completing the square to get perfect squares, we obtain $(5m - 3n)^2 + 26n^2 = 9925$. Taking the equation (mod 13) to eliminate the $26n^2$, we have $(5m - 3n)^2 \equiv 6 \pmod{13}$. But the squares mod 13 are 0, 1, 4, 9, 3, 12, and 10; since 6 is not a square, there can be no such m and n.

421. The even leg of such a primitive Pythagorean triple is $2rs = 28$, or $rs = 14$. We thus have $r = 7$ and $s = 2$ or $r = 14$ and $s = 1$. In the first case, the hypotenuse is $7^2 + 2^2 = 53$; in the second case, the hypotenuse is $14^2 + 1^2 = 197$. The sum of these two possible values is $\mathbf{250}$.

422. Suppose there are such a and b; then $25a^2 + 30ab + 35b^2 = 5 \cdot 1993$, or $(5a + 3b)^2 + 26b^2 = 5 \cdot 1993$. Clearly $5a + 3b$ is odd, since $26b^2$ is even and $5 \cdot 1993$ is odd. We let $5a + 3b = 2k + 1$, so that $5 \cdot 1993 - 26b^2 = (2k + 1)^2 = 4k^2 + 4k + 1 = 8s + 1$ for some s, yielding $4982 - 13b^2 = 4s$. Since 4982 and $4s$ are both even, then $13b^2$ must be even as well. Since b is thus even, b^2 is divisible by 4. But we now have a contradiction, because $13b^2$ and $4s$ are both divisible by 4 but 4982 is not. Thus there are no such a and b.

423. Any three consecutive numbers are congruent to 0, 1, and 2 (mod 3). Their squares are thus congruent to 0, 1, and 1 (mod 3), so their sum is congruent to 2 (mod 3). But all squares are congruent to 0 or 1 (mod 3), so this sum cannot be a square.

424. Taking the equation (mod D), we have $x^2 \equiv -1 \pmod D$. This only has a solution if -1 is a quadratic residue.

425. Let (x_0, y_0, z_0) be the solution of $x^3 + 3y^3 = 9z^3$ with the smallest z. Since $3y_0^3$ and $9z_0^3$ are both divisible by 3, x_0^3 must also be divisible by 3. Thus we let $x_0 = 3x_1$, so that $27x_1^3 + 3y_0^3 = 9z_0^3$. Since $27x_1^3$ and $9z_0^3$ are both divisible by 9, $3y_0^3$ must be also, so that y_0 is divisible by 3. Letting $y_0 = 3y_1$, we have $27x_1^3 + 81y_1^3 = 9z_0^3$. Since $27x_1^3$ and $81y_1^3$ are divisible by 27, $9z_0^3$ must be also, so that z_0 is divisible by 3. Letting $z_0 = 3z_1$, we have $27x_1^3 + 81y_1^3 = 243z_1^3$. Dividing out a factor of 27, we have $x_1^3 + 3y_1^3 = 9z_1^3$. But this is a solution of the original equation with $z_1 < z_0$, contradicting our assertion that (x_0, y_0, z_0) had the smallest z value. Thus we have a contradiction, so the equation has no solutions.

426. If all three of x, y, and z are odd, then all seven terms of $x^3 + y^3 + z^3 + x^2y + y^2z + z^2x + xyz$ are odd, so the sum itself is odd. Since 0 is even, the equation cannot be satisfied in this case.

If exactly two of x, y and z are odd, then three terms of $x^3 + y^3 + z^3 + x^2y + y^2z + z^2x + xyz$ are odd, so the sum itself is odd. (For example, if x and y are odd then x^3, y^3, and x^2y are odd.) Again, the equation cannot be solved in this case.

If exactly one of x, y, and z is odd, then one term of $x^3 + y^3 + z^3 + x^2y + y^2z + z^2x + xyz$ is odd, so again the sum is odd and the equation has no solution.

Thus the only way the equation can have a solution is if x, y, and z are all even. Letting $x = 2x_1$, $y = 2y_1$, and $z = 2z_1$, the equation becomes

$$8x_1^3 + 8y_1^3 + 8z_1^3 + 8x_1^2y_1 + 8y_1^2z_1 + 8z_1^2x_1 + 8x_1y_1z_1 = 0.$$

Dividing out by 8, we find that (x_1, y_1, z_1) is a solution to the original equation. But this means that x_1, y_1, and z_1 are all even, so that $x_1 = 2x_2$, $y_1 = 2y_2$, and $z_1 = 2z_2$. But then (x_2, y_2, z_2) is a solution, so all these are even, and so on. Since we can find a smaller solution for any given solution, there can be no solution at all.

Chapter 25

Graph Theory

Solutions to Exercises

25-1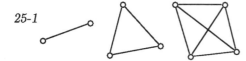

25-2 There are as many edges as there are pairs of vertices, which from combinatorics is $\binom{n}{2} = n(n-1)/2$.

25-3 The vertices comprising the largest clique, of size **3**, have been colored black in the graph at right; the vertices of the largest independent set, size **5**, are squares. (The black square is in both.) Can you prove that there is no bigger independent set in this graph?

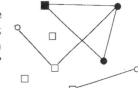

25-4 We have tried at left; however, the last edge cannot be drawn, since it would intersect one of the other edges we drew.

25-5 Some four of the vertices can always be formed into a square. The fifth vertex may be either inside the square or outside it. If the fifth vertex is inside the square, then the two edges connecting opposite vertices of the square must both lie outside the square. This cannot be. Similarly, if the fifth vertex is outside the square, the two edges connecting opposite vertices of the square must both lie inside the square, another impossibility.

25-6 It has **4** faces, where we make sure to count the unbounded face.

25-7 If we add up the degrees of all the faces, we count each edge twice, so that $D = 2E$. Substituting this into $D \geq 3F$, $E \geq 3F/2$ is immediate.

25-8 Some ways to add an edge *look* different, because the edge goes into or through the unbounded face. But these are the same basic ways.

25-9 Just do it.

25-10 If we add up the degrees of all the vertices, we get a total of dV. In doing so, we have counted each edge twice, so that $2E = dV$, or $E = dV/2$.

25-11 Since there are f edges around each face, we can add up the numbers of edges around all the faces to get fF. Since this counts each edge twice, we have $fF = 2E$, or $F = 2E/f$. Substituting in $E = dV/2$ from the previous exercise, we thus have $F = dV/f$, as desired.

25-12 From the inequality $(d-2)(f-2) < 4$, we can write $(d-2)(f-2) = 1$, $(d-2)(f-2) = 2$, or $(d-2)(f-2) = 3$. In the first case, we must have $d-2 = f-2 = 1$, so that $d = f = 3$. In the second case we can have $d-2 = 1$, $f-2 = 2$, so that $d = 3$ and $f = 4$, or $d-2 = 2$, $f-2 = 1$, so that $d = 4$ and $f = 3$. In the last case we can have $d-2 = 1$, $f-2 = 3$, so that $d = 3$ and $f = 5$, or $d-2 = 1$, $f-2 = 3$, so that $d = 5$ and $f = 3$. Thus the five solution pairs are $(\mathbf{3,3})$, $(\mathbf{3,4})$, $(\mathbf{4,3})$, $(\mathbf{3,5})$, and $(\mathbf{5,3})$.

25-13 Looking at the graph, this is fairly clear.

25-14 The pair $(3,3)$ corresponds to the tetrahedron, $(3,4)$ to the cube, $(3,5)$ to the dodecahedron, and $(5,3)$ to the icosahedron, as you can see by counting edges around the faces and edges emerging from the vertices of the corresponding solids. (For pictures of the five Platonic solids, see Volume 1.)

25-15 From left to right below, we have the path $BCADE$, the trail $ABCADE$, which is not a path because it goes through A twice, and the walk $CABCADE$, which is not a trail because it passes through edge CA twice.

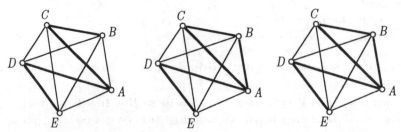

25-16 There are n edges, since we take n steps by walking around the cycle, passing through every edge once.

25-17 There are $n-1$ edges, since each of the n vertices, except the very top one, has one edge above it in the "levels" structure described in the text.

25-18 Try to think about the "why" before you read the explanation in the text.

25-19 Since Q has leftover edges, we can move out from it on an unused edge. Since we have passed through every vertex an even number of times, and every vertex started with even degree, each vertex has an even number of unused edges. Thus the vertex we go to from Q must have an unused edge besides the one we came in on, and similarly for each edge in the trail—if the path ended on a vertex, that vertex would have to have odd degree. (This is exactly the same as our original argument that the path has to end up at its starting point.) Thus the path can always keep going on unused edges until it gets back to Q.

25-20 A graph with exactly two odd degree vertices will always have an Euler trail, and an Euler trail of such a graph will always start and end on the odd-degree vertices. To see that the graph has an Euler trail, imagine an edge between the two odd-degree vertices. Since adding this edge increases the degree of each by 1, their degrees are then even. Since the entire graph is now even-degree, we can use our previous method to draw an Euler trail which starts and ends at the same place. Cutting the added edge back out, we have an Euler trail which starts on one odd-degree vertex and ends on the other.

To see that any Euler trail of the graph must start and end on odd-degree vertices, recall that the unused degree of a vertex goes down by 2 each time we pass through the vertex. Thus if the walk did not start or end on one of the odd-degree vertices, the unused degree of that odd-degree edge would go $2n + 1 \rightarrow 2n - 1 \rightarrow 2n - 3 \rightarrow \cdots \rightarrow 1$, and would never hit 0. Thus some edge connected to that vertex would never be used in the walk.

25-21 Each vertex corresponds to the country it sits in.

25-22 Any two vertices which are connected together must have different colors. Thus if a graph has any edges at all, it has $\chi \geq 2$! The only graphs with $\chi = 1$ are null graphs.

25-23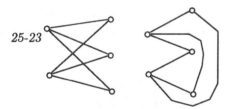

25-24 The normal way is easy. If you try to draw $K_{3,3}$ with no edges crossing, though, you will find it impossible.

25-25 $K_{3,3}$ has $E = 9$ and $V = 6$. Thus $3V - 6 = 10$, so $E \leq 3V - 6$ is indeed satisfied. However, this does NOT mean $K_{3,3}$ is planar. It just passes one test of being planar.

25-26 $K_{s,t}$ has $E = st$ and $V = s + t$. To satisfy $E \leq 2V - 4$, we must thus have $st \leq 2s + 2t - 4$. Rearranging and factoring, this yields $(s - 2)(t - 2) \leq 0$. This inequality is a necessary condition for $K_{s,t}$ to be planar, but it cannot be satisied for $s, t \geq 3$.

25-27 Put the set of t vertices on a line, and put one of the set of 2 vertices on each side of the line. It is clear that all the desired connections can be drawn without crossing, as shown at right.

25-28 Since every face has at least g edges around it, we can count the edges around all the faces to get a total of at least Fg. Since this sum counts every edge twice, we have

$Fg \leq 2E$, or $F \leq 2E/g$. Substituting this into Euler's formula, we have $V - E + 2E/g \geq 2$, or $E \leq (V - 2)/(1 - 2/g)$. (Verify that we get familiar inequalities for $g = 3$ and $g = 4$.)

Solutions to Problems

427. When we add up the degrees of all the vertices, each edge gets counted twice—once for each of its endpoints. Thus the total sum is equal to twice the number of edges.

428. If we add up the degrees of all the vertices, we get a sum Vd, where d is the common degree. This sum counts each edge twice, so $Vd = 2E = 40$. Thus our graph could have 2 vertices of degree 20, 4 vertices of degree 10, and so on. However, the degree of a vertex must be less than the total number of vertices, so the only real possibilities are $V = 40$, $d = 1$; $V = 20$, $d = 2$; $V = 10$, $d = 4$; and $V = 8$, $d = 5$.

Are all these graphs possible? The first is: just divide the 40 vertices into 20 pairs and connect the pairs—then each vertex has degree 1 and there are a total of 20 edges. The second combination is similarly attainable, with a cycle of length 20. How about the third? We can construct a graph with 10 degree-four vertices as at upper right, arranging the points in a circle and connecting every point to its two nearest neighbors and its two next-nearest neighbors. We can construct a graph with 8 degree-five vertices in the same way, except additionally connecting each point to the one directly opposite, as at lower right. Hence all our candidates are possible graphs, and the answers are **40, 20, 10, and 8**.

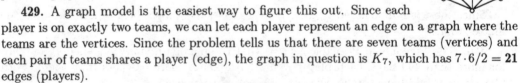

429. A graph model is the easiest way to figure this out. Since each player is on exactly two teams, we can let each player represent an edge on a graph where the teams are the vertices. Since the problem tells us that there are seven teams (vertices) and each pair of teams shares a player (edge), the graph in question is K_7, which has $7 \cdot 6/2 = \mathbf{21}$ edges (players).

430. To get the most edges out of the fewest vertices, we let our graph be K_n for some n. It then has $n(n - 1)/2$ vertices. Since $10(9)/2 = 45$ and $11(10)/2 = 55$, our smallest graph has **11** vertices. (How close does our graph come to being K_{11}?)

431. Here we cannot take K_n, because K_n is not planar for $n \geq 5$. Recalling the restriction that $E \leq 3V - 6$ for planar graphs, we find $V \geq 56/3$, so the smallest possible V is 19. This is only a candidate, though; we need to show that a planar graph with 19 vertices and 50 edges exists. Experimentation shows that it does, so we're done. (Can you draw such a graph?)

432.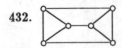

433. Let's assume, for the sake of contradiction, that all V vertices of some planar graph have degree ≥ 6. The sum of the degrees of all the vertices is equal to $2E$, as we have seen repeatedly, so $2E \geq 6V$, or $E \geq 3V$. But we know that in any planar graph, $E \leq 3V - 6$, so we get $3V \leq 3V - 6$, a contradiction.

434. This looks like a job for Euler's formula. Since the sum of the degrees of the vertices is $4V$, we have $E = 2V$. Then Euler's formula gives $V - E + F = V - 2V + 10 = 2$, so $V = 8$. Find a generalization to the case of V vertices, each with degree k, and F faces.

435. Without loss of generality, suppose segment BC is red. We consider three cases.

Case I: At least three of the edges BA_i are red. Let three red edges be BA_r, BA_s, and BA_t. At least one of the sides of the triangle $A_r A_s A_t$, say $A_s A_t$, is a diagonal of the base, so is colored. If $A_s A_t$ is red, then triangle $BA_s A_t$ is all red. Moreover, if CA_s or CA_t is red, then triangle BCA_s or BCA_t is all red. Thus all of $A_s A_t$, CA_s and CA_t must be blue to avoid an all-red triangle; but this makes $CA_s A_t$ and all-blue triangle. Thus we must always have a unicolored triangle in this case.

Case II: Exactly two of the edges BA_i are red. Let the two edges be A_s and A_t, and consider two subcases. If $A_s A_t$ is a diagonal of the base, then we can reason exactly as in Case I above. Otherwise, we can without loss of generality suppose that $s = 1$ and $t = 2$, which means that BA_i is blue for $i \neq 1, 2$. Consider the three base vertices A_3, A_5, and A_7. Since BA_3, BA_5, and BA_7 are all blue, the diagonals $A_3 A_5$, $A_5 A_7$, and $A_7 A_3$ must all be red to avoid an all-blue triangle with B. But these edges all being red forces the all-red triangle $A_3 A_5 A_7$. Thus we must always have a unicolored triangle in this case.

Case III: Exactly one edge BA_i is red. Let the red edge be BA_1, so that BA_i is blue for all $i \neq 1$. We can repeat the argument of Case II on A_3, A_5, and A_7 to show that there is always a unicolored triangle in this case.

Since there is a unicolored triangle in every case, there must be a unicolored triangle no matter what.

436. The Pigeonhole Principle tells us that the maximum answer is 499. If we played for more than 499 days, each player would have 500 or more partners from the 499 other players, so would have to play with some other player twice.

The tough part is to show that a 499 day tournament is possible. To do this, we arrange 499 of the players around a circle with one player at the center. We can choose any player on the circumference to play with the central player, then pair up the other players using lines perpendicular to the line connecting this first pair. (The procedure is shown as right using 10 players instead of 500.) By rotating the resulting figure, we can get 499 different pairings so that no player 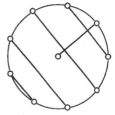 plays with the same other player twice. Since we have shown that we can get 499, and that nothing greater than 499 is possible, **499** is the answer.

Chapter 26

Parting Shots

Solutions to Problems

437. Rewriting and factoring, we have

$$(\ln x)^3 - \ln x^4 = (\ln x)^3 - 4\ln x = (\ln x)(\ln x - 2)(\ln x + 2) = 0.$$

Hence $\ln x = 0$, $\ln x = 2$, or $\ln x = -2$ and the solutions are $\mathbf{1}$, $\mathbf{e^2}$, and $\mathbf{1/e^2}$.

438. A function has a well defined inverse if there is one and only one element x for which $f(x) = y$ for all y. This means that our function must assign a different element of A to each element of A. Let $A = \{a_1, \ldots, a_{13}\}$. If all the $f(a_i)$ are to be distinct, so there are 13 choices for $f(a_1)$, leaving 12 choices for $f(a_2)$, then 11 for $f(a_3)$, and so on, for a total of 13! different functions with a well-defined inverse. Since in defining a function from A to A we have 13 choices for each $f(a_i)$, there are 13^{13} functions from A to A and our desired fraction is $13!/13^{13} = \mathbf{12!/13^{12}}$.

439. Let there be s steers and c cows. Thus, $25s + 26c = 1000$. Since $26c = 1000 - 25s = 25(40 - s)$ and s and c are integers, c must be divisible by 25. Since $c > 1$ and $c < 50$ (since $(26)(50) > 1000$), $c = \mathbf{25}$.

440. Since $\ln b - \ln a = 1$, $\ln b/a = 1$, so $b/a = e$. Similarly, we can show $d = ec = e^2b = e^3a$, so a, b, c, d is a geometric sequence with ratio e.

441. Since $3x^2 + 9x + 17 = (3x^2 + 9x + 7) + 10$, our given expression is equal to

$$1 + \frac{10}{3x^2 + 9x + 7}.$$

To maximize this, we must minimize the denominator of the second term. Completing the square of the denominator yields $3x^2 + 9x + 7 = 3(x + 3/2)^2 + 1/4$. The minimum value of this is clearly $1/4$ (when $x = -3/2$). Thus, the maximum value of our given expression is $1 + 10/(1/4) = $ **41**.

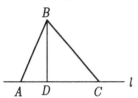

442. The figure formed upon rotation is a pair of cones joined at the base. If we draw altitude BD of the triangle, we see that in the solid formed by rotation, BD is the radius of the cones. Segment DC is the altitude of the right hand cone and AD is the altitude of the left cone. Thus, our problem is now finding BD, AD, and DC. We find the altitude by determining $[ABC]$ in two ways, as $(AC)(BD)/2$ and by using Heron's formula. Heron yields $[ABC] = 84$ and from this we find $BD = 12$. Since $AB = 13$ and $BC = 15$, $AD = 5$ and $DC = 9$. Hence, our desired volume is

$$\frac{(12^2)(5)\pi}{3} + \frac{(12^2)(9)\pi}{3} = \mathbf{672\pi}.$$

443. Shown is the case where $n = 4$. We see that the $2n$ radii divide the circle into $2n$ regions. As shown in our diagram, we can always draw a secant that passes through $n + 1$ of these regions, cutting each of them into two regions and thus forming $n + 1$ new regions in addition to the original $2n$. Our answer therefore is $\mathbf{3n+1}$.

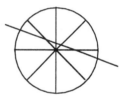

444. Writing

$$f(n+1) = \frac{5 + 3\sqrt{5}}{10}\left(\frac{1 + \sqrt{5}}{2}\right)^{n+1} + \frac{5 - 3\sqrt{5}}{10}\left(\frac{1 - \sqrt{5}}{2}\right)^{n+1}$$

$$f(n-1) = \frac{5 + 3\sqrt{5}}{10}\left(\frac{1 + \sqrt{5}}{2}\right)^{n-1} + \frac{5 - 3\sqrt{5}}{10}\left(\frac{1 - \sqrt{5}}{2}\right)^{n-1},$$

we have

$$\left(\frac{5 + 3\sqrt{5}}{10}\right)\left(\left(\frac{1 + \sqrt{5}}{2}\right)^2 - 1\right)\left(\frac{1 + \sqrt{5}}{2}\right)^{n-1} +$$

$$\left(\frac{5 - 3\sqrt{5}}{10}\right)\left(\left(\frac{1 - \sqrt{5}}{2}\right)^2 - 1\right)\left(\frac{1 - \sqrt{5}}{2}\right)^{n-1}$$

as the desired expression. Evaluating the inner term in each of the above products, we find that $f(n+1) - f(n-1) = f(n)$.

445. If we write the point (x, y) in polar coordinates, s and c are $\sin\theta$ and $\cos\theta$, respectively. Since $\sin^2\theta - \cos^2\theta = \cos 2\theta$, $s^2 - c^2$ can range from -1 to 1, inclusive, or $-1 \le s^2 - c^2 \le 1$.

446. Writing the number with just twos and threes as bases it is $2^6 3^6 + 2^{12} + 3^{12}$. This problem gets a bit tricky; recall from Volume 1 that $x^2 + xy + y^2 = (x+y)^2 - xy$. Let's try this here, with $x = 2^6$ and $y = 3^6$:

$$
\begin{aligned}
2^{12} + 2^6 3^6 + 3^{12} &= 2^{12} + 2(2^6 3^6) + 3^{12} - 2^6 3^6 \\
&= \left(2^6 + 3^6\right)^2 - 2^6 3^6 \\
&= \left(2^6 + 3^6\right)^2 - \left(2^3 3^3\right)^2 \\
&= \left(2^6 + 2^3 3^3 + 3^6\right)\left(2^6 - 2^3 3^3 + 3^6\right)
\end{aligned}
$$

Thus, our numbers are **1009** and **577**.

447. Squaring the second quantity and multiplying by the first, we have

$$
z^3 = \left(\frac{x^2}{y^2}\right)\left(\frac{8y}{x}\right)^2 = 64.
$$

Thus, the possible values of z are the cube roots of 64, which, by DeMoivre's Theorem, are **4, $-2 + 2i\sqrt{3}$**, and **$-2 - 2i\sqrt{3}$**.

448. Note that $z(1 + x + xy) = z + xz + xyz = 1 + z + xz$. Similarly, we note that we can get a common denominator of the three fractions by multiplying the first term top and bottom by z and the second term top and bottom by xz, yielding:

$$
\frac{z}{z + xz + 1} + \frac{xz}{xz + 1 + z} + \frac{1}{1 + z + zx} = 1.
$$

449. First we write each of P, S, and S' in closed form:

$$
P = a(ar)(ar^2)\cdots(ar^{n-1}) = a^n r^{(n-1)(n)/2},
$$

$$
S = a + ar + ar^2 + \cdots + ar^{n-1} = \frac{a - ar^n}{1 - r} = a\frac{1 - r^n}{1 - r}, \text{ and}
$$

$$
S' = \frac{1}{a} + \frac{1}{ar} + \frac{1}{ar^2} + \cdots + \frac{1}{ar^{n-1}} = \left(\frac{1}{a}\right)\frac{1 - r^{-n}}{1 - r^{-1}} = \left(\frac{1}{ar^{n-1}}\right)\frac{1 - r^n}{1 - r},
$$

where in evaluating S' we have noted that it is a geometric series with first term $1/a$ and ratio r^{-1}. Thus the quotient S/S' (which gets rid of the $(1 - r^n)/(1 - r)$ term) is $a^2 r^{n-1}$. Comparing this to our expression for P, we see that

$$
(S/S')^{n/2} = (a^2 r^{n-1})^{n/2} = a^n r^{n(n-1)/2} = P.
$$

450. Since $\cos(180° + x) = \cos 180° \cos x - \sin 180° \sin x = -\cos x$, we see that $\cos 45° = i^2 \cos 225° = i^4 \cos 315° = \cdots = i^{40} \cos 3645°$. Similarly, we can show that the second, fourth, etc. terms are the same. Hence, our sum becomes $21 \cos 45° + 20i \cos 135° =$ **$21\sqrt{2}/2 - 10i\sqrt{2}$**.

451. The expression $\sqrt{x^2 + y^2}$ is the distance of the point (x, y) from the origin. The point on the line $5x + 12y = 60$ which minimizes this quantity is the closest point on the line to the origin, and the desired minimum is the distance of this line from the origin, or $|5(0) + 12(0) - 60|/\sqrt{5^2 + 12^2} = $ **$60/13$**.

452. The center of the circle is on the side shared by the two bottom squares (by the symmetry of the figure). Let the distance OC be x. By the Pythagorean Theorem,

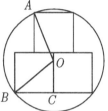

$$\sqrt{x^2 + 1^2} = OB = OA = \sqrt{(2 - x)^2 + (1/2)^2},$$

where the final expression comes from considering the vertical and horizontal distances between O and A. Equating these expressions for x, we find $x = 13/16$. Using the above expression to find OB, our desired radius is **$5\sqrt{17}/16$**.

453. When omitting one number between 1 and n inclusive, the highest average that could occur happens when 1 is the number erased, leaving $n - 1$ numbers with an average of $(n - 1)(n + 2)/2(n - 1) = (n + 2)/2$ (since the $n - 1$ numbers form an arithmetic sequence). Similarly, the lowest average occurs when n is erased, leaving $n - 1$ integers with an average of $n(n - 1)/2(n - 1) = n/2$. Since 18.8 must fall between these values, we have $n/2 \leq 18.8 \leq (n + 2)/2$, or

$$n \leq 37.6 \leq n + 2.$$

For this to be true, n must be 36 or 37. Since the average of the $n - 1$ remaining numbers is 18.8, n cannot be 37, since division by $37 - 1 = 36$ cannot yield a decimal of .8. Hence, there were 36 numbers originally. The sum of these was $36(37)/2 = 666$. Let the number omitted be x. From the given information, $(666 - x)/35 = 18.8$ and we find $x = $ **8**.

454. From the second equation, we have $c(a + b) = 23$. Since 23 is prime, either $c = 23$ and $(a + b) = 1$ or $c = 1$ and $(a + b) = 23$. The former case is impossible since a and b are positive integers, so $c = 1$ and $a + b = 23$. Using this in the first equation, we have $ab + b = 44$. Substituting $a = 23 - b$ for a, we find $b^2 - 24b + 44 = 0$. Thus, $b = 2$ or $b = 22$, which give the solutions $(21, 2, 1)$ and $(1, 22, 1)$. There are **2** solutions.

455. Letting N be the initial population, we have

$$N = x^2 \quad N + 100 = y^2 + 1 \quad N + 200 = z^2.$$

Subtracting the first two equations, we find $(y - x)(y + x) = 99$. Since $y > x$ and both are positive integers, we have the following possibilites:

$$y - x = 1 \text{ and } y + x = 99 \qquad y - x = 3 \text{ and } y + x = 33$$

$$y - x = 9 \text{ and } y + x = 11.$$

From these, our possibilities for (x,y) are $(49,50)$, $(15,18)$, and $(1,10)$. For the last two of these, $x^2 + 200$ is not a perfect square, so these cases must be eliminated. The first case checks out, as $49^2 + 200 = 51^2$. Hence, $N = 49^2 = \mathbf{2401}$.

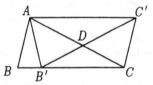

456. Since $AB = AB'$, $\angle ABB' = \angle AB'B$ and by AA similarity, $\triangle BAB' \sim \triangle ACB$. Since $\angle C'AB' = \angle CAB$, we have $\angle CAC' = \angle BAB' = \angle ACB$. Thus, by SAS congruency we have $\triangle CAC' \cong \triangle ACB \cong \triangle AC'B'$. From these congruencies, $AC' = BC$ and $AB = CC'$, so $ABCC'$ is a parallelogram (part ii). Since $AC' \parallel BC$, $\angle CB'C' = \angle B'C'A = \angle ACB$, so $\triangle B'DC$ is isosceles (part i). Since $AC = AC'$ and $\triangle ADC' \sim \triangle B'DC$, $DB'/CB' = AD/AC' = AD/AC$ (part iii). Since $\angle C'B'C = \angle ACB' = \angle CAC'$, $AC'CB'$ is a cyclic quadrilateral (part iv). Finally, since $\triangle BAB' \sim \triangle ACB$, $AB/BB' = BC/AB$ so that $AB^2 = (BB')(BC)$. By the converse of the Power of a Point Theorem, this means that AB is tangent to the circumcircle of $AB'CC'$ (part v).

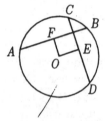

457. Let the chords be $AB = 8$ and $CD = 7$ and their midpoints be F and E, respectively. The perpendicular bisector of any chord passes through the center of the circle, so the center of the circle is intersection of the perpendicular bisectors of the chords. Let the chords intersect at X (not labelled). Hence $OE = AB/2 - XB = 2$ and $CE = CD/2 = 7/2$. From the Pythagorean Theorem, $OC = \sqrt{OE^2 + CE^2} = \sqrt{65}/2$. Hence, the diameter is $\sqrt{\mathbf{65}}$.

458. First we must show that in any group of 4 points, no three of which are collinear and no three of which form a right triangle, there is some group of three points which forms an obtuse triangle. This is a simple exercise in contradiction. If the four points form a convex quadrilateral and all its angles are acute, then the sum of the angles would be less than $360°$, a contradiction. If the points form a concave quadrilateral (i.e. three points form a triangle containing the fourth), the three angles formed at the interior point when connected to the vertices of the triangle must add to $360°$. If all three of these are acute, the sum will be less than $270°$.

Now we can move on. Each obtuse triangle which can be formed among the n points is contained in $n-3$ groups of 4 of the n points (since we can choose any of $n-3$ other points to include with the three triangle vertices). Thus, if there are T obtuse triangles, then there are at most $T(n-3)$ groups of four points which contain obtuse triangles. If less than $1/4$ of the triangles formed among the n points are obtuse, then $T < (1/4)\binom{n}{3}$. Hence,

$$T(n-3) < \frac{n(n-1)(n-2)(n-3)}{1(2)(3)(4)} = \binom{n}{4}.$$

Thus, the maximum possible number of groups of four points which contain an obtuse triangle is less than the total number of groups of 4 points. This means there is some group of 4 points among the n for which we cannot form an obtuse triangle by connecting any 3 of the 4 vertices. This is a contradiction to our initial proved assertion, so our assumption that less than $1/4$ of the triangles formed by choosing 3 of the n points are obtuse must be false. Our proof is complete.

459. Starting from $(0,0)$, every time the line passes through either a vertical line, $x = n$ for some integer n, or a horizontal line, $y = m$ for some integer m, it passes into a new square. Since it crosses 118 vertical lines ($x = 1$ through $x = 118$) and 152 horizontal ones, we have $118 + 152 = 270$. In this count, we have not included the unit square with $(0,0)$ as its lower left vertex, so this gives us 271. Unfortunately, we are still not right because every time the line passes through a lattice point, it enters a new square, but we have counted it as passing through two new squares, one for the horizontal and one for the vertical line. Hence, by the Principle of Inclusion-Exclusion, we subtract the number of lattice points (besides the initial and final points) through which the line passes. The given line is described by $119y = 153x$, or $7y = 9x$. Hence, we have one lattice point on the line for each x that is a multiple of 7. Since there are 16 positive multiples of 7 less than 119, the line passes through 16 lattice points besides the endpoints. Finally, our total number of lattice squares is $271 - 16 = \mathbf{255}$.

460. Since at $x = 0$ we have $0 f(-1) = -3P(0)$, $x = 0$ is a root of $P(x)$. At $x = 3$, we find that $3P(2) = 0$, so $x = 2$ is a root of $P(x)$ as well. Using $x = 2$ in the given equation gives $2P(1) = -P(2) = 0$, so $x = 1$ is a root. Putting this together, we find $P(x) = \boldsymbol{x(x-1)(x-2)}$, which does satisfy the restrictions of the problem.

461. If a fraction is reducible, so is its reciprocal. Using long division on $(5n+6)/(n-13)$ as in our chapter on polynomials, we find

$$\frac{5n + 6}{n - 13} = 5 + \frac{71}{n - 13}.$$

Hence $(5n + 6)/(n - 13)$ is reducible if and only if $71/(n - 13)$ is. (Make sure you see why.) Since 71 is prime, the smallest n for which $71/(n - 13)$ can be reduced is $n = \mathbf{84}$.

462. Since $(x^3 + 1/x^3)^2 = x^6 + 1/x^6 + 2$, we can factor the numerator as a difference of squares:

$$
\begin{aligned}
f(x) &= \frac{\left(x + \frac{1}{x}\right)^6 - \left(x^6 + \frac{1}{x^6}\right) - 2}{\left(x + \frac{1}{x}\right)^3 + \left(x^3 + \frac{1}{x^3}\right)} \\[2mm]
&= \frac{\left[\left(x + \frac{1}{x}\right)^3\right]^2 - \left(x^3 + \frac{1}{x^3}\right)^2}{\left(x + \frac{1}{x}\right)^3 + \left(x^3 + \frac{1}{x^3}\right)} \\[2mm]
&= \frac{\left[\left(x + \frac{1}{x}\right)^3 - \left(x^3 + \frac{1}{x^3}\right)\right]\left[\left(x + \frac{1}{x}\right)^3 + \left(x^3 + \frac{1}{x^3}\right)\right]}{\left(x + \frac{1}{x}\right)^3 + \left(x^3 + \frac{1}{x^3}\right)} \\[2mm]
&= \left(x + \frac{1}{x}\right)^3 - \left(x^3 + \frac{1}{x^3}\right)
\end{aligned}
$$

$$= 3\left(x + \frac{1}{x}\right).$$

From AM-GM, we have $x + \frac{1}{x} \geq 2$, so that the minimum value of $f(x)$ is **6**.

463. The sum of the smallest three sides of a quadrilateral must be greater than the fourth side, so that $F_a + F_b + F_c > F_d$. If $c < d-1$, then $F_b + F_c \leq F_{d-1}$, so $F_a + F_b + F_c \leq F_a + F_{d-1} \leq F_d$. Hence $c = d-1$. Similarly, we can show that $b = d-2$. Hence, $d - b$ must be **2**.

464. As suggested in the chapter on trigonometry, square both equations, yielding

$$\sin^2 A + \sin^2 B + 2\sin A \sin B = 1/9$$
$$\cos^2 A + \cos^2 B + 2\cos A \cos B = 16/9.$$

Adding these and noting that $\cos^2 x + \sin^2 x = 1$ gives

$$2 + 2(\sin A \sin B + \cos A \cos B) = 2 + 2\cos(A - B) = 17/9,$$

so that $\cos(A - B) = -1/18$.

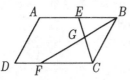

465. First, $[ABC] = [ABCD]/2 = 126$. Since $\triangle ABC$ and $\triangle EBC$ share an altitude, $[EBC]/[ABC] = EB/AB$, so $[EBC] = 126/2 = 63$. Similarly, we find $[FBC] = (2/3)(126) = 84$. Since $AB \parallel CD$, we have $\triangle EBG \sim \triangle CFG$. Since $EB/AB = 1/2$ and $FC/CD = 2/3$, we find $(EB/AB)(CD/FC) = EB/FC = 3/4$. From our similar triangles, $GC/EG = 4/3$, so $GC/EC = 4/7$. Thus, $[GBC] = (4/7)[EBC] = 36$. Now we can find $[EGFCB]$:

$$[EGFCB] = [EGB] + [BFC] = [EBC] - [BGC] + [BFC] = 63 - 36 + 84 = 111.$$

Finally, $[AEGFD] = [ABCD] - [EGFCB] = $ **141**.

466. Lots of equal angles means lots of similar triangles. Namely, we determine that $\triangle ADM \sim \triangle ACD$ and $\triangle BCM \sim \triangle ACB$. Hence, $AD/AC = AM/AD$, $BC/CM = CA/BC$, and

$$AD^2 + BC^2 = (AM)(AC) + (MC)(AC) = (AM + MC)(AC) = AC^2,$$

completing our proof, since AD, BC, and AC satisfy the Pythagorean Theorem.

467. We can prove a number is not a complete square by proving that it is always between a pair of consecutive perfect squares. The given quadratic suggests placing the number between $(n-10)^2$ and $(n-9)^2$. Since $(n-9)^2 - (n^2 - 19n + 89) = n - 8$, $(n-9)^2 > n^2 - 19n + 89$ for all $n > 8$. Similarly, $(n - 10)^2 < n^2 - 19n + 89$ if and only if $n > 11$. Thus, for all $n > 11$, $(n - 9)^2 > n^2 - 19n + 89 > (n - 10)^2$, showing that the expression cannot be a perfect square since it is always between two consecutive squares.

468. Through the two parts we are proving that for any square set we can make a new set by adding a certain element or by replacing one of the elements with a certain new element. The proofs that follow are largely algebraic and a good exercise in manipulation. Let x^2 be the sum of the products of all pairs in the set and s be the sum of the elements of the set so that $b = s + 2x$. For the new set $\{a_1, a_2, \ldots, a_n, b\}$, we have

$$
\begin{aligned}
a_1 a_2 + a_1 a_3 + \cdots + a_{n-1} a_n + b(a_1 + a_2 + \cdots + a_n) &= x^2 + b(s) \\
&= x^2 + (s + 2x)(s) = (x + s)^2,
\end{aligned}
$$

so that the new set is a square set. For the second part, suppose a_i is the element replaced by b. Now in our sum of products of pairs of a's, we must remove all the terms involving a_i. We can write this as

$$
a_1 a_2 + a_1 a_3 + \cdots + a_{n-1} a_n - a_i(s - a_i),
$$

where the last term 'erases' the a_i terms from the sum. Hence our sum of the products of pairs in the new set is

$$
\begin{aligned}
a_1 a_2 + \cdots + a_{n-1} a_n - a_i(s - a_i) + b(a_1 + \cdots + a_n) - ba_i &= x^2 - a_i(s - a_i) + b(s - a_i) \\
&= x^2 + (b - a_i)(s - a_i) \\
&= x^2 + (s + 2x - a_i)(s - a_i) \\
&= x^2 + 2x(s - a_i) + (s - a_i)^2 \\
&= (x + s - a_i)^2.
\end{aligned}
$$

Thus the new set is a square set as well.

469. Since $(e^{ai})^7 = e^{7ai} = \cos 7a + i \sin 7a$, we have

$$
(\cos a + i \sin a)^7 = \cos 7a + i \sin 7a.
$$

To find $\cos 7a$ in terms of $\cos a$, we equate the real parts of the equation above:

$$
\cos 7a = \cos^7 a + \binom{7}{2} i^2 \cos^5 a \sin^2 a + \cdots + \binom{7}{6} i^6 \cos a \sin^6 a.
$$

We can convert the right hand side to a polynomial in $\cos a$ by noting $\sin^2 a = 1 - \cos^2 a$. Letting $x = \cos a$ we have the polynomial desired in the problem. Looking at the polynomial above, it is clear that we will only have odd powers of $\cos a$, so that the coefficient of $\cos^2 a$, or x^2 in terms of the problem, is **0**.

470. Clearly there are $\binom{13}{3}$ sets of three numbers we can choose. Let's look at the chosen numbers mod 4. The sum of the three integers is divisible by four if the resulting set (after evaluating each number mod 4) is congruent to $\{0, 0, 0\}$, $\{0, 2, 2\}$, $\{0, 1, 3\}$, $\{1, 1, 2\}$, or $\{2, 3, 3\}$. These can be done in respectively $\binom{3}{3}$, $3 \cdot \binom{3}{2}$, $3(4)(3)$, $\binom{4}{2} \cdot 3$, and $3 \cdot \binom{3}{2}$ ways. Thus, our probability is

$$\frac{1 + 9 + 36 + 18 + 9}{\frac{13 \cdot 12 \cdot 11}{3 \cdot 2 \cdot 1}} = \frac{73}{286}.$$

471. Expanding the given equation, we have

$$x^2 + 2xy\sqrt{2} + 2y^2 + z^2 + 2zt\sqrt{2} + 2t^2 = 5 + 4\sqrt{2}.$$

Just like when dealing with imaginary numbers, the rational part of the left equals that on the right and the irrational part on the left equals that on the right. Hence, we can change the sign of the irrational parts and equality still holds (just like taking the conjugate of a complex number). Thus, we can write

$$x^2 - 2xy\sqrt{2} + 2y^2 + z^2 - 2zt\sqrt{2} + 2t^2 = 5 - 4\sqrt{2},$$

from which we have

$$(x - y\sqrt{2})^2 + (z - t\sqrt{2})^2 = 5 - 4\sqrt{2}.$$

Since $(5^2) < (4\sqrt{2})^2$, the number on the right is negative and thus cannot be the sum of squares of real numbers. Hence, the initial equation has no rational solutions.

472. We are given

$$F_1 = \frac{3}{R_1} + \frac{7}{R_1^2} + \frac{3}{R_1^3} + \frac{7}{R_1^4} + \cdots, \text{ and}$$

$$F_2 = \frac{7}{R_1} + \frac{3}{R_1^2} + \frac{7}{R_1^3} + \frac{3}{R_1^4} + \cdots.$$

Finding the sum and difference of these, we find

$$F_1 + F_2 = 10 \left(\frac{1}{R_1} + \frac{1}{R_1^2} + \frac{1}{R_1^3} + \cdots \right) \text{ and}$$

$$F_2 - F_1 = 4 \left(\frac{1}{R_1} - \frac{1}{R_1^2} + \frac{1}{R_1^3} - \frac{1}{R_1^4} + \cdots \right).$$

Doing the same with base R_2, we find

$$F_1 + F_2 = 7 \left(\frac{1}{R_2} + \frac{1}{R_2^2} + \frac{1}{R_2^3} + \cdots \right) \text{ and}$$

$$F_2 - F_1 = 3 \left(\frac{1}{R_2} - \frac{1}{R_2^2} + \frac{1}{R_2^3} - \frac{1}{R_2^4} + \cdots \right)$$

We can set the two expressions for $F_1 + F_2$ and $F_2 - F_1$ equal and evaluate the series as geometric series, yielding

$$F_1 + F_2 = \frac{10}{R_1 - 1} = \frac{7}{R_2 - 1} \text{ and}$$

$$F_2 - F_1 = \frac{4}{R_1 + 1} = \frac{3}{R_2 + 1}.$$

Hence, we have two linear equations in R_1 and R_2. Solving this system for (R_1, R_2), we find $(R_1, R_2) = (11, 8)$ and our desired sum is **19**.

473. Draw the incircle and label the equal tangents as shown. Now we can find the area of the triangle in two ways, with Heron's formula and as rs. Hence, $rs = 4(14 + x) = \sqrt{(14 + x)(6)(8)(x)}$ (since the tangent lengths x, 8, and 6 are $s - a$, $s - b$, and $s - c$). Dividing each side by $4\sqrt{14 + x}$ gives $\sqrt{14 + x} = \sqrt{3x}$. Hence, $x = 7$ and the sides of the triangle have lengths 13, 14, and 15. The shortest is obviously **13**.

474. From Heron's formula, the area of $\triangle ABC$ is $4\sqrt{5}$. We find XY by finding the area of $\triangle AXC$ in two ways. First, from the Angle Bisector Theorem, $XC/BX = AC/AB = 6/3 = 2$, so $[AXC]/[ABC] = XC/BC = 2/3$. Hence, $[AXC] = 8\sqrt{5}/3$. Since $[AXC] = (AC)(XY)/2$, we solve for XY and find $XY = \mathbf{8\sqrt{5}/9}$.

475. Any number whose digits are all the same is the product of a single digit and a number consisting only of ones, i.e. we can write the number as $k(11\cdots11)$. Either $k = 7$ and $11\cdots11$ is a multiple of 7 or $11\cdots11$ is a multiple of 49. From direct checking we can find that the lowest number consisting only of ones which is also a multiple of 7 is 111111. Unfortunately, this is not also a multiple of 49, so we must multiply by 7 to get a multiple of 49. Our desired number is **777777**.

476. For any integer n which is not a multiple of 3, make the list n, $3n$, $9n$, etc. Clearly we make our maximal subset by including n and every other member of each list (since no member of one list can be three times a member of a different list). Thus, our maximal subset contains all numbers which are not multiples of 3, all multiples of 9 which are not multiples of 27, and the number 81, for a total of $(100 - 33) + (11 - 3) + 1 = 67 + 8 + 1 = \mathbf{76}$.

477. First we attack $n = 1$. We factor the resulting polynomial in x:

$$\begin{aligned} y^2 &= x(x^{1991} - x^{1989} + x^2 - 1) = x(x - 1)(x^{1990} + x^{1989} + x + 1) \\ &= x(x - 1)(x + 1)(x^{1989} + 1) = x(x - 1)(x + 1)^2(x^{1988} - x^{1987} + x^{1986} - \cdots + 1). \end{aligned}$$

Since $(x + 1)^2$ is a perfect square, the remaining product, $x(x - 1)(x^{1988} - \cdots + 1)$ is a perfect square. Now we compare the three terms of this product. The last two terms differ by 1 from a multiple of x and therefore cannot share any factors with x. Similarly, the final two factors do not share any factors. Thus, the three factors are relatively prime numbers whose product is a perfect square and as such each factor must be a perfect square. Since x and $x - 1$ can both be perfect squares only if $x = 1$, the only solution to the equation is $(x, y) = (1, 0)$. Since we want solutions in positive integers, we discard this and move on to $n = 2$.

Again we factor, getting $x(x^{1991} - x^{1989} + 3x^2 - 1) = y^2$. And again, our factors are relatively prime, so we must have $x^{1991} - x^{1989} + 3x^2 - 1 = z^2$ for some integer z. Attacking this mod 3 to eliminate the $3x^2$ term, we find

$$x^{1991} - x^{1989} \equiv z^2 + 1 \quad (\text{mod } 3).$$

Since $x^{1991} - x^{1989} = x^{1989}(x^2 - 1)$, we see that $x^{1991} - x^{1989}$ is congruent to 0 mod 3 (try $x \equiv 0, 1, 2 \ (\text{mod } 3)$). However, $z^2 + 1$ can never be conruent to 0 mod 3 since no square is congruent to 2 mod 3. Thus, the equation has no solutions in positive integers for $n = 2$.

478. Let the greater part have length 1 so that the lesser part has length R. Thus, we have

$$\frac{R}{1} = \frac{1}{R + 1},$$

so that $R^2 + R = 1$. Returning to the desired expression, we want to find $R^2 + R^{-1}$. From above we find $R^{-1} = R + 1$, so that $0 = R^2 + R - 1 = R^2 + R^{-1} - 2$. Thus, we have $R^2 + R^{-1} = 2$. Using this repeatedly, we find

$$R^{\left[R^{(R^2 + R^{-1})} + R^{-1}\right]} + R^{-1} = R^{(R^2 + R^{-1})} + R^{-1} = R^2 + R^{-1} = \mathbf{2}.$$

479. Let point M be some point on the extension of AB past B. We will prove that $A_1 B_1$ and $B_1 C_1$ are the bisectors of $\angle BB_1 C$ and $\angle BB_1 A$. Since BB_1 bisects $\angle ABC$, we have

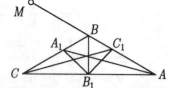

$$\angle MBA_1 = \angle A_1 BB_1 = \angle B_1 BA = 60°.$$

Since a point on the angle bisector of an angle is equidistant from the sides of the angle, we find that A_1 is equidistant from AM and BB_1 (since BA_1 bisects $\angle MBB_1$) and also equidistant from AB and AC (from angle bisector AA_1). Hence, A_1 is equidistant from BB_1 and AC, from which we deduce that $B_1 A_1$ bisects $\angle BB_1 C$. Similarly, we can show that $B_1 C_1$ bisects $\angle BB_1 A$. Finally,

$$\angle A_1 B_1 C_1 = \angle A_1 B_1 B + \angle BB_1 C_1 = \frac{\angle CB_1 B + \angle AB_1 B}{2} = 90°.$$

480. We can draw a simple one-to-one correspondence between the numbers in base three which have no 2's and numbers written in base two. In other words, we can interpret each base three number with no 2's as a base two number. Clearly for each base two number there is exactly one corresponding base three number with no 2's. Hence our task is to find the largest base three number less than or equal to 1992 which has no 2's, then interpret that as a base two number. Since $1992_{10} = 2201122_3$, the largest number in base three less than 1992_{10} which contains no 2's is 1111111_3. Evaluating this in base two, we have $1111111_2 = 127$. For all base two numbers less than this there is exactly one corresponding base three number with no 2's. Thus, as we discussed above, there must be **127** base three numbers from 1 to 1992 with no 2's.

481. Seeing products of cosines, we think of all of our trigonometric identities involving products. We also note that many of the angles in the product are twice those of other angles in the product. Hence, we come to the identity $\sin 2x = 2 \sin x \cos x$, but with no sines, this doesn't look helpful; however, we can always put one in. Let the product be P. Hence, we have (notice that we'll use $\cos(180° - x) = -\cos x$ and $\sin(180° - x) = \sin x$ among our manipulations to use acute angles as much as possible)

$$
\begin{aligned}
P \sin \frac{\pi}{7} &= \sin \frac{\pi}{7} \cos \frac{\pi}{7} \cos \frac{2\pi}{7} \cos \frac{3\pi}{7} \cos \frac{4\pi}{7} \cos \frac{5\pi}{7} \cos \frac{6\pi}{7} \\
&= \frac{1}{2} \sin \frac{2\pi}{7} \cos \frac{2\pi}{7} \cos \frac{3\pi}{7} \cos \frac{4\pi}{7} \cos \frac{5\pi}{7} \cos \frac{6\pi}{7} \\
&= -\frac{1}{4} \sin \frac{4\pi}{7} \cos \frac{3\pi}{7} \cos \frac{3\pi}{7} \cos \frac{2\pi}{7} \cos \frac{\pi}{7} \\
&= -\frac{1}{4} \sin \frac{3\pi}{7} \cos \frac{3\pi}{7} \cos \frac{3\pi}{7} \cos \frac{2\pi}{7} \cos \frac{\pi}{7} \\
&= -\frac{1}{8} \sin \frac{6\pi}{7} \cos \frac{3\pi}{7} \cos \frac{2\pi}{7} \cos \frac{\pi}{7} \\
&= -\frac{1}{8} \sin \frac{\pi}{7} \cos \frac{3\pi}{7} \cos \frac{2\pi}{7} \cos \frac{\pi}{7} = -\frac{1}{16} \sin \frac{2\pi}{7} \cos \frac{3\pi}{7} \cos \frac{2\pi}{7} \\
&= -\frac{1}{32} \sin \frac{4\pi}{7} \cos \frac{3\pi}{7} = -\frac{1}{32} \sin \frac{3\pi}{7} \cos \frac{3\pi}{7} = -\frac{1}{64} \sin \frac{6\pi}{7}.
\end{aligned}
$$

Hence, $P \sin \frac{\pi}{7} = -\frac{1}{64} \sin \frac{6\pi}{7} = -\frac{1}{64} \sin \frac{\pi}{7}$, or $P = -\frac{1}{64}$.

482. Let $x(i,j)$ be the number appearing on the card in row i and column j after both rearrangements. Suppose that the $x(i,j)$ do not increase from left to right. Then for some i, j, we have $x(i,j) > x(i,j+1)$. Since column j is ordered from top to bottom, there are exactly $i-1$ entries in the column less than $x(i,j)$. Hence, there are at most $i-1$ entries in column j which are less than $x(i,j+1)$. Now consider the first i entries in column $j+1$. At most $i-1$ of the entries in column j are not greater than all of these i elements. Thus, one of the original rows before the column rearrangement must not have been in order, a contradiction. (The smallest i entries in column $j+1$ cannot be paired with i elements in column j so that each element in column $j+1$ is greater than the corresponding element in column j.)

483. We use a Principle of Inclusion-Exclusion approach to this problem. We can get $\triangle XYZ$ by starting with $\triangle ABC$ and cutting out $\triangle CBF$, $\triangle AEB$, and $\triangle ACD$. In doing this we cut out triangles CDY, FZB and AEX twice, so we must add these pieces back in. Since $CD/CB = 1/3$, we have $[ADC] = [ABC]/3$ and similarly for the initial triangles removed. Since $YD/AD = 1/7$, we have $[CYD] = [ACD]/7 = [ABC]/21$ and similarly for the other two triangles added back in. Hence we have

$$[XYZ] = [ABC] - 3([ABC]/3) + 3([ABC]/21) = [ABC]/7.$$

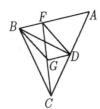

484. Since CF bisects BD at E, we can form a parallelogram by selecting the point G on CF such that $EF = EG$, since then GF and BD bisect each other. Remember that introducing parallel lines or parallelograms is often very helpful! Since $DG \parallel AF$, we have $\triangle CGD \sim \triangle CFA$. Since $CD/CA = 1/2$, we have $AF = 2(DG) = 2(BF) = 10$ and $AB = AF + FB = \mathbf{15}$.

485. We can use the Pythagorean Theorem to determine $AB = 5$ and $DB = 13$. The desired ratio is just $\sin \angle DBE$. Since $\angle DBE + \angle DBC = 180°$, we have $\sin \angle DBE = \sin \angle DBC$. Angle DBC is composed of two angles in easily determined right triangles. Hence, we write

$$
\begin{aligned}
\sin \angle DBC &= \sin(\angle DBA + \angle ABC) \\
&= \sin \angle DBA \cos \angle ABC + \sin \angle ABC \cos \angle DBA \\
&= (AD/DB)(CB/AB) + (AC/AB)(AB/DB) = 48/65 + 15/65 = \mathbf{63/65}.
\end{aligned}
$$

486. From the relationships between the roots of a polynomial and its coefficients, we have $a^2 + b^2 + c^2 = P$ and $a^2b^2c^2 = R$. Seeing cosines in the desired sum, we apply the law of cosines to $\triangle ABC$ and our desired sum becomes

$$\frac{b^2 + c^2 - a^2}{2abc} + \frac{a^2 + c^2 - b^2}{2abc} + \frac{a^2 + b^2 - c^2}{2abc} = \frac{a^2 + b^2 + c^2}{2abc} = \frac{P}{2\sqrt{R}}.$$

487. As in a prior problem, the equality $(5 + 3\sqrt{2})^m = (3 + 5\sqrt{2})^n$ holds if and only the equality $(5 - 3\sqrt{2})^m = (3 - 5\sqrt{2})^n$ holds. Since $0 < 5 - 3\sqrt{2} < 1$ and $|3 - 5\sqrt{2}| > 1$, the magnitude of $(5 - 3\sqrt{2})^m$ is always less than one and the magnitude of $(3 - 5\sqrt{2})^n$ is always greater than 1. Hence, the two can never be equal and the initial equation therefore has no solutions in positive integers.

488. From the given limit and recursion definition, we can write

$$3 = \lim_{n \to \infty} \left(\frac{bu_{n-1} + cu_{n-2}}{u_{n-1}} \right) = \lim_{n \to \infty} \left(b + c\frac{u_{n-2}}{u_{n-1}} \right).$$

From our limit, we have $\lim_{n \to \infty} (u_{n-1}/u_{n-2}) = \lim_{n \to \infty} (u_n/u_{n-1}) = 3$, so $\lim_{n \to \infty} (u_{n-2}/u_{n-1}) = 1/3$. Hence, b and c must satisfy $3 = b + c/3$. Since b and c are nonnegative integers, our possible solutions then are $(0, 9)$, $(1, 6)$, $(2, 3)$, and $(3, 0)$. The last three are valid solutions, but the first yields the sequence 1, 1, 9, 9, 81, etc. The limit $\lim_{n \to \infty} (u_n/u_{n-1})$ is not defined for this sequence.

489. Seeing only even numbers available for our desired representation, we think of doubling or halving. Since $n/2$ is an integer, it can be written in normal base three using 0's, 1's, and 2's. Doubling this representation for $n/2$ gives us a base three representation for n consisting of 0's, 2's, and 4's. For example, $5 = 1 \cdot 3^1 + 2 \cdot 3^0$, so $2 \cdot 5 = 10 = 2 \cdot 3^1 + 4 \cdot 3^0$.

490. Let the highest degree term of $f(x)$ be $a_n x^n$. Hence, the highest degree of the three given expressions are $a_n x^{2n}$, $a_n^2 x^{2n}$, and $a_n^{n+1} x^{n^2}$, respectively. Equating these, we find $2n = n^2$ and $a_n = a_n^2$. Since n and a_n are nonzero integers, we have $n = 2$ and $a_n = 1$. Thus, $f(x) = x^2 + bx + c$ for some b and c. Putting this in the given equality $f(x^2) = [f(x)]^2$ gives

$$x^4 + bx^2 + c = x^4 + 2bx^3 + (b^2 + 2c)x^2 + 2bcx + c^2.$$

Equating coefficients of x^3 gives $b = 0$ and the coefficients of x^2 then give $c = 0$. Hence, only **one** function satisfies the problem, $f(x) = x^2$.

491. We've already seen that we can write any even number in a base three representation with only 0's, 2's, and 4's, so how can we use this to get a representation with only -1's, 1's, and 3's? We can get the latter by subtracting 1 from each digit of a representation with just 0's, 2's, and 4's. For example,

$$4 \cdot 3^3 + 2 \cdot 3^2 + 0 \cdot 3^1 + 2 \cdot 3^0 - 1111_3 = 3 \cdot 3^3 + 1 \cdot 3^2 + (-1) \cdot 3^1 + 1 \cdot 3^0.$$

Now how do we form the first number above with the 4's, 2's and 0's? Since we want to get our original n by subtracting $11 \cdots 11_3$ from this number, we must add $11 \cdots 11_3$ to n to get the number we write with 4's, 2's and 0's. We must be careful, however, because the sum $11 \cdots 11_3 + n$ must be even in order to write it in base 3 with 0's, 2's, and 4's, and we must have at least as many 1's in $11 \cdots 11_3$ as there are digits in the normal base three representation of n; otherwise, when subtracting it from the even number, we won't be able to change all the 0's, 2's, and 4's to odd numbers. Hence, we can write n as suggested by following this method: write n in base 3; then choose a number of the form $11 \cdots 11_3$ which is of the same parity (odd or even) as n; add these two and express the sum in base three with 4's, 2's, and 0's as in the prior example; finally subtract the $11 \cdots 11_3$ from this to get the representation for n. Let's try it for $n = 18$. Hence, n in base three is 200_3. Thus, we add 1111_3 (since 111_3 is odd, we can't use it). We find $n + 1111_3 = 18 + 40 = 58$. Hence, we have

$$58 = 2(1 \cdot 3^3 + 0 \cdot 3^2 + 0 \cdot 3^1 + 2 \cdot 3^0) = 2 \cdot 3^3 + 0 \cdot 3^2 + 0 \cdot 3^1 + 4 \cdot 3^0.$$

Subtracting 1111_3 from this, we have

$$18 = 1 \cdot 3^3 + (-1) \cdot 3^2 + (-1) \cdot 3^1 + 3 \cdot 3^0$$

as the desired representation for 18.

492. We find the area of the pentagon in two ways. First, connecting O to each of the vertices of the pentagon forms five triangles congruent to $\triangle ODC$. Hence, we have $[ABCDE] = 5[ODC] = 5(OP)(DC)/2 = 5x/2$, where x is the side length of the pentagon. Second, we have

$$[ABCDE] = [ACD] + [ABC] + [ADE] = (AP)(DC)/2 + (AQ)(BC)/2 + (AR)(DE)/2$$
$$= (x/2)(AO + AQ + AR + 1),$$

where we have used $AP = AO + OP = AO + 1$. Setting this expression equal to $5x/2$, we find our desired sum is **4**.

493. We could divide, but that would take a long time. Instead, let $f(x) = x^2 - x + a$ and $g(x) = x^8 + 5x^6 + 13x^4 + 20x^2 + 36$. Since $f(x)$ divides $g(x)$ evenly, then for any integer n, $f(n)$ divides $g(n)$. Hence, $f(0) = a$ divides $g(0) = 36$. Since $f(1) = a$, a divides $g(1) = 75$. Comparing the common factors of 36 and 75, we find that a is 1 or 3 (since a is known to be positive). Trying one or two more integers can determine which of these is the answer. For example, since $f(-2) = a + 6$ and $g(-2) = 900$, we exclude $a = 1$ because 900 is not divisible by $1 + 6 = 7$. Hence, the answer is **3**.

494. Proceed by induction. The case where $n = 3$ is obvious; the closest pair shoot each other and the third person remains dry. Now suppose any group of $2m - 1$ are such that at least one person is left dry. We shall prove the same is true for $2m + 1$ people. Consider the two people among the $2m + 1$ who are closest to each other. These two shoot each other. If someone else shoots one of these two, there are then $2m - 2$ shots left and $2m - 1$ dry people, so someone will be dry at the end. Otherwise, we are left with $2m - 1$ dry people and $2m - 1$ shots among them. By our induction hypothesis, someone will be left dry then. Hence, someone will be left dry if there is an odd number of people.

495. This one's a bit tricky! If we expand $(\sqrt{7} + \sqrt{5})^6$, we find that the odd powered terms contain $\sqrt{35}$. Since we are looking for an integer, we would do well to eliminate these odd powered terms. In $(\sqrt{7} + \sqrt{5})^6$ these terms are positive, but if we expand $(\sqrt{7} - \sqrt{5})^6$, these terms are negative. Hence, if we add the two, we find

$$(\sqrt{7} + \sqrt{5})^6 + (\sqrt{7} - \sqrt{5})^6 = 2\left((\sqrt{7})^6 + \binom{6}{2}(\sqrt{7})^4(\sqrt{5})^2 + \binom{6}{4}(\sqrt{7})^2(\sqrt{5})^4 + (\sqrt{5})^6\right)$$
$$= 13536.$$

Since $(\sqrt{7} - \sqrt{5}) < 1$, we have

$$(\sqrt{7} + \sqrt{5})^6 = 13536 - (\sqrt{7} - \sqrt{5})^6 > 13535.$$

Since $13535 < (\sqrt{7} - \sqrt{5})^6 < 13536$, the answer is **13535**.

496. Seeing the circumcircles involved, we think of the expression $R = abc/4K$ for the circumradius. Hence, the sum of the desired areas is

$$\pi(R^2_{\triangle ABX} + R^2_{\triangle AXC}) = \pi \left(\frac{(AX)^2(BX)^2(AB)^2}{16[ABX]^2} + \frac{(AX)^2(CX)^2(AC)^2}{16[ACX]^2} \right).$$

Since $\triangle ABC$ and $\triangle ABX$ share an altitude from A, $[ABX] = (BX/BC)[ABC]$. Finding a similar expression for $[ACX]$, our sum becomes

$$\frac{(BC^2)(AX^2)\pi}{16[ABC]^2} \left(AB^2 + AC^2 \right).$$

The only quantity which varies in this expression is AX^2. Hence, our desired area is at a minimum when AX is minimized, or when AX is an altitude. (Why?) From Heron's formula, the area of $\triangle ABC$ is $6\sqrt{6}$, so $(AX)(BC) = 2(6\sqrt{6})$ and $AX = 12\sqrt{6}/7$. From the Pythagorean Theorem, we then find $BX = \mathbf{19/7}$.

497. The value of y/x at a point in the plane is equal to the slope of the line through the origin and the point (x, y). Hence, we seek the point on the circle for which this slope is the greatest. Clearly this point will be such that the line through the origin and (x, y) is tangent to the circle as shown. Since $XY = \sqrt{6}$ and $OY = 3\sqrt{2}$, we have $OX = \sqrt{18 - 6} = 2\sqrt{3}$ and $\tan \angle YOX = \sqrt{2}/2$. The value of y/x at point X is the slope of the line through O and X, which is in turn equal to the tangent of the angle formed by OX and the positive x axis. Since this angle is $45° + \angle YOX$, we have

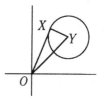

$$\frac{y}{x} = \tan(45° + \angle YOX) = \frac{1 + \tan \angle YOX}{1 - (1)(\tan \angle YOX)} = \mathbf{3 + 2\sqrt{2}}.$$

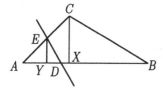

498. First we establish that E is on AC by showing that if DE passes through C, then $[AED] > [BED]$, so we have to move DE towards A to get equal areas. If DE goes through C, we have $BD = CD < AD$ (by looking at the angles of $\triangle ACD$ and $\triangle BCD$). Hence we have the desired $[ADC] > [BCD]$ since the two triangles share an altitude. Now we draw altitudes CX and EY and assume that $CX = 1$. Thus, $AX = 1$ and $BX = \sqrt{3}$ (since $\angle CAX = 45°$ and $\angle CBX = 30°$), so $[ABC] = (1 + \sqrt{3})/2$. Letting $EY = x$, we find $AY = x$ and $YD = x\sqrt{3}/3$, so $[AED] = x^2(1 + \sqrt{3}/3)/2$. Since $2[AED] = [ABC]$, we have $x^2(1 + \sqrt{3}/3) = (1 + \sqrt{3})/2$. Solving for x, we find $x = \sqrt[4]{3/4}$. Our desired ratio then is $AD/AB = x(1 + \sqrt{3}/3)/(1 + \sqrt{3}) = \mathbf{1/\sqrt[4]{12}}$.

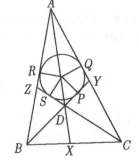

499. Lemma: Quadrilateral $DYAZ$ is circumscriptible if and only if

$$BD - CD = AB - AC.$$

Proof: If $DYAZ$ is circumscriptible, then let the shown points be the points of tangency. Then since $SD = DP$, $BP = BR$, and $CS = CQ$, we have

$$BD - CD = (BD + DP) - (CD + DS) = BP - CS = BR - CQ.$$

Since $AR = AQ$, we have $BR - CQ = (BR + RA) - (CQ + QA) = AB - AC$, as desired. We can prove the converse by assuming that the line from C tangent to the incircle of $\triangle ABY$ intersects BY at some point E different from D. As above we have $AB - AC = BE - EC$. Let $BE = BD + \alpha DE$, where $\alpha = \pm 1$. Combining $AB - AC = BE - EC$ with the obvious $EC = CD + (EC - CD)$, we find

$$AB - AC = BD - CD + (\alpha DE - EC + CD).$$

This last expression equals zero only when $\triangle DEC$ is degenerate, i.e. when point D and E are the same. If points D and E are the same, $DYAZ$ is circumscriptible. Hence, $AB - AC = BD - CD$ if and only if $DYAZ$ is circumscriptible.

Applying this to our problem, we find that we must prove that if $AB - AC = BD - CD$ and $BC - AB = CD - AD$, then we have $AC - BC = AD - BD$. This is clearly true (just add the two given equations to get the desired one), so our lemma proves the problem completely.

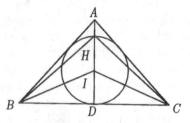

500. In the figure, H is the orthocenter, I is the incenter, and D is the midpoint of BC. If we continue BH to meet AC at M and CH to meet AB at N, we will find from cyclic quadrilateral $AMHN$ that $\angle CHB = \angle MHN = 180° - \angle A$. Similarly, $\angle BIC = 180° - (\angle B + \angle C)/2 = 180° - (180° - \angle A)/2 = 90° + \angle A/2$. Letting $IH = ID = 1$, we note that $BD = 2\tan \angle BHD = \tan \angle BID$ from right triangles BHD and BID. Letting $x = \angle A/4$, this equation becomes

$$2\tan(90° - 2x) = \tan(45° + x),$$

where $\angle BHD = \angle BHC/2$ and $\angle BID = \angle BIC/2$. Applying various trigonometric identities (such as $\tan(90° - 2x) = \sin(90° - 2x)/\cos(90° - 2x) = \cos 2x/\sin 2x = 1/\tan 2x$), we find

$$\frac{2}{\tan 2x} = \frac{1 - \tan^2 x}{\tan x} = \frac{1 + \tan x}{1 - \tan x} = \frac{\tan 45° + \tan x}{1 - \tan 45° \tan x}.$$

Writing $\tan x = (\sin x)/(\cos x)$, we work through much algebra (be careful!) to find $3\cos x \sin x = 1$ or

$$\sin 2x = \frac{2}{3}.$$

Since $\sin 2x = \sin(A/2) = \sqrt{(1 - \cos A)/2} = 2/3$, we find $\cos A = 1/9$.

501. First note that from the AM-GM Inequality we have

$$\frac{n + 17/n}{2} \geq \sqrt{17}$$

for any positive n. Hence, if $x > 0$, then $2y = (x + 17/x) \geq 2\sqrt{17}$. From this we get $z \geq \sqrt{17}$, then $w \geq \sqrt{17}$, and $x \geq \sqrt{17}$. We can rewrite the first equality in the problem as

$$y - \sqrt{17} = \frac{x^2 + 17}{2x} - \sqrt{17} = \left(\frac{x - \sqrt{17}}{2x}\right)(x - \sqrt{17}).$$

Since $(x - \sqrt{17})/2x = 1/2 - \sqrt{17}/2x$, $(x - \sqrt{17})/2x \leq 1/2$ and we have $y - \sqrt{17} \leq (x - \sqrt{17})/2$. Rearranging this we have $x - y \geq y - \sqrt{17}$. Since $y \geq \sqrt{17}$, $x - y \geq 0$, so $x \geq y$. Similarly we can show $y \geq z$, $z \geq w$, and $w \geq x$, so that $x \geq y \geq z \geq w \geq x$. Thus, $x = y = z = w = \sqrt{17}$ is the only possible positive solution. We check it and find that it works. Since $(-w, -x, -y, -z)$ is a solution if and only if (w, x, y, z) is, our only solutions are $(\sqrt{17}, \sqrt{17}, \sqrt{17}, \sqrt{17})$ and $(-\sqrt{17}, -\sqrt{17}, -\sqrt{17}, -\sqrt{17})$.

502. Look at x in base 2. The recursion in the problem is then equivalent to sliding the decimal place over to the right and chopping off any integer part. For example, let $x_0 = 0.010111_2$. Hence, $x_1 = 2x_0 = 0.10111_2$, $x_2 = 2x_1 - 1 = 0.0111_2$ (since $2x_1 > 1$), $x_3 = 2x_2 = 0.111_2$, etc. As we can see, the number of decimal places of x_i decreases as i increases unless x_0 repeats indefinitely. Since $x_0 = x_5$, x_0 must go on indefinitely. Since the 0th and 5th term differ by sliding the decimal 5 places to the right, x_0 must consist of a block of 5 digits repeating indefinitely in order for x_0 and x_5 to be the same. Since each of these digits can be 0 or 1, there are $2^5 = 32$ possible blocks. However, since the block $x_0 = 0.\overline{11111}$ is equal to 1 and $x_0 < 1$, we exclude this from our count of 32. Thus, there are **31** x_0 such that $x_0 = x_5$.

503. For the first part, Let k be one of the elements and S_k the sum of the remaining elements. The sum of all the elements is $k + S_k$. Since $S_k/k = d$, where d is an integer, $(S_k + k)/k = d + 1$ and k divides the sum of all the elements.

Since 1 is an element of the set in the second part, the greatest common divisor of all the numbers in the set is clearly 1. The sum of all the members of the set is $1 + 1 + 2 + \cdots + 2^n = 1 + 2^{n+1} - 1 = 2^{n+1}$. Hence, for any member of the set 2^k we have $(2^{n+1} - 2^k)/2^k = 2^{n+1-k} - 1$, so any element of the set divides the sum of the remaining elements and the set is magical.

Let n be the perfect number whose proper divisors form our set. The sum of the numbers in the set is then n. Let k be the number removed from the set. The sum of the remaining elements is $n - k$. Since n is a multiple of k, $n - k$ is also a multiple of k and the set is thus magical.

For the fourth part, let the members of the set be a, b, and c with $a \leq b \leq c$. Since $a + b$ must be a multiple of c for the set to magical and $a + b \leq 2c$, we must have either $a + b = c$

or $a + b = 2c$. The latter set is easy, since in this case if $a \leq b \leq c$ and $a + b = 2c$, then $a = b = c$. Since the greatest common factor of the three numbers must be 1, the only set of this type is $\{1, 1, 1\}$. For the case $a + b = c$, a and b cannot both be even, or then all three will have the common factor 2. Thus, let a be odd and b even. We know that $a|b + a + b$ and $b|a + b + a$, or $a|2b$ and $b|2a$. Since b is even, we let $b = 2k$, so $a|4k$ and $2k|2a$. Since a is odd we find $a|k$ and $k|a$, so $k = a$ and our set is $\{a, 2a, 3a\}$. Since the greatest common factor of these is 1, our set is $\{1, 2, 3\}$. Finally, if a and b are odd we go through exactly the same steps as above to show $a|b$ and $b|a$ so $a = b$ and we thus find the solution $\{1, 1, 2\}$.

Let $n \geq m$. Since the set is magical, we have $n|m + 4$, so $4 + m = kn$ for some k. Since $n \geq m$, we have $kn \geq km$, so $4 + m \geq km$. Solving for k, we have $k \leq 1 + 4/m$. Since $m \geq 3$, k can only be 1 or 2. For $k = 1$, our set is $\{1, 3, m, m + 4\}$. Thus, $m|8 + m$ or $m|8$. Since $m \geq 3$, $m = 4$ or $m = 8$. Only the latter leads to a magical set, namely $\{1, 3, 8, 12\}$. For $k = 2$, from $k \leq 1 + 4/m$, we must have $m = 3$ or 4. Only the value $m = 4$ leads to a magical set, namely $\{1, 3, 4, 4\}$.

Finally, for the last part, we can easily see that adding the sum S of the elements in the original set we form a new magical set. The proof that this new set is magical is straightforward. Let k be an element of the original set. Since $k|S$, k will also divide $2S$. Hence, we need only prove that S divides the sum of the elements of the new set. Since S clearly divides $2S$, we have shown that all the elements of the new set divides the sum of the elements of the set. Thus, the new set is magical.

504. Remove the barriers. Instead of standing still at the barrier, let the particle move beyond it according to the toss of the coin. Hence, if the particle ever goes to $(n, n + k)$ from point $(n - 1, n + k)$ without barriers, then it would have gone to (n, n) in $2n + k$ moves with barriers since it would stay stuck on the north barrier for the k moves it takes to get up to the $(n + k)$th row. (Why don't we consider the case where the non-barriered particle gets to $(n, n + k)$ from $(n, n + k - 1)$? Because then with barriers, it would have taken less than $2n + k$ moves to get to (n, n).) Thus, we remove the barriers and find the probability that the particle goes through $(n, n + k)$ from $(n - 1, n + k)$. It can get to $(n - 1, n + k)$ by taking $n - 1$ east steps out of $2n + k - 1$. Hence, the probability that the particle gets to $(n - 1, n + k)$ is

$$\binom{2n + k - 1}{n - 1} \left(\frac{1}{2}\right)^{2n+k-1}$$

There is a 1/2 chance that the particle will then take the right step from this point to $(n, n + k)$, so our probability is

$$P = \frac{1}{2}\binom{2n + k - 1}{n - 1} \left(\frac{1}{2}\right)^{2n+k-1}$$

We're not quite done; if the unbarriered particle gets to $(n + k, n)$ via point $(n + k, n - 1)$, then it would have gotten to (n, n) in $2n + k$ steps as well. These paths to (n, n) are just the mirror images of the paths to $(n, n + k)$, so the probability of this course is the same as for the one to $(n, n+k)$ via $(n-1, n+k)$. Hence, our final probability of getting to (n, n) in $2n + k$ moves is $2P$, or

$$\binom{2n+k-1}{n-1} \left(\frac{1}{2}\right)^{2n+k-1}$$

505. Let the numbers be $a_1, a_2, \ldots, a_7$. Since the range of $\tan x$ for $-\pi/2 < x < \pi/2$ is all real numbers, then for each a_i there is an x_i such that $a_i = \tan x_i$. If we divide the interval $(-\pi/2, \pi/2)$ into six equal subintervals, there are two of the x_i in one of the subintervals by the Pigeonhole Principle. Let these two be x_k and x_j with x_k the larger of the two. Hence we have $0 \le x_k - x_j < \pi/6$. Since $\tan x$ increases over the interval $(0, \pi/6)$, this inequality becomes $\tan 0 \le \tan(x_k - x_j) < \tan \pi/6$, or

$$0 \le \frac{\tan x_k - \tan x_j}{1 + \tan x_k \tan x_j} < \frac{1}{\sqrt{3}}.$$

Hence we have

$$0 \le \frac{a_k - a_j}{1 + a_k a_j} < \frac{1}{\sqrt{3}},$$

as desired.

506. Since $\angle AED + \angle AFD = 180°$, $AEDF$ is a cyclic quadrilateral. Since these two angles are right angles, AD is a diameter of this circle. Hence, the circumradius of $\triangle AEF$ has length $AD/2$. The circumradius of $\triangle ABC$ is $abc/4[ABC]$. Since $(AD)(a/2) = [ABC]$, the product of these circumradii is

$$\left(\frac{AD}{2}\right)\left(\frac{abc}{4[ABC]}\right) = \left(\frac{[ABC]}{a}\right)\left(\frac{abc}{4[ABC]}\right) = \frac{bc}{4}.$$

Thus, we have $[ABC] = bc/4$. Since we want $\angle A$, we write $[ABC] = (bc/2)\sin A$ and we find $\sin A = 1/2$, so $\angle A = 30°$ since $\triangle ABC$ is acute.

507. The coin could end up heads $0, 2, 4, \ldots,$ or 50 times to satisfy the problem. Hence, our probability is

$$\binom{50}{0}\left(\frac{2}{3}\right)^0\left(\frac{1}{3}\right)^{50} + \binom{50}{2}\left(\frac{2}{3}\right)^2\left(\frac{1}{3}\right)^{48} + \cdots + \binom{50}{48}\left(\frac{2}{3}\right)^{48}\left(\frac{1}{3}\right)^2 + \binom{50}{50}\left(\frac{2}{3}\right)^{50}\left(\frac{1}{3}\right)^0.$$

This sum is the the sum of the even powered terms of $(1/3 + 2/3)^{50}$. To isolate the even powered terms, we note that the odd powered terms of $(1/3 - 2/3)^{50}$ are negative. Hence, adding $(1/3 + 2/3)^{50}$ and $(1/3 - 2/3)^{50}$ eliminates all the odd terms and leaves us with double the sum of the even terms. Our probability then is

$$P = \frac{(1/3 + 2/3)^{50} + (1/3 - 2/3)^{50}}{2} = \frac{1 + (1/3)^{50}}{2}.$$

508. This is a tough one, so pay close attention. First we draw the tangents MX and MY. Since $\angle ACM = \angle MYA = \angle MXA = 90°$, points A, Y, C, M, and X are all on a circle as shown below. Since $AY = AX$, we have $\overparen{AY} = \overparen{AX}$, so $\angle AYX = \angle AXY = \angle ACY$ and $\triangle AYC \sim \triangle AKY$, so $AK = AY^2/AC$. Since $AB = AY$, we find $AK = AB^2/AC = (4/5)AB$. Hence, point K is fixed. Since $MY = MX$, the orthocenter H of $\triangle YMX$ is on line AM and $YH = XH$. Since YH and AX are both perpendicular to XM, they are parallel. Similarly, $AY \parallel HX$ and $AYHX$ is a parallelogram. Since $AY = AX$, $AYHX$ is a rhombus. Let point L be the intersection of the diagonals of $AYHX$. Since $\angle ALK = 90°$ (the diagonals of a rhombus are perpendicular), as M moves, point L moves around the circle Γ with diameter AK. Since $AH = 2(AL)$ (why?), point H is on the circle homothetic to Γ with ratio $2:1$ and center of homothecy A. Thus, the locus of H is the circle through A with center K (except point A). To show that all these points are in the locus, we note that for any point H on the circle, we draw AH through to CM in the diagram to determine the point J such that the tangents to circle A from J form the triangle with orthocenter H as the problem requires.

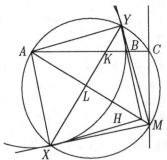

509. First we recall that the interior angles of a regular n-gon have measure $180(n-2)/n$. Hence, let's consider the case where we fit 3 polygons about a point. Let the polygons have a, b, and c sides, where $a \geq b \geq c \geq 3$. Since the sum of the angles about a point is $360°$, we have

$$\frac{180(a-2)}{a} + \frac{180(b-2)}{b} + \frac{180(c-2)}{c} = 360.$$

Simplifying this equation we find

$$\frac{1}{a} + \frac{1}{b} + \frac{1}{c} = \frac{1}{2}.$$

Note that if $c \geq 7$, then the sum on the left will always be less than or equal to $3/7$. Hence, $c = 3, 4, 5,$ or 6. These lead to $1/a+1/b = 1/6, 1/4, 3/10,$ or $1/3$. Now we need a systematic way to solve equations of the form

$$\frac{1}{a} + \frac{1}{b} = \frac{p}{q},$$

where p and q are relatively prime and a and b are integers. Write the left side of this as $(a+b)/ab$. Let $a = (m+q)/p$ and $b = (n+q)/p$. Hence,

$$\frac{a+b}{ab} = p \cdot \frac{m+n+2q}{q^2 + (m+n)q + mn} = \frac{p}{q}.$$

Thus, we see that the big fraction must equal $1/q$. Thus, $q(m+n+2q) = q^2+(m+n)q+mn$, so $mn = q^2$. Hence, we have a way to generate our solutions: list all ways to write q^2 as a product mn of integers, keep only those for which p divides $q+m$ and $q+n$ (since a and b must be integers), and the solutions are $(m+q)/p$ and $b = (n+q)/p$. Coming back to our above values for $1/a + 1/b$, we thus generate the solutions $(42, 7, 3)$; $(24, 8, 3)$; $(18, 9, 3)$; $(15, 10, 3)$; $(12, 12, 3)$; $(20, 5, 4)$; $(12, 6, 4)$; $(8, 8, 4)$; $(10, 5, 5)$; and $(6, 6, 6)$.

For four polygons, we have $a \geq b \geq c \geq d \geq 3$ and working through the algebra as above we get $1/a + 1/b + 1/c + 1/d = 1$. Hence, if $d \geq 5$, the sum is less than 1. We thus consider $d = 3$ and $d = 4$. For $d = 4$ we have only $(4, 4, 4, 4)$. For $d = 3$, we get $1/a+1/b+1/c = 2/3$. Again, we deduce $c \geq 5$ is impossible. We then let $c = 3$ or 4. Thus we get $1/a + 1/b = 1/3$ and $5/12$, which we then solve with our process to get $(12, 4, 3, 3)$; $(6, 6, 3, 3)$; and $(6, 4, 4, 3)$.

The same processes work for the cases of five or six polygons (or we can find these by inspection), and we get $(6, 3, 3, 3, 3)$; $(4, 4, 3, 3, 3)$; and $(3, 3, 3, 3, 3, 3)$ as the solutions. Clearly there can't be more than six polygons since the smallest angle possible among the polygons is $60°$. Hence there are a total of **17** solutions.

This is a very difficult problem to do without the use of a computer. The authors of this problem (the authors of this text together with Sam Vandervelde) used a computer to determine there are indeed 17 solutions before developing a methodical method to find the solutions without a computer. Therefore, don't feel too bad if you had to resort to peeking at the solutions to solve this one!